ACTS AND OTHER EVENTS

CONTEMPORARY PHILOSOPHY

General Editor
Max Black, Cornell University

ACTS AND OTHER EVENTS

Judith Jarvis Thomson

Cornell University Press

ITHACA AND LONDON

International Standard Book Number 0-8014-1050-9
Library of Congress Catalog Card Number 77-4791
Printed in the United States of America by Vail-Ballou Press, Inc.
*Librarians: Library of Congress cataloging information
appears on the last page of the book.*

For James

Preface

I began this book because I wanted to know what acts are. It soon became plain, however, that finding out what acts are requires finding out what their parts are, and that finding out what their parts are requires finding out what are the parts of events generally. Hence my interest in events that are not acts as well as in events that are.

I wanted to know what acts are, in part because it seemed to me that ethics has suffered for lack of an acceptable ontology of action. But while I think that some of what is done here will be found useful by a moral philosopher, I do not discuss how. The prospective reader should take warning now that the morals I draw are all metaphysical.

It should also be said here that although I make liberal use of the notion 'cause' in giving an account of events and their parts, I have given no account of what it is for one event to cause another. Since it is not at all clear what it is for one event to cause another, it may seem, and at times does seem to me, like building on stilts to proceed as I did. If I had been competent to take on the question of what it is for one event to cause another, I would certainly have done so. But perhaps there may be some interest for others, as there was for me, in asking whether a plausible account of events can be got to issue from a limited and (I hope) prima facie plausible set of assumptions about causality.

7

Preface

I am most deeply indebted to George Boolos, who read and criticized the entire final draft. I am particularly grateful to him for his suggestions for revision in Chapters V through VII.

An earlier draft of Chapters I through IX was read and criticized by Gilbert Harman, and by the members of MIT's seminar on Theory of Action, spring 1975 (Ali Akhtar, David Auerbach, Anne Ellison, Lena Goldberg, Fred Katz, Barbara Klein, Jeffrey Poland, Alan Sparer).

The previous year, Scott Soames went through the long manuscript that later became Chapters I through III.

Robert M. Harnish and I jointly conducted MIT's Theory of Action seminar in the spring of 1971. I am sure that some of his ideas have found their way into this book—my not citing him is owing to the embarrassing fact that I cannot now remember which they are.

I think it was some time before then that the idea for thesis-schema (T-S$_7$) of Chapter XIV surfaced in a talk I had with James Thomson. I thought at the time that it was a lovely idea, and I still do; moreover, it was with that idea that this book began. My thanks to him for the idea, if it was his, and in any case for that and all the other good talks over the years.

JUDITH JARVIS THOMSON

Cambridge, Massachusetts

8

Contents

ACTS AND OTHER EVENTS

I

Method (I)

An essay by a mineralogist, or a physiologist, on (as it might be) emeralds, or brains, need hardly open with an argument to the effect that there are such things; no one doubts it. But an essay by a philosopher on acts might well be expected to begin by establishing that it has a subject-matter, for some philosophers are suspicious of everything but physical objects (such as emeralds and brains) and think acts—indeed, events generally—may well be mere fancy.

Short arguments for their existence are easy enough to come by. Here is one I rather like.

(1)   Sirhan killed Kennedy

is true; and surely it is equivalent to

(1')   There was a killing of Kennedy by Sirhan,

which is therefore also true. But if there was at any time an entity that was a killing, there was an act at that time. So there was at least one act. So there (tenselessly) are acts.

However those who are suspicious of acts are most unlikely to be moved by this little argument. One possible reply is this: "No doubt if there was an entity that was a killing, there was an act. And no doubt (1') looks as if it says there was an entity that was a killing. But does it? Does

There was a shortage of beef recently

Acts and Other Events

say there was an entity that was a shortage? Surely the fact that a sentence begins with "There was a . . ." does not by itself show anything: surely

There was a superfluity of sugar in the tea Mary gave John

does not say there was an entity that was a superfluity. But if (1') does not say there was an entity that was a killing, how should proving the truth of (1') be proving that there are acts?" Alas, the argument now looks rather less attractive.

My own view is that there plainly are acts and that proof is not necessary. *Of course* there is such a thing as Sirhan's killing of Kennedy; it took place in June 1968. *Of course* there is such a thing as my typing of the sentence I am now typing; it is taking place now. The question whether there are any acts seems to me an easy one to answer. The question what acts are seems to me the hard one; it is the one anyway that will occupy us throughout most of this book. In fact, I suspect that those who are suspicious of acts are so precisely because they think that latter question has no answer, or is at least peculiarly difficult. Consider, for example, a student who had stopped in to say he was not at all sure there are any acts. Not having much time, I presented him with the following (even shorter) argument: "Here is one hand-waving [while saying that, I waved one hand], and here is another [while saying that, I waved the other hand]; therefore there are acts." My student said, with what on a closer look was not really irrelevance, "But what *are* hand-wavings?"

Curiously enough, however, it will pay us to attend to yet another argument for the existence of acts. Consideration of it will bring us to what seems to me a good place at which to begin an investigation into the nature of acts.

The argument I have in mind is Donald Davidson's.[1] Davidson was not in search of an argument for the existence of acts; what he was looking for was, rather, an explanation of what he takes to be entailment-relations among certain sentences, which he called "action sentences". But what he found was reason to think that (1)—and so of course also (1')—really does say there was an entity that was a killing,

---

[1] See his "Logical Form of Action Sentences," in *The Logic of Decision and Action*, ed. Nicholas Rescher (Pittsburgh: University of Pittsburgh Press, 1967), and "The Individuation of Events," in *Essays in Honor of Carl G. Hempel*, ed. Nicholas Rescher et al. (Dordrecht, Holland: D. Reidel, 1970).

14

from which it follows that there was an act; indeed, if he is right about (1), what he found is a proof that there are acts.

Davidson's proposal is well known by now, and I shall give only a quick summary of it. Consider, for example,

(2)   Sirhan killed Kennedy with a gun.

Davidson says, and seems to be quite right in saying, that (2) entails (1). By what rule or rules of logic does it do so? Davidson asks us to notice what happens if we *first* suppose (1) says there is an entity x that has a certain relation to Kennedy and Sirhan, viz., the relation that x, y, and z have just in case x is a killing of y by z; i.e., if we suppose (1) may be rewritten as

(1.1.) $(\exists x)$ [Kills$_3$ $(x,$ Kennedy, Sirhan)].[2]

(I insert the subscript to mark that the predicate in (1.1) has three argument-places.) And if we *second* suppose (2) says both this and also that that entity x has a certain relation to a gun, viz., the relation that x has to y just in case x is performed with y; i.e., if we suppose (2) may be rewritten as

(2.1) $(\exists x)$ $(\exists y)$ [Kills$_3$ $(x,$ Kennedy, Sirhan) & With (x, y) & Gun (y)].

If we suppose these two things, we have in hand an explanation of the fact that (2) entails (1). For if (2) may be rewritten as (2.1) and (1) as (1.1), then (2) entails (1) by the rules of first-order logic.

The idea is ingenious and powerful: proceeding in a similar way we are able to explain a great many of what certainly appear to be entailment-relations among a great many sentences. So, for a further example, it certainly looks as if (1) and

(3)   Sirhan shot Kennedy

are both entailed by

(4)   Sirhan killed Kennedy by shooting him.

Let us suppose, by analogy with (1), that (3) may be rewritten as

(3.1) $(\exists x)$ [Shoots$_3$ $(x,$ Kennedy, Sirhan)].

(4) tells us that shooting was the method or means by which Sirhan killed Kennedy. So let us suppose that (4) says a shooting of Kennedy by Sirhan and a killing of Kennedy by Sirhan have a certain relation to each other, which we can call the 'method-relation', viz., the rela-

---

[2] (1) is in the past tense and (1.1) has no tense, so of course (1) cannot really be rewritten as (1.1). There is no general agreement on how best to handle tense, and since tense is irrelevant for my purposes, I simply ignore it throughout—by "may be rewritten" I shall mean "may, if you ignore tense, be rewritten".

tion that x has to y just in case y is performed by performing x; i.e., that (4) may be rewritten as

(4.1) $(\exists x)\,(\exists y)$ [Shoots$_3$ $(x,$ Kennedy, Sirhan) & Kills$_3$ $(y,$ Kennedy, Sirhan) & Method (x, y)].

Then we can explain the fact that (4) entails (1) and (3). For if (4), (1), and (3) may be rewritten as (4.1), (1.1), and (3.1), respectively, then (4) entails (1) and (3) by the rules of first-order logic.

Now Davidson seems to think not merely that (2) entails (1), and not merely that (2) entails (1) if (2) and (1) may be rewritten as (2.1) and (1.1); he seems to think also that (2) entails (1) only if they are rewritable in this way. If he is right, then we have in hand as good a proof of the existence of acts as anyone could want. First premise (supposing Davidson to be right): (2) entails (1). Second premise (again supposing Davidson to be right): (2) entails (1) only if (1) may be rewritten as (1.1). Third premise: (1) is true. Fourth premise: if S is true, and S may be rewritten as S', S' is true. Conclusion: (1.1) is true. But then there *are* acts. For if there actually is an entity that is a killing, there actually is an entity that is an act.

Is Davidson right? Some philosophers think he is not. One group thinks he is mistaken in thinking that the sentences he draws our attention to have the entailment-relations he says they have: in particular, they would deny that (2) entails (1).[3] A second group thinks that the sentences do have the entailment-relations he says they have, but that there must be a better way of explaining their entailment-relations than the one he offers.[4] I am inclined to think that the second group is right. I think in particular that (2) entails (1), and that (4) entails (1) and (3), and I shall assume so throughout. I think also—and shall explain why I think—that (1) and (3) are rewritable as (1.1) and (3.1). But I think also—and shall explain why I think—that (2) and (4) are *not* rewritable as (2.1) and (4.1). I think therefore that we cannot explain these entailments in a manner that requires rewriting (1) through (4) as (1.1) through (4.1), and that if there is to be any explaining of these entailments at all, there must be a better way. But I hasten to say that I shall not try to provide one. I shall have a good bit more to say about (4) in particular, but nothing about 'the logic of

---

[3] See, e.g., Richmond H. Thomason and Robert C. Stalnaker, "A Semantic Theory of Adverbs," *Linguistic Inquiry*, 4 (1973), 195–220.

[4] See, e.g., Romane Clark, "Concerning the Logic of Predicate Modifiers," *Nous*, 4 (1970), 311–335.

action sentences' in general. For my purposes it is not necessary that we take a stand on it. And as I said earlier, I think it is not necessary to prove that there are acts, but that we can freely suppose that there are, even if Davidson's argument is no proof of it.

If there are acts, as I think there are, then it does no harm to suppose that (1) is rewritable as (1.1). If there are acts, there presumably are killings, for killings surely are paradigm acts. And if there are killings, then it may be presumed that there is a killing of *B* by *A* if and only if *A* kills *B*. So if there are acts, (1) is true if and only if there was an entity that was a killing of Kennedy by Sirhan. Now, that there is an entity that is a killing of Kennedy by Sirhan is precisely what (1.1) says. It does not, of course, follow from the fact that a sentence *S* is equivalent to a sentence *S'* that what *S* says is what *S'* says; so we could not conclude from this that what (1) says is—if you ignore its tense—what (1.1) says. Nevertheless, it seems to me that it does no harm (if there are acts) to suppose that what (1) says *is*—if you ignore its tense—what (1.1) says.

By analogy, if there are acts, then it does no harm to suppose that what (3) says is what (3.1) says. For if there are acts, there presumably are shootings, for shootings are surely paradigm acts too. And if there are shootings, then it may be presumed that there is a shooting of *B* by *A* if and only if *A* shoots *B*.

The situation is different, however, in the case of (2) and (4). Let us concentrate now on (4); we will come back to (2) in the following chapters. To accept that what (4) says is what (4.1) says is to commit oneself to an answer to a very important question about the nature of acts—anyway, about the nature of a very important and large class of acts. Very many of the things we do, we do *by* doing things. If I break a window, I presumably break it by doing something, for instance, by throwing a rock at it. If you sink a ship, you presumably sink it by doing something, for instance, by torpedoing it. One who kills a man presumably kills him by doing something, for instance shooting him. Now it is an important question, to which any theory of action ought to supply an answer, just what it *is* to do something by doing something. To take (4) to be rewritable as (4.1) is to suppose that for Sirhan to have killed Kennedy by shooting him is for there to have been something that was Sirhan's shooting of Kennedy, and something that was Sirhan's killing of Kennedy, and for the former to have a certain relation to the latter, viz., the relation that *x* has to *y* just in case *y* is performed by performing x. And this suggests we ought to give the following quite general answer to that general question: for a person to do something by doing something is for there to be an entity x that has that relation to an entity y.

Is this true? One thing that is plain is that it really will not do to say what the 'method-relation' is in the manner in which I just did, thus as follows:

(D$_{1a}$)   Method (x, y) just in case y is performed by performing x.

Consider Sirhan's shooting of Kennedy: that is supposed to have this relation to Sirhan's killing of Kennedy. But is

> Sirhan's killing of Kennedy was performed by performing Sirhan's shooting of Kennedy

true? It does not even seem to make sense. One might naturally suppose that "was performed by" is the passive of "performed", and that it therefore must be followed by a noun-phrase which refers to whatever it was that performed the thing. Thus, for example, one might say "Beethoven's Ninth was performed by the Boston Symphony", or "The dance was performed by John Jones". But "performing Sirhan's shooting of Kennedy" can hardly be taken to refer to a thing that performed Sirhan's killing of Kennedy.

A shift to the active, viz., to

(D$_{1b}$)   Method (x, y) just in case whatever performs y performs y by performing x

would eliminate this difficulty, but leave us with another. Did Sirhan, for example, *perform* his killing of Kennedy? Did he perform his shooting of Kennedy? An orchestra might perform a symphony; does it perform its own performing of that symphony? We shall come back to this again in Chapter II.

Perhaps we should in any case shift gears. Sirhan killed Kennedy by shooting him; and doesn't this mean that Sirhan's shooting of Kennedy *was* his killing of Kennedy? After all, once Sirhan had shot Kennedy, there was nothing more he needed to do in order to kill Kennedy; the shooting itself was enough; after the shooting, Sirhan himself could have done anything or nothing, he could have stood on his head, or died, and still the killing would have occurred. And it may strike one that perhaps this is always the case when a man does something by doing something: having done the one thing, there is nothing further he needs to do in order to have done the other. So perhaps we should say—it is, I think, natural to want to say—that this

Method (I)

'method-relation' just is identity. Or perhaps better, it is the relation that x has to y just in case x and y are events, and x is identical with y. In other words, that

(D_{1c})   Method (x, y) just in case x and y are events, and x is identical with y.

But a second glance makes plain it will not do. If "Method (x, y)" is defined as in (D_{1c}), then "Method (x, y)" is equivalent to "Method (y, x)", and (4.1) is equivalent to

($\exists x$) ($\exists y$) [Shoots$_3$ $(x$, Kennedy, Sirhan) & Kills$_3$ $(y$, Kennedy, Sirhan) & Method (y, x)],

and therefore to

(4.1*)   ($\exists y$) ($\exists x$) [Kills$_3$ $(y$, Kennedy, Sirhan) & Shoots$_3$ $(x$, Kennedy, Sirhan) & Method (y, x)].

Now there is no reason to think that (4) may be rewritten as (4.1), which is not also reason to think that

(4*)   Sirhan shot Kennedy by killing him

may be rewritten as (4.1*). So if "Method (x, y)" is defined as in (D_{1c}), (4) is equivalent to (4*). Which it quite certainly is not.

I am inclined to think that no account of what it is to do something by doing something will be satisfactory unless it makes room for, and indeed explains, those things that make us want to say that for a man to do something by doing something is for his doing of the one thing to be identical with his doing of the other, and in particular, that for Sirhan to have killed Kennedy by shooting him is for the shooting to have been identical with the killing. So I shall return to this later. But we cannot accept it as giving the meaning of "Method (x, y)".

I doubt that causality will do any better than identity did. Pretty plainly it will not do to say

(D_{1d})   Method (x, y) just in case y causes x:

Sirhan's killing of Kennedy certainly did not cause his shooting of Kennedy. But it also will not do to say

(D_{1e})   Method (x, y) just in case x causes y:

it seems equally certain that the shooting did not cause the killing. A shooting might cause a killing: e.g., you might shoot, and thereby frighten an elephant, who, from fright, breaks out of his cage and steps on somebody, thereby killing him. But it was not like that with Sirhan. *His* shooting did not cause any killing. Causality does seem to be involved, and I am inclined to think that no account of what it is to do something by doing something will be satisfactory unless it makes clear how causality is involved. But no straightforward account of this 'method-relation' in terms of causality seems likely to succeed.

It is important to stress that I am not merely being disagreeable. It has been proposed that (4) may be rewritten as (4.1); and we cannot possibly tell whether or not this proposal is true if we do not know what (4.1) means—in particular, if we do not know what its last clause, "Method (x, y)", means. Another way to put the point is this: according to the logic of the notation used in (4.1), (4.1) entails "$(\exists x)$ $(\exists y)$ Method (x, y)". So if (4.1) is a mere rewriting of (4), (4) entails this too. And if we do not know what it means, how on earth can we tell if (4) entails it?

My own inclination is to think that this 'by of method' is syncategorematic, and that what method involves begins to come out when we notice that (4) is equivalent to

(4′)   There was a shooting of Kennedy by Sirhan, which killed Kennedy.

There is a quite general thesis lurking in here, which we shall be looking at later. For the time being it is enough if two things can be granted. First, that if (4′) is true, (4) is true: if your shooting of a man kills him, then you kill him, and indeed kill him by shooting him. A little generalizing will do no harm: if your stabbing of a man, or your dunking him in tea, kills him, then you kill him, and kill him by stabbing or dunking him. Whatever you do to a man, if your doing it to him kills him, you kill him by doing it to him. And second, that if (4) is true, (4′) is true: if you kill a man by shooting him, then your shooting of him kills him. That by which you kill, itself kills.

A possible first reaction may be that we cannot really, truly, say of what is an event that it killed a man: only an animate being can kill. But a second thought surely convinces that this is wrong. Hearing bad news might kill a man; the fall of a tree on a man's head might kill him; explosions of bombs have killed vast numbers of people. In fact we may truly say of inanimate objects of a great many different kinds that they killed: consider meningitis, for example, and poison gas. Indeed, I think that if you had been there at the death, and had then pointed to the right bullet, and then to the right wound, and said of them

(5)   That bullet killed Kennedy,

(6)   That wound killed Kennedy,

you would have been speaking with as much truth as you do when you say (1)—*and* when you say (4'). The fact that Sirhan (a man), a shooting of Kennedy (an event), a certain bullet (an inanimate physical object), and a certain wound (whatever a wound is) are entities of very different kinds seems to me no ground at all for thinking that these are not all true.

Certainly anyone who believes that "kill" is definable as "cause to die" is committed to agreeing that (4'), (5), and (6) are truths along with (1). For Sirhan is not the only thing that caused Kennedy's death—his shooting of Kennedy caused it, and so also did that bullet and that wound (if you have fastened on the right bullet and wound). There is, I think, a fairly widespread tendency to think that it can be of at most one thing that we can truly say "It caused E"; and so perhaps also that it can be of at most one thing that we can truly say "It killed P". But this seems to me a mistake. Mostly one would not *say* of more than one thing that it caused John's death, or of more than one thing that it killed John; but this is because in saying these things we are mostly responding to a request to fix responsibility, or blame. But what is expected in this or that context is certainly not all that can be truly said; and what is responsible for, or to blame for, the coming about of a certain event is not all that can truly be said to have caused it. Now I do not myself think that "kill" is definable as "cause to die", and will return to the proposal that it is later. I merely draw attention here to the fact that anyone who does think that "kill" is definable as "cause to die" must agree with me on the truth-value of (4'), (5), and (6).

Perhaps at this point there will be a retreat to a weaker claim, viz., that while these things may be true of what is not an animate being, they are not true of such a thing in the same sense of the word "kill" as that in which they are true of animate beings. According to this weaker claim, we can truly say of what is an event that it killed, but not in the straightforward, literal, ordinary sense in which we can truly say of a man that he killed. Now I see no good reason to think that even this weaker claim is true. But it should be noted that even if it is true we could still have it that (4) is equivalent to (4'): we need only add that "killed" in (4) is to be taken in the sense appropriate to animate beings, and that "killed" in (4') is to be taken in the sense appropriate to inanimate objects.

If I am right in thinking we can safely say that (4) is equivalent to (4'), then anyone who wishes to have it that (4) entails (1) and (3) by the rules of first-order logic can have that it does without committing himself to (4)'s saying, among other things, that something has the 'method-relation' to something. How?

If (4') predicates of a shooting exactly what (1) predicates of Sirhan, there is as much reason to take (4') to entail

(4.2)   ($\exists z$) [Kills$_3$ (z, Kennedy, a shooting of Kennedy by Sirhan)]

as there was to take (1) to entail

(1.1)   ($\exists x$) [Kills$_3$ (x, Kennedy, Sirhan)]

A shooting of Kennedy by Sirhan is just an event y such that
        Shoots$_3$ (y, Kennedy, Sirhan);
so we can take (4.2), and therefore (4') itself, to entail

(4.3)   ($\exists y$) $\exists z$) [Shoots$_3$ (y, Kennedy, Sirhan) & Kills$_3$ (z, Kennedy, y)].

(4.3) entails

(3.1)   ($\exists x$) [Shoots$_3$ (x, Kennedy, Sirhan)],

so, so far so good: since (3) is rewritable as (3.1), (4') entails (3) within first-order logic. Now let us suppose that (4') is equivalent to (4). Then since, as I am supposing, (4) entails (1), (4') must also entail (1). We can have that (4') entails (1)—and indeed have that it entails (1) within first-order logic—if we take (4') to be rewritable, not as (4.3) itself, but rather as

(4.4)   ($\exists x$) ($\exists y$) ($\exists z$) [Kills$_3$ (x, Kennedy, Sirhan) & Shoots$_3$ (y, Kennedy, Sirhan) & Kills$_3$ (z, Kennedy, y)],

which entails (1.1) as well as (3.1). And if we wish to have that (4) entails both (1) and (3) within first-order logic, we need only take it that (4) too is rewritable as (4.4).

Of course, if "kill" is ambiguous, and cannot be predicated of an event in the same sense in which it can be predicated of a man, then (4')—and (4) too—had better be rewritten, not as (4.4), but rather as

(4.4')   ($\exists x$) ($\exists y$) ($\exists z$) [Kills$_3$ (x, Kennedy, Sirhan) & Shoots$_3$ (y, Kennedy, Sirhan) & Kills$_3$' (z, Kennedy, y)],

in which the superscript marks that it is the sense of "kill" appropriate to inanimate objects which is to be assigned to the predicate in the third clause. All the same, so rewritten, (4) entails (1) and (3) within first-order logic.

As I said earlier, I am not going to try to give an account of 'the logic of action sentences'. But as I also said, it seems to me that if there are acts, then it does no harm to rewrite (1) as (1.1) and (3) as (3.1). I suggest here that if there are acts, then it does no harm also to

Method (I)

rewrite (4) as (4.4) or (4.4'). As (4.4), in fact, since it seems to me that "kill" is not ambiguous in the manner indicated. But what should be said about 'the logic of action sentences' in general is another thing, and I shall have nothing to say about it.

Indeed, what should be said about method in general is another thing too. I said that there was a general thesis lurking in here; we shall be trying to extract it in Chapters XIV and XVII below.

Meanwhile, however, we ought to take a closer look at one possible source of dissatisfaction with what I have been saying about what (4) says. There is something behind the inclination to say that no inanimate object can really kill a man, or at least that no inanimate object can kill a man in the sense in which a man can kill a man. I do not for a moment say that what lies behind this inclination is good reason to think that inanimate objects do not kill, or that inanimate objects do not kill in the sense in which a man can kill. But I do think we should see what it is.

II

Agency: The Verbs "Do" and "Perform"

What I have in mind is the thought that a man's killing of a man is an 'exercise of agency', whereas an inanimate object's killing of a man is not. What is an 'exercise of agency'? A 'thing done', an event with an 'agent'. A man (it is said) may be 'agent of' a killing; an inanimate object—an event, bullet, or wound—may perhaps kill a man, but is not agent of any killing.

Moreover, it is thought that we can single the acts out from all other events in this way: acts are those events that have agents—all other events are 'mere happenings'. Thus it is thought we should say:

(D$_{2a}$)   Act (y) just in case y is an event and there is an x such that Agent (x, y).

But it is not at all plain just what it is for something to be agent of an event. It is plain enough that only animate beings are to be agents of events, but what else is required? *You*, after all, are animate, and are surely not agent of the event that was Sirhan's killing of Kennedy. Why not?

It used to be thought that agency could be explained by use of the verb "do". For isn't the answer to the question I just asked that you did not *do* Sirhan's killing of Kennedy? If acts are 'things done', then the agent of an event is surely the thing that *does* it. What this suggests is that we should say:

(D₃ₐ)   Agent (x, y) just in case x does y.

But on the one hand, (D₃ₐ) seems not to rule out that *in*animate things are agents of events. For surely hurricanes do things. Surely events, bullets, and wounds do things. We should have to add the requirement ". . . and x is an animate being" to (D₃ₐ) if these are to be ruled out as not agents of events.

And on the other hand, suppose a man falls asleep. His falling asleep is presumably an event, but not an act of his—it should presumably turn out not to be a 'thing done', but rather a thing that 'merely happens'; so he should turn out not to be its agent. By contrast, Sirhan (not you) should turn out to be agent of Sirhan's killing of Kennedy. So it should turn out that

    John did his falling asleep

is false, whereas

    Sirhan did his killing of Kennedy

is true. In fact, however, both look equally awful—what on earth is one to make of either of them?

Though I think no one any longer hopes to define agency by appeal to the verb "do", it still is used in peculiar ways in writings on action. I think it will pay us to look more closely at it. We shall see not only where writers on action go wrong with it, but also why it reappears, again and again, in just the very constructions in which (as it seems to me) it cannot appear.

1. Let us begin with this: though it does not seem to be acceptable English to say

(1)   Sirhan did Sirhan's killing of Kennedy,

there *are* perfectly good pieces of English of the form "x does y" in which a name replaces "x" and a singular referring expression replaces "y". Consider, for example,

(2)   John did my dining room floor.

Or again,

    Tom did the house,
    Mary did her face,
    Dick did the play.

"Do" in these sentences seems to be in *some* sense a dummy verb, a 'stand-in' for some more specific verb or verb-phrase. Thus if you

know I have hired a team to wax my floors, and want to know which man waxed which floor, my reply *may* begin
(3)   John waxed my dining room floor, . . . ;
or, since I know that you know that waxing is in question, and that all you want to know is who waxed what, my reply *may* instead begin with (2). In the latter case I use "did" because there is no need to use the more informative "waxed".

Again, if you ask me who built (designed, painted, put the shutters on) my house, I may reply that Tom built (designed, painted, put the shutters on) my house; but I may reply, simply, "Tom did the house". If you ask how quickly Mary made her face up this morning, I may reply, simply, "She did her face in three minutes flat." Someone might ask "Who did the play?" and it be perfectly plain all round that what he wants to know is who wrote (staged, directed, designed the costumes for) it; and we may reply "Dick did the play", and it be perfectly plain all round that what we mean is that Dick wrote (staged, directed, designed the costumes for) it.

What *we* mean; not what the words mean. Plainly (2) does not mean the same as (3); plainly "Dick did the play" does not mean the same as "Dick wrote the play"—else we could not reply "Dick did the play" when what we have been asked is who designed the costumes for it.

But in what sense precisely is the "do" in (2) a stand-in?

Perhaps the simplest way of accounting for the facts pointed to so far is to say that (2) is elliptical, on one occasion for
(4)   John did wax my dining room floor,
which is equivalent to (3), on another occasion, perhaps, for
        John did refinish my dining room floor,
or for
        John did wash my dining room floor,
or for some other sentence of the form "John did verb my dining room floor"; and thus that knowing what *I* mean when I say (2) on some occasion is knowing what (2) is elliptical for on that occasion. Since on this view (2) is arrived at by deletion of the verb following "did" in some such sentence, and since "did" in such a sentence is an auxiliary—its role being merely this: by writing "did" before a verb one constructs a past tense of that verb—the "did" in (2) is itself just that auxiliary.

But this idea becomes implausible when we notice that it would

Agency: "Do" and "Perform"

commit us to a curious asymmetry. For consider sentences of the form "John will verb my dining room floor"—e.g.,

(5)   John will wax my dining room floor,

John will refinish my dining room floor,

and

John will wash my dining room floor.

Sentences of this form differ from sentences of the form "John did verb my dining room floor" only in tense; and the "will" in them is also an auxiliary—its role in such a sentence being merely this: by writing "will" before a verb one constructs a future tense of that verb. Now suppose that (2) is the result of deleting "wax" from (4), so that the verb in (2) is the auxiliary "did"; why is it that there is no sentence which is the result of deleting "wax" from (5), and whose verb is the auxiliary "will"? For there is no such sentence as

(6)   John will my dining room floor:

(6) is not a sentence. [1]

Notice, moreover, that just as there is in English, not merely the sentence (3), but also the sentence (4), so also is there in English, not merely the sentence (2), but also the sentence

(7)   John did do my dining room floor.

And while (6) is not a sentence of English,

(8)   John will do my dining room floor

plainly is. Now *neither* (7) *nor* (8) is at all plausibly construable as elliptical, on any occasion of utterance, for some such sentences as

John did do wax my dining room floor,

or

John will do wax my dining room floor:

these strings of words are not sentences.

But aren't the "did" of (2) and the "did do" of (7) just two past tenses of the verb "do"?—as "waxed" and "did wax" are two past tenses of "wax", and "refinished" and "did refinish" are two past tenses of "refinish", and "washed" and "did wash" are two past tenses of "wash", and so on. If we so take it, and I think it eminently plausible to do so, then the "did" in (2) is *not* an auxiliary; and (2) is no more the result of deleting "wax" than (7) is. Or than (8) is.

If we take the "did" in (2) as a past tense of the verb "do", we can in

---

[1] Janet Dean Fodor drew my attention to the fact that construing (2) as elliptical commits one to this asymmetry. I am indebted to her, and to James Thomson and Scott Soames, throughout these remarks on "do".

27

fact explain why there is no such sentence as (6): "will" is never a future tense of "do". What I mean is this: while "did" sometimes functions as an auxiliary, it sometimes functions as a past tense of "do": hence (2) is possible as well as (7). By contrast, "will" never functions as a future tense of "do": hence only (8) is possible, (6) is not.

So I think that we had better not take (2) to be elliptical, and that we had better find an account of the role of "did" in (2) which makes it, not an auxiliary, but—like the "did do" of (7)—a past tense of the verb "do". The account must, of course, be such as to allow of a symmetrical account of the "will do" of (8).

What I think we should do is to take the term "stand-in" seriously: that we should take the "do" in these sentences to be a pro-form, a 'pro-verb', as we might call it. That is, that we should say that

(2)   John did my dining room floor

is related to

(3)   John waxed my dining room floor

as

        He waxed my dining room floor

is related to (3); and that

(7)   John did do my dining room floor

is related to

(4)   John did wax my dining room floor

as

        He did wax my dining room floor

is related to it; and that

(8)   John will do my dining room floor

is related to

(5)   John will wax my dining room floor

as

        He will wax my dining room floor

is related to it. That is, that just as the pronoun "he" may be used instead of the name "John" where everyone knows it is John who is being talked about, so may the verb "do" (a past, future, or present tense of it, whichever is relevant) be used as a pro-verb instead of the verb "wax" where everyone knows it is waxing that is being talked about.

It has often enough been suggested that the verb "do" sometimes functions as a pro-verb; but I think that the reasons most commonly given are not good ones. It is said, for example, that the verb "do" in

Agency: "Do" and "Perform"

(9)   Alfred waxed my dining room floor, and Bert did too

is a pro-verb: that "did" in (9) is a past tense of "do", and stands in for "waxed my dining room floor". It should be noticed, however, that it is open to us to say that the "did" in (9) is not a past tense of "do", but that it is an auxiliary, i.e., that (9) is elliptical for

> Alfred waxed my dining room floor, and Bert did wax my dining room floor too,

and the result of deleting "wax my dining room floor" from it. At any rate, we are not committed to the asymmetry I mentioned earlier if we do say this, for

(10)   Alfred will wax my dining room floor, and Bert will too

is a perfectly respectable sentence of English, and can equally well be seen as elliptical for

> Alfred will wax my dining room floor, and Bert will wax my dining room floor too.

[Compare "Alfred is eating, and Bert is too". On anyone's view this is elliptical: surely the verb "be" *never* functions as a pro-verb.]

Moreover, if we say that (9) is *not* elliptical—if we say that the "did" in it is not an auxiliary, but is, rather, a past tense of "do"—then what shall we say of the second token of "will" in (10)? Shall we say that it too is not an auxiliary, but is, rather, a future tense of "do"? If we do, we shall have to say that while "did" has both transitive and intransitive past tense occurrences, since (2) and (9) are both sentences of English, "will" has only intransitive future tense occurrences, since while (10) is a sentence, (6) is not.

It does not really matter for our purposes what is said of the role of "do" in (9) and (10). Careful readers will see that I have already committed myself to taking the second token of "will" in (10) to be an auxiliary rather than a future tense of "do" [and thus to taking (10) to be elliptical], for I said earlier that "will" is never a future tense of "do". And if the second token of "will" is an auxiliary in (10), it seems right to take the "did" in (9) also to be an auxiliary [and thus to take (9) also to be elliptical]. Indeed, I shall assume this throughout the following. But in fact nothing theoretically important will turn on our making this assumption. And in any case, what matters for our purposes now is only the role of the verb "do" in sentences of the form "x does y". (2) is a sentence of this form; and (as I said) I suggest we should take the "did" in it not to be an auxiliary, but rather to be a past tense of "do" functioning as a pro-verb.

Acts and Other Events

"He" may stand in only for a referring expression that refers to a male; and there are also limits on the use of "do" as a pro-verb. It is not at all clear precisely what those limits are. I suppose that "do" cannot stand in for a 'state' verb,[2] such as "know", "love", and "admire". For notice that while if I am asked "Who waxed your dining room floor?" I can reply

(2)   John did my dining room floor,

"did" standing in for "waxed", if I am asked "Who knew the name of the sixteenth President?" I cannot reply

John did the name of the sixteenth President,

"did" standing in for "knew". (It is not, of course, that this cannot *ever* be said. If I am asked "Who embroidered the names of the presidents on your pillow?" I may say "Well, Jim did the name of the first president, Tom the name of the second, . . ." In that case, however, "did" stands in for "embroidered".)

But beyond this, things become murky. I think there are further limits. Mary comes home and finds somebody ate the baked apple she had made and was saving to eat later. She investigates, and we then ask her "Have you found out who ate your apple?" She cannot, I think, reply

Yes: John did my apple,

"did" standing in for "ate".

This is not, I think, because "do" can never stand in for "eat". I think it can, though we have to stretch a bit for an example. Imagine that the government pays a team of people to be Testers. You and I are apple-growers; we have been trying new insecticides, and the rule is this: we are each to give an apple to a Tester, who is to eat it, and then if he does not die within six months, we may go to market. I later ask you "Who ate your apple?" "Tom," you reply. "Ah," I say, "John did mine". It is arguable of course that "did" in what I said stood in for "tested" rather than for "ate"; but it is not obvious that we have to agree.

This seems to suggest that "do" can stand in for a verb only when if you asserted the original sentence (in which the verb itself, and not a stand-in for it, appears) you would be reporting on the doing of some job. If asked "Who killed Kennedy?" one presumably would not reply

<hr/>

[2] See Zeno Vendler, "Verbs and Times," *Linguistics in Philosophy* (Ithaca, N.Y.: Cornell University Press, 1967).

Agency: "Do" and "Perform"

"Sirhan did Kennedy".[3] But if Sirhan had been part of an assassination team, and the team's head has been on vacation, so that he does not know which member of the team killed which public figure, he might ask on his return "Who did Kennedy? Who was assigned to do Wallace, and failed? . . ." And the man who was acting head in his absence might reply "Sirhan did Kennedy, and Bremer was assigned to do Wallace. . . ."

"Job" is presumably too strong: it might well not be Mary's *job* to make up her face in the morning, and yet we might report that she made it up, and quickly at that, in the words "Mary did her face in three minutes flat this morning". But I think it is only if we see making up her face as a task she carries out that we do. Eating an apple, by contrast, is normally neither a job nor a task.

In any case, and whatever precisely may set these limits, if it is right to take the "do" in (2), (7), and (8) as a pro-verb, it plainly does not stand for a relation. It stands in for some verb that stands for a relation, just as "he" may stand in for some name that stands for a person. But there is no one relation that it stands for, just as there is no one man that "he" stands for.

And then if the "do" of (D_{3a}) is the pro-verb "do" of (2), (7), and (8), then there is no one relation that it stands for, and so no relation that (D_{3a}) defines.

Interestingly enough, if it is right to take the "do" in (2), (7), and (8) as a pro-verb, we can see why something I said earlier was wrong.

On page 25 above, I drew attention to a number of sentences constructed by replacing "x" and "y" in "x does y" by, respectively, a name and a referring expression. The referring expressions I chose were chosen in order to bring out (i) that one can 'do a physical object' (a floor, a face) where 'doing the object' is doing a job (waxing the floor), or merely carrying out some task (making up the face); (ii) that one can 'do a physical object' that pre-exists one's 'doing of it' (the floor, the face), or such that 'doing it' consists in bringing it into existence (the house—the "did" in "Tom did the house" might stand in for "built"); and (iii) that one can 'do' something that is not a physical object at all (the play). We should notice now that one can also 'do' an event. I suppose that Princess Anne's wedding was an event. And the

---

[3] Though note the slang "Sirhan did Kennedy in". Cf. also "John did me out of forty dollars."

31

reporter from *Variety* might ask "Who did the wedding?" wanting to know who staged it; the reporter from *Women's Wear Daily* might ask "Who did the wedding?" wanting to know who designed the clothes for it; the reporter from *TV Guide* might ask "Who did the wedding?" wanting to know who covered it for NBC. And the correct reply might be

John did the wedding,

where "did" stands in for, respectively, "staged", "designed the clothes for", and "covered . . . for NBC".

Once we notice this, however, it becomes plain that

(1)   Sirhan did Sirhan's killing of Kennedy

is *not* after all unacceptable English. Let us imagine that Sirhan was a reporter for the *Daily Assassinator*. Being the best, he was sent out to cover all the major assassinations. So, for example, Sirhan did (i.e., covered) Oswald's killing of J. F. Kennedy; and indeed he did (i.e., covered) his own killing of R. F. Kennedy—there being no better reporter, he was assigned to do (i.e., cover) his own killing of R. F. Kennedy the moment the managing editor learned of his plan. Nothing in this, I take it, is unacceptable English.

So there do, after all, seem to be pieces of English that result from replacing "*x*" by a name and "*y*" by an expression that refers to an event in "*x* does *y*". But I suggest—it seems to be a very plausible hypothesis—that the verb "do" in *every* such sentence is the pro-verb "do" of (2), (7), and (8).

Consider what seems a possible countercase. No doubt there is *a* reading of

(11)   John did his shopping

in which "do" is a pro-verb: John, a celebrity, whose public appearances are newsworthy, might have been so short of funds as to have been willing to cover for a newspaper the event that consisted in his shopping; and after the fact, the managing editor might say (11) to the editor-in-chief, meaning to say that John did do what he was willing to do. But there is available a second reading of (11), a reading under which the "do" in it is not functioning as a pro-verb. What I have in mind is a reading under which it does not require for its truth that John did anything to or with or on or in respect of an event that consisted in his shopping. What I have in mind is a reading of (11) under which it requires for its truth only that John had some shopping to do, and he did it. Now it could be argued that the "do" in (11), when (11) is read in this second way—as also the "do" in the sentence which immediately precedes this one—is *not* a pro-verb, and that it stands for a particular relation. Perhaps, indeed, that 'agent-relation' which (D_{3a}) purported to define.

But does "his shopping" in (11) refer to an *event* when (11) is read in the second way? Suppose you say (11), and it is plain to me your words are to be taken in this second way. But suppose I think that, taken in this second way, they are false: No, I say, you're mistaken,

(12)   *Mary* did John's shopping.

Is there an entity such that you said John did it, and I said Mary did it? If so, it presumably is not an event that consists in John's shopping. (Indeed, if *I* am right, there may have been no event that consisted in John's shopping at the time we speak of.) It presumably is not an event at all. If there is an entity such that you said John did it, and I said Mary did it, it presumably is a job or task, which John had to carry out, but which Mary might have carried out for him. So the possibility of a second reading of (11)—and of course of (12) as well—is no countercase to the hypothesis I said seemed very plausible.

It now appears, however, that what I said earlier was doubly wrong. It came out that

(1)   Sirhan did Sirhan's killing of Kennedy

is not after all unacceptable English: there is a reading of it under which the "do" in it is a pro-verb, which might on a given occasion stand in for "covered for a newspaper". But it now comes out that there is a second possible reading for it, a reading under which it does not require for its truth that Sirhan did anything to or with or on or in respect of the event that consisted in his killing of Kennedy. What this second reading is comes out best I think, if we look first at

(13)   Sirhan did Bremer's killing of Wallace.

There is a reading of (13) under which the "do" in it is a pro-verb. But there is a second reading of it available. Suppose that Sirhan and Bremer had been members of an assassination team; and suppose also that Bremer had been assigned the job of killing Wallace. Now in fact he failed; he did not kill Wallace. Sirhan, on his release from jail, might then volunteer to do Bremer's job for him, i.e., kill Wallace for Bremer. And let us suppose he does. We might then report on the matter, after the fact, by saying (13); and under the second reading of it, what we say would be true. If, under this second reading of (13), "Bremer's killing of Wallace" stands for something, it stands for a job or task, not an event; and (13) says that Sirhan has to it the very same relation that (11) says John, and (12) says Mary, have to the job or task that "John's shopping" stands for.

And (1) can presumably be read in this way too. Sirhan might say to the head of the team: "Certainly I did my killing of Kennedy—I can be counted on, when given a job I do it!" But so read, "Sirhan's killing of Kennedy" does not refer to an event: if it refers to anything at all, it refers to a job or task.

Now I suppose it is arguable that under the second reading of (11), (12), (13), and (1), the "do" in them stands for a particular relation, viz., the relation of 'carrying out' that a man has to a job or task he carries out. But we cannot take the "do" of (D_{3a}) to stand for that relation—if we wish to define "act" as in (D_{2a}). For there is no *event* to which you can have the relation of 'carrying out' that you have to the jobs and tasks you have carried out. So if the "do" in (D_{3a}) stands for that relation, it follows, by (D_{2a}), that there are no acts at all.

I suspect, in fact, that those who have concerned themselves with the notion have intended that it should be of events, and only of events, that an animate being is agent. (*Not* floors or faces, jobs or tasks.) Perhaps, in order to secure this, (D_{3a}) had best be replaced by

(D_{3b}) Agent (x, y) just in case y is an event and x does y.

But—if I am right—(D_{3b}) defines no relation at all. For, as I said above, it seems to me a very plausible hypothesis that the "do" in every sentence that results from replacing "x" by a name, and "y" by an expression that refers to an *event*, in "x does y", is the pro-verb "do" of (2), (7), and (8).[4] And while a pro-verb may stand in for a verb that stands for a relation, there is no one relation that it stands for.

---

[4] John Robert Ross argues on purely linguistic grounds that "every verb of action is embedded in the object complement of a two-place predicate whose subject is identical to the subject of the action verb, and whose phonological realization in English is *do*" ["Act," in *Semantics of Natural Language*, ed. Donald Davidson and Gilbert Harman (Dordrecht, Holland: D. Reidel, 1972), p. 70]. I am not competent to assess the evidence he presents for this conclusion. I am not even sure I understand the conclusion. Thus I take it he wishes to say that underlying such a sentence as, for example, "Sirhan killed Kennedy" is a structure indicated by "Sirhan did Sirhan killed Kennedy"; but I do not know if he would say this implies that there is an English sentence, viz., "Sirhan did Sirhan's killing of Kennedy," which can be read in such a way that "Sirhan's killing of Kennedy" refers to an event, and "did" is a two-place predicate that is not a 'propredicate'. That "Sirhan did Sirhan's killing of Kennedy" *cannot* be read in this way is what I suggest in the text above. There will be more to say about the verb "do" in Chapter VIII.

Agency: "Do" and "Perform"

If I am right, it should be no wonder at all, then, that it turned out to be impossible to define agency by appeal to the verb "do".

2. The verb "perform" appears just about as often in writings on action as the verb "do" does. Acts are said to be things done (as opposed to things that merely happen), not things performed; but we are, I think, at least as often said to *perform* our acts as to do them. And we might as well have been offered

(D_{3c})   Agent (x, y) just in case x performs y

as (D_{3a}).

Presumably hurricanes, events, bullets, and wounds do not *perform* things, so (D_{3c}) is not open to attack from that side. But what about the other side? John's falling asleep, I said, is presumably an event, but not an act of John's; so he should turn out not to be its agent. By contrast, Sirhan should turn out to be agent of his killing of Kennedy. So it should turn out that

John performed his falling asleep

is false, whereas

Sirhan performed his killing of Kennedy

is true. But both are really equally awful.

"Perform" is very different from "do": it has far fewer uses than "do", and is nowhere, ever, to be read as a pro-verb.

What can one perform? Well, symphonies, operas, plays, and ballets; also operations, miracles, and marriage ceremonies. (It is perhaps just worth noticing that while the theater company performs *Hamlet* the play, its star does not perform Hamlet the character: the star *plays* Hamlet.) But can one perform an *event?*

One doctor may ask another, "Who performed the operation in Operating Room 14 this morning?" Is the operation they are talking about an *event?* If "the operation" refers to something that was also being performed at the same time in an operating room in another hospital, if it refers to something that will be performed in Operating Room 14 again tomorrow morning, then it presumably does not refer to an event. (Consider: "Jones has by now performed the heart transplant operation five times.") But it seems to me unclear. Perhaps the words "the operation" in the question do refer to an event. "It was quite a performance," the first doctor may say, "the tidiest performance of the heart transplant I've ever seen." So perhaps there are events that are performed.

Acts and Other Events

"Who performed the wedding in the chapel this morning?" Is it an *event* they are talking about? I suppose it might be.

I am inclined to think that an event is performed only if (but perhaps not also if) the event is itself a performance, thus a performance *of* something. Which are the things such that an event can be a performance *of* one or another of them? Beethoven's Ninth Symphony is one. The heart transplant operation is another. The Episcopalian wedding ceremony is another. I think that this much is clear about these things: while an event can be a performance of one or another of them, none of them is itself an event.

In any case, while it *may* be that some events are performed—viz., those that are performances *of* something—there certainly are others that are not; and among those are a great many events that we should wish to have turn out to be acts. My typing the preceding sentence just now: that was not a performance of anything, and I surely did not perform it. Also your putting on your left shoe this morning. Also, I should think, Sirhan's killing of Kennedy.

3. If the meaning of "perform" is such that we are able to say of at most a limited class of acts that so-and-so performed one of them; if "do" must be read as a pro-verb in any sentence of the form "*x* does *y*" in which the expression that replaces "*y*" refers to an event; *why* is it again and again said that acts are 'things done', and that a man performs his acts?

I am inclined to think that it is largely because "do" and "perform" accept so many adverbial modifiers.

The way people talk nowadays is this. We are confronted with a sentence containing an adverbial modifier, e.g.,

> Sirhan killed Kennedy with a gun

or

> Sirhan killed Kennedy by shooting him.

Davidson's procedure for explaining the entailment-relations among 'action-sentences' is so ingenious and powerful that we straightway turn the adverbial modifiers into event-predicates—e.g., "With (x, y)" and "Method (x, y)". And then we explain the meaning of these new predicates by attaching the adverbial modifier, not to the verb in the sentence we started with, but rather to a dummy verb. Thus we say

> With (x, y) just in case x is performed with y

Agency: "Do" and "Perform"

and
>Method (x, y) just in case y is performed by performing x,

as I did in Chapter I, or
>With (x, y) just in case x is done with y

and
>Method (x, y) just in case y is done by doing x.

Why are "perform" and "do" the dummy verbs of choice? Well, notice that an orchestra can perform a symphony by . . . , with . . . , at . . . , on . . . , before . . . , under . . . , in . . . , and so on. (It can also perform a symphony slowly and intentionally, but these modifiers are not given the same treatment.) And you can do the dishes by . . . , with . . . , at . . . , on . . . , before . . . , under . . . , in . . . , and so on. (And you can do them slowly and intentionally too.)

"Perform" and "do" unfortunately will not accept all adverbial modifiers: an orchestra presumably cannot perform a symphony *toward* anything, and you presumably cannot do the dishes *toward* anything (where "toward" is taken spatially rather than temporally). But they will accept many more of them than some other expressions often met in these writings—I have "occurred" and "took place" in mind in particular. An event can have occurred or taken place at such and such a time, and in such and such a place (and perhaps also slowly); but an event cannot have occurred or taken place with a gun, or by shooting anyone (or intentionally). Hence the appeal of "do" and "perform".

Now if you can perform an event with a knife, you can presumably perform an event; and aren't your acts just those events that you perform? If you can do an event with a knife, presumably an event may be a thing done with a knife; and aren't acts just 'things done'?

But it has to be noticed that if I did not perform my typing of the preceding sentence at all, I certainly did not perform it with a typewriter, or by depressing the keys of a typewriter. And it has to be noticed also that just as "do" is a pro-verb in every sentence of the form "x does y" in which the expression that replaces "y" refers to an event, so also is it a pro-verb in every sentence of the form "x does y with a z", or "x does y by doing z", in which the expression that replaces "y" refers to an event. We might well say that John did the wedding with a Leica, or that John did the wedding by wiring the altar with a voice-sensitive camera—"did" standing in for "photographed". But a stand-in is what "do" has to be in such sentences. So what I wrote no more defines the 'with-relation', and the 'method-relation', than (D_{3a}) and (D_{3b}) define the 'agent-relation'.

This has an obvious bearing on the suggestion looked at in the preceding chapter, viz., that

(1)   Sirhan killed Kennedy with a gun

is rewritable as

(1.1) $(\exists x)\,(\exists y)\,[\text{Kills}_3\,(x,\,\text{Kennedy},\,\text{Sirhan})\,\&\,\text{With}\,(x,\,y)\,\&\,\text{Gun}\,(y)]$.

If "With $(x,\,y)$" has to mean

        x is performed with y

then (1.1) is false, since Sirhan's killing of Kennedy was not performed at all, and a fortiori was not performed with a gun. If "With $(x,\,y)$" has to mean

        x is done with y

then the truth-value of (1.1) turns on the question what "do" stands in for. Either way, (1), which is true, is therefore certainly not rewritable as (1.1).

4. There are, I think, two further reasons why "do" in particular plays so large a role in writings on action, and why acts are so often said to be 'things done'. One of them I save for Chapter VIII; the other comes out as follows. An act is an event. But which events are acts? Well, a typing, a putting on, a killing of something is an act; also a waxing, washing, shooting, or eating of something. Now "do" can stand in for many (if not all) verbs such that we may be inclined to think that the result of replacing a third-person singular, past tense, of the verb for "verbed" in

        John verbed something

is true just in case there was an *act*, which the result of replacing the gerund of the verb for "verbing" in

        John's verbing of something

may be used to refer to. So it may be felt that "do" is simply a very general 'action-verb': not many acts are killings, but many (if not all) acts are 'doings'. Now my suspicion is that some people conclude from this that an act is a 'thing done'; and therefore that the agent of an act is the person who does it, and therefore that the verb "do" stands for the 'agent-relation'.

But this is sheer mess.

Agency: "Do" and "Perform"

If I am right, the verb "do" is *not* a very general 'action-verb'. When someone asks "Who waxed the floors?" and I reply "Well, John did the dining room floor", I am not giving a very general answer, which would be true if John had waxed *or* washed *or* shot *or* eaten *or* . . . the dining room floor. What I said was that John waxed the dining room floor, the "did" in the sentence I asserted having been a stand-in for "waxed". (Compare the fact that if someone asks "What did John wax?" and I reply "Well, he waxed the dining room floor", I am not giving a very general answer, which would be true if John *or* Jim *or* George *or* . . . waxed the dining room floor. What I said was that John waxed the dining room floor, the "he" in the sentence I asserted having been a stand-in for "John".)

Moreover, even if "do" were a very general 'action-verb', and if acts were, then, 'doings', it would certainly not follow that acts are 'things done'. Sirhan's killing of Kennedy, for example, is a killing; but it certainly does not follow from this that it is a thing killed.

And lastly, if "do" were a very general 'action-verb' it could not possibly stand for the 'agent-relation'. Suppose "do" is a very general 'action-verb'. Then

Sirhan did Sirhan's killing of Kennedy

is true if and only if Sirhan waxed *or* washed *or* shot *or* ate *or* . . . Sirhan's killing of Kennedy. But then "do" does not stand for the 'agent-relation': for it surely does not follow from the fact that a man waxes or washes or shoots or eats or . . . a thing that he is agent of it. Even if the thing is an event. I should imagine that "photograph" is an 'action-verb', so that if "do" is a very general 'action-verb',

John did Princess Anne's wedding

is true if John photographed it. But it surely does not follow from the fact (supposing it a fact) that John photographed Princess Anne's wedding that he was agent of it.

III

Agency: Causality (I)

So if acts are to be singled out from all other events by

(D_{2a})   Act (y) just in case y is an event and there is an x such that
Agent (x, y),

we must do better at saying what this 'agent-relation' is than we have
done so far.

It seems plain that

(D_{3d})   Agent (x, y) just in case x causes y

will not do: lots of inanimate things cause things, and only animate
beings are to be agents, only animate beings are to *act*. But it will not
do any better, really, to say

(D_{3e})   Agent (x, y) just in case x causes y, and x is an animate
being.

On the one hand, it lets in far too much. You might cause your falling asleep, by taking seconal; and a person's falling asleep is not supposed to be an act—it is often put forward as a paradigm of a 'mere
happening'. Indeed, you might cause the fall of a tree, by chopping at
it with an axe; yet the fall of a tree must surely not turn out to be an
act.

And on the other hand, it lets in too little. We noted above (page
19) that it is possible that a killing should have a cause. It seems possible even that a man should cause his own killing of someone. For example, you might take a drug in order to get some great new high, in

40

the course of which, and because of which, you kill someone; if you do, I suppose you cause your own killing of that person. Some people might even argue that if you decide to kill a man, and then, for that reason, kill him, your deciding to kill him causes your killing of him; and they might add that if your deciding to kill a man causes your killing of him, *you* cause your killing of him. (Just as if your shooting of a man, or your stabbing him, or your dunking him in tea, kills him, *you* kill him.) But even if it is often the case that a man who kills a person causes his own killing of the person he kills, it is often not the case. A man may kill while in an epileptic fit, or while asleep—and not only not have decided to kill, but not have caused his having that fit, or caused his falling asleep, indeed not have done anything at all that could be said to have caused his killing of his victim, and hence not have caused his killing of his victim. Yet a man must surely turn out to be agent of his killing of another; and killings are often put forward as paradigm acts.

A somewhat more subtle proposal is:

(D_{3f})   Agent (x, y) just in case y is an event, and x causes every-
           thing y causes,

or, perhaps better,

(D_{3g})   Agent (x, y) just in case y is an event, and x causes every-
           thing y causes, and x is an animate being.

By (D_{3g}), a man need not have caused his killing of another in order to be agent of it, and for it therefore to be an act: it is enough if he causes everything that his killing of that person causes. And I should imagine that everyone who kills does do this: i.e., if your killing of a man causes grief, then *you* cause grief, if your killing of a man causes a war, then *you* cause that war, and so on.

But it will not really do. Some people think it obvious that causality is transitive. Others think it obvious that causality is not transitive. My own view is that causality is transitive. I have no argument that it is (though I shall have more to say on the matter at the beginning of Chapter V), and I am merely going to assume that it is, here and throughout. If I am right to do so, then it is plain that it will not do to define agency as in (D_{3g}). For suppose you cause your falling asleep. Causality being transitive, you cause everything your falling asleep causes. It follows, by (D_{3g}), that you are agent of your falling asleep. But your falling asleep is not supposed to turn out to be an event you are agent of—*it* is not supposed to be an act.

A modification that might, then, suggest itself is this:

(D$_{3h}$)   Agent (x, y) just in case y is an event, and x causes everything y causes, and x is an animate being, and x does not cause y.

If you cause your falling asleep, then, causality being transitive, you cause everything it causes, and therefore are agent of it by (D$_{3g}$); but since you cause *it*, you are not agent of it by (D$_{3h}$).

But the further condition that was added to (D$_{3g}$) to produce (D$_{3h}$) is far too strong. As I said, you might cause your own killing of a man. And a man must surely turn out to be agent of his own killing of another, killings being paradigm acts.

Nevertheless, the relation defined in (D$_{3f}$) is a very interesting one, and we shall make good use of it, and of certain relations like it, later. Since we cannot take either (D$_{3f}$) or (D$_{3g}$) or (D$_{3h}$) to say what the 'agent-relation' is, I shall give the relation I mean a new name: I shall speak of 'event-ownership', and say

(D$_4$)   Owns (x, y) just in case y is an event, and x causes everything y causes.

We shall, as I say, come back to this later.

Meanwhile, however, it ought to be noted that I have implicitly been concerning myself with only one of the two, quite distinct, notions of 'agency' that are to be found in the literature on action. I said above that a man who kills while in an epileptic fit, or while asleep, nevertheless is agent of the event that is his killing of his victim; killings, I said, are often put forward as paradigm acts. But only by some writers. Other writers take the view that intentionality is the mark of action; on their view, a man who kills while in an epileptic fit, or while asleep, is *not* agent of the event that is his killing of his victim, and that event is *not* an act.

It is unfortunately no easier to see just how this second group of writers is to explain 'agency' than it is to see how the first group is. I suspect they may have thought it possible to do so as follows:

Agent (x, y) just in case y is an event, and x does (or: performs) y intentionally.

Well, perhaps this would not suit them: it issues in a familiar difficulty about intensionality. Suppose I drink some coffee intentionally; I suppose, then, that on this view I 'do' my drinking of some coffee intentionally, and I am therefore agent of my drinking of some coffee. But suppose that, although I do not know it, the coffee I drink is *your* coffee; I suppose, then, that on this view I do not 'do' my drinking of *your* coffee intentionally—for I do not drink your coffee intentionally. But isn't the event that is my drinking of some coffee identical with the event that is my drinking of your coffee, if the coffee I drink *is* yours? If so, we should have the result that I both am and am not agent of the one event. Of course, some of the writers I speak of may simply deny the identity-claim. Those who do not, however, may be presumed to prefer to say, instead,

> Agent (x, y) just in case y is an event, and for some z such that $z = y$, x does (or: performs) z intentionally. [1]

By this account of the matter, I *am* agent of my drinking of your coffee: for I 'do' my drinking of some coffee intentionally, and my drinking of some coffee is my drinking of your coffee.

But in any case, we can now see that neither of these will do. If I am right, "does" in "x does y intentionally", as in "x does y", must be a pro-verb if "y" is replaced by an expression that refers to an event; and if it is a pro-verb, there is trouble for these accounts of agency—John, for example, might have done (i.e., photographed) Princess Anne's wedding intentionally, and yet is surely not on any view agent of it. And as for the use of "performs" here, there are too many acts, i.e., events that we had therefore better be agents of, that are not performed at all, and *a fortiori* not performed intentionally. Consider, for example, my typing the preceding sentence, and your putting on your left shoe this morning. [We would do well to compare turning the adverbial modifier "intentionally" into the event-predicate "done (or: performed) intentionally" with turning the adverbial modifiers "with a gun" and "by shooting" into the event-predicates "done (or: performed) with a gun" and "done (or: performed) by shooting"—cf. pages 36–37 above.]

Of course they might simply drop 'agency', and go straight for acts—e.g., as follows:

(D_{2b})   Act (y) just in case y is an event, and y is intentional.

Or, to avoid that difficulty about intensionality, as follows:

(D_{2c})   Act (y) just in case y is an event, and for some z such that $z = y$, z is intentional.

But surely there is worse trouble still for this proposal. For do we really

---

[1] This seems to be the most plausible way of expressing Donald Davidson's view: see his "Agency," in *Agent, Action, and Reason*, ed. Robert Binkley, Richard Bronaugh, and Ausonio Marras (Toronto: University of Toronto Press, 1971), p. 7.

Acts and Other Events

understand what we are to do with the question whether or not some given event is intentional? Suppose I knock my copy of *Principia Ethica* off the top shelf of my bookcase; and suppose someone asks, "Was *Principia*'s fall intentional?" I suppose I am likely to say: "If you mean did I knock *Principia* off the shelf intentionally, then the answer is yes. If you mean did *Principia* fall intentionally, then the answer is no. (Books don't do anything intentionally, and so certainly don't fall intentionally.)" But consider the reply: "The words 'Was *Principia*'s fall intentional?' don't mean the same as the words 'Did you knock *Principia* off the shelf intentionally,' and they don't mean the same as the words 'Did *Principia* fall intentionally', and I mean what the words mean. What I want to know is: Was *Principia*'s fall intentional?" [Passing from the fact that "intentionally" is a quite respectable adverbial modifier to the supposition that "intentional" may be meaningfully used, by itself, as an event-predicate would be like passing from the fact that "with a gun" and "by shooting" are perfectly respectable adverbial modifiers to the supposition that they may be meaningfully used, by themselves, as event-predicates—thus that a given event might meaningfully be said to be with a gun or by shooting. And this should remaind us again of the suggestion looked at in Chapter I, viz., that

(1)   Sirhan killed Kennedy with a gun

is rewritable as

(1.1) $(\exists x)(\exists y)$ [Kills$_3$ $(x,$ Kennedy, Sirhan$)$ & With (x, y) & Gun (y)].

We saw (page 38) that if "With (x, y)" has to mean either of

x is performed with y

or

x is done with y,

then (1) is not rewritable as (1.1). It should be plain also that if "With (x, y)" has to mean

x is with y,

then (1.1) is nonsense, and (1), which is true, is therefore certainly not rewritable as (1.1). I do not go so far as to say—as I did in the case of the 'by of method'—that the 'with of equipment' is syncategorematic; I do say that in the absence of a better account of the meaning of "With (x, y)" it really does look as if (1) just is not rewritable as (1.1).]

My suspicion is that those who think intentionality is the mark of action would do best to give up the idea of defining either "act" or

Agency: Causality (I)

"agent". This need not leave them speechless: there would still be available the option of offering us a thesis-schema, viz.,

> x's verb-phrasing is an act if it is an intentional verb-phrasing,

from which any number of sufficient conditions could be constructed in an obvious way—thus, e.g.,

> My drinking of some coffee is an act if it is an intentional drinking of some coffee,
>
> My drinking of your coffee is an act if it is an intentional drinking of your coffee,
>
> Sirhan's killing of Kennedy is an act if it is an intentional killing of Kennedy,
>
> *Principia*'s falling is an act if it is an intentional falling,

and so on. My drinking of some coffee, then, turns out to be an act, since it is an intentional drinking of some coffee. My drinking of *your* coffee also turns out to be an act, for although it is not an intentional drinking of *your* coffee, it is identical (I suppose) with my drinking of some coffee, which is, by hypothesis, an intentional drinking of some coffee. Sirhan's killing of Kennedy is an act, since it is an intentional killing of Kennedy. Any event that is identical with Sirhan's killing of Kennedy is an act, since any event that is identical with Sirhan's killing of Kennedy is an intentional killing of Kennedy. And these results are as they should be. Unfortunately, while we know that *Principa*'s fall is not an intentional falling, nothing so far said—indeed, nothing further sayable along these lines—rules out that *Principa*'s fall is an act. But, at any rate, nothing so far said rules *in* that *Principia*'s fall is an act, and while it may not be glorious to not get a false result, it is not nothing either.

Now, is the first group of writers right to say that a man who kills in an epileptic fit, or while asleep, is agent of the event that is his killing of his victim? Is the first group right to say that such a killing is an act? Or is the second group of writers right to say that a man who kills in an epileptic fit, or while asleep, is not agent of the event that is his killing of his victim, and that such a killing is not an act—since such a man does nothing at all intentionally?[2] It seems to me that neither is right and neither is wrong and that there simply are two quite distinct

[2] It is of interest to notice that while Davidson—in "Agency"—is plainly in the second group, his commentator in the same book, James Cornman, appears to be in the first group.

notions of 'agency' at work here. Which is not to say there are not very many cases that fall under both—Sirhan is presumably agent of his killing of Kennedy and his killing of Kennedy an act, whichever notion of 'agency' is in question, and a book is presumably not agent of its falling and its falling not an act, whichever notion of 'agency' is in question.

The question what it is for a coffee-drinking or a killing to be an intentional coffee-drinking or an intentional killing does seem to me an interesting and important one, and we shall return to it in the concluding chapter. So anyone who wishes to opt for the second of the two notions of 'agency' will find it has not been wholly neglected.

But I think the first notion is at least as interesting—the intuition it issues from seems right. It really does seem as if a man's killing of a man—whether in an epileptic fit, or while asleep, on the one hand, *or* fully intentionally, on the other hand—is a very different sort of event from a man's falling asleep, and from the fall of a book or a tree. There really does seem to be *some* sense in which a man who kills another is plausibly said to be agent of an event, whereas a man who merely falls asleep is not; and *some* sense in which a killing is plausibly said to be an act and a falling asleep is not. It is worth trying to see if we can find such senses.

I suggest that we shall want to appeal to causality to make them out, and that the best way to begin is with this:

(D_{3i})   Agent (x, y) just in case y is a causing of something by x.

But in order to show that this is so much as *a* way of beginning, we need to see what is the difference between (D_{3i}) and

(D_{3d})   Agent (x, y) just in case x causes y:

i.e., we need to see what is the difference between x's causing of y and y's being a causing of something by x. And in order to do this, we need to see what it is for one event to be part of another.

IV

On Some Parts
of Some Events

There is yet another reason why we need to see what it is for one event to be part of another.

We took note in Chapter I of the inclination to think that for Sirhan to have killed Kennedy by shooting him was for Sirhan's shooting of Kennedy to have *been* Sirhan's killing of Kennedy. After all, once Sirhan had shot Kennedy, he needed to do nothing more in order to kill Kennedy; the shooting itself was enough; after the shooting, Sirhan himself could have done anything or nothing, he could have stood on his head, or died, and all the same, the killing would have occurred. As we saw on page 19 however, it is not possible to take "Method (x, y)" to mean "x and y are events, and x is identical with y" if

(1)   Sirhan killed Kennedy by shooting him

is to be rewritable as

(1.1) $(\exists x)$ $(\exists y)$ [Shoots$_3$ $(x,$ Kennedy, Sirhan) & Kills$_3$ $(y,$ Kennedy, Sirhan) & Method (x, y)].

We cannot, that is, take (1) to say that Sirhan's shooting of Kennedy was Sirhan's killing of Kennedy. But—in light of the considerations I just mentioned—perhaps *we* should say that Sirhan's shooting of Kennedy was Sirhan's killing of Kennedy.

There are some, by now very familiar, objections to identifying

Acts and Other Events

Sirhan's shooting of Kennedy with his killing of Kennedy. There are, first, those that issue from temporal considerations.[1] Suppose that Sirhan shot Kennedy at T. I have marked T in the following diagram as a rectangle rather than a point, making T a time-stretch rather than a time-point, for shooting someone *takes* time. And let us also suppose that Kennedy's death occurred at T'. Some people might argue that the time of Kennedy's death was also a time-stretch; others might say that death is the termination of a process and that it happened at an instant. It does not matter for present purposes, and I shall mark it on the diagram with a small dot.

T	T'
Sirhan's shooting of Kennedy	Kennedy's death

Now by hypothesis,

(2)   Sirhan's shooting of Kennedy occurred at T

is true. So if

(3)   Sirhan's shooting of Kennedy is Sirhan's killing of Kennedy

is also to be true,

(4)   Sirhan's killing of Kennedy occurred at T

must be true also. But surely Sirhan's killing of Kennedy *did not* occur at T. Suppose that T' was n hours after T. Surely it would be simply false to say that Kennedy's death occurred n hours after Sirhan's killing of Kennedy occurred.

Suppose a man is shot, fatally, in January. Suppose then, not knowing that the wound is fatal, he goes south, to Miami, in hope of recuperating. And suppose this does him no good: he dies in June. So he was not merely shot, he was killed. It could hardly be said that after the killing occurred in January, he went south, to Miami, in hope of recuperating, but alas died in June.

Second, there are those objections which issue from considerations of causality. Suppose that it went like this: Sirhan's shooting of Kennedy caused the onset of a hemorrhage, which caused Kennedy's death. Then by hypothesis

(5)   Sirhan's shooting of Kennedy caused the onset of that hemorrhage

[1] For a survey of them, see Judith Jarvis Thomson, "The Time of a Killing," *The Journal of Philosophy*, 68 (1971), 115–132.

On Some Parts of Some Events

is true. So if (3) is to be true,

(6)   Sirhan's killing of Kennedy caused the onset of that hemorrhage

must be true also. But surely Sirhan's *killing* of Kennedy did not cause the onset of that hemorrhage.[2]

But these arguments do not seem to have settled the matter.[3] It has been granted that it would be misleading to say that Sirhan's killing of Kennedy occurred at *T*, and very odd indeed to say that Sirhan's killing of Kennedy caused the onset of the hemorrhage that caused Kennedy's death. But it has been asked what reason there is to think these things not merely misleading or odd, but false.

It is no surprise, I think, that these arguments from time and causality have not settled the matter. For if the shooting is not identical with the killing, then how *are* they related to each other? And how shall we account for the fact that the shooting itself was enough? In the absence of an alternative account of how the shooting is related to the killing, it is no surprise that people are reluctant to give up the only clear one so far in the field.

Now it seems to me that the shooting is not identical with the killing, but is part of it.

We talk sometimes as if events were atoms, little solid nuggets, without internal structure, and this is surely wrong. Consider the event that consisted in my typing the preceding sentence: it began with an event that consisted in my typing a "W", which was followed, moments later, by an event that consisted in my typing an "e", which was followed, moments later. . . . Some people have felt strongly inclined to say that Sirhan's shooting of Kennedy was his killing of Kennedy; *no one* could plausibly say that my typing a "W", or my typing an "e", was my typing the sentence—these were surely only parts of my typing the sentence. We are going to need to be able to say that one event is part of another, and therefore to be able to give an account of what it is for this to be true of a pair of events, anyway. I am inclined to think, in fact, that we do not have a theory of action at all unless we have an answer to the general question, Under what condi-

---

[2] For a similar example, put forward by way of objection to a claim similar to (3), see Alvin I. Goldman, *A Theory of Human Action* (Englewood Cliffs, N.J.: Prentice-Hall, 1970), p. 2.

[3] For ways of side-stepping at least the temporal argument, see Thomson, "Time of a Killing," section IV, and Jonathan Bennett, "Shooting, Killing and Dying," Canadian Journal of Philosophy, 2 (1973), 315–323.

tions is an event *x* part of an event *y*? Once we have the answer in hand, we shall also be able to say—what in any case I think to be independently plausible—that the shooting, though not identical with the killing, is part of it.

1. Let us look a bit more closely at a much more complicated event: my cleaning of the house last Friday. That may be carved into parts in a number of ways. We can say that it had among its parts

> my cleaning of the living room, my cleaning of the dining room, my cleaning of the kitchen, . . .

and we can *also* say that it had among its parts

> my dusting of the wood surfaces, my vacuuming of the carpets, my cleaning of the kitchen floor. . . .

Plainly the events on the second list overlap, i.e., have parts in common with, the events on the first list. Thus, for example, the event that was my dusting of the wood surfaces in the living room was part of both the event that was my cleaning of the living room and also the event that was my dusting of the wood surfaces.

In passing, we can *also* say that the house-cleaning had among its parts

> my cleaning of the living-room, my cleaning of the dining-room, my cleaning of the kitchen, my dusting of the wood surfaces, my vacuuming of the carpets, my cleaning of the kitchen floor. . . .

I here combined the two lists. That events on this list overlap one another leaves it still true that everything on the list is part of that house-cleaning.

Suppose now that on Thursday I bought a new vacuum cleaner, in preparation for Friday's house-cleaning. Presumably my buying the new vacuum cleaner was *not* part of my house-cleaning: the house-cleaning did not start until after the vacuum-cleaner-buying occurred. Certainly if I had said, at the time of buying the new vacuum cleaner, "I am now cleaning the house", I would have spoken falsely.

Suppose that on Friday night, I walked about the house, admiring its cleanliness. Presumably my walking about the house, admiring its cleanliness, was not part of my house-cleaning: the house-cleaning had already occurred before it started. Certainly if I had said, at the time of walking about the house, admiring its cleanliness, "I am now cleaning the house", I would have spoken falsely.

On Some Parts of Some Events

But obviously not every event that occurred at a time throughout which I would have spoken truly if I had said "I am now cleaning the house" was part of the house-cleaning. Lots of events occurred during that time, and they were not parts of my house-cleaning. A truck went by in the street outside while I was dusting; the truck's going by was no part of my house-cleaning. Suppose that while I was dusting I was grumbling; I should imagine that my grumbling—though it accompanied the dusting, and perhaps was even caused by it—was no part of the house-cleaning. It seems intuitively, to have played no part in my getting the house clean and therefore seems intuitively, not to have been part of it.

Are there any events that are parts of the house-cleaning that occur at times during which I would have spoken falsely if I had said "I am now cleaning the house?" The answer you will give depends on how strict a speaker you are. Suppose that the way I cleaned my kitchen floor was this: I poured all over it a certain stuff, commercially known as "Stuff", which dissolves dirt—you just pour Stuff on, and let it evaporate, after which there is nothing but a light sifting of dust to be swept up. (No scrubbing.) Now suppose also that after I poured Stuff on, and while I was waiting for it to evaporate, *you* telephoned and asked what I was doing. "I'm cleaning the house", I say. Do I speak falsely? *I* think I speak truly. But we all know people who are capable of replying: "Well, strictly speaking, you're not cleaning the house *now*; you're talking to me on the telephone now".

But whether or not I speak truly, there *is* a part of my house-cleaning that is occurring throughout the time I speak on the telephone, viz., Stuff's dissolving the dirt on my kitchen floor. On any view, the event that is Stuff's dissolving that dirt played a part in my getting the house clean—it is an event that I caused, by pouring Stuff on the floor, and caused precisely in order to bring about that the kitchen floor should be clean, and getting the kitchen floor clean is part of getting the house clean. We might put it: it was 'on my route to' a clean house. So it seems plausible to take it that the event that is Stuff's dissolving that dirt is part of my cleaning of the floor and therefore of my cleaning of the house.

My cleaning of the house is an event that is an act of mine; Stuff's dissolving that dirt is an event that is not an act of mine. So if Stuff's dissolving the dirt is part of my cleaning of the house, there are events that are acts of mine that have among their parts events that are not themselves acts of mine. But this is no ground for objection. An event may presumably have only events as parts, and an act may therefore have only events as parts, but why should we suppose that acts of mine may have only acts of mine as parts? A tin cup must be all tin; but there is no reason why it should be supposed that a tin cup may have only tin cups as parts. A typing of a sentence plainly does not have only typings of sentences as parts. And in any case, it must surely be granted, by *any* remotely plausible view of action, that a person's acts may have among their parts events that are not acts of his. Take Alfred's raising of his arm just now. All sorts of tickings and clickings went on in his cells while he did that; and at least some of them (those that went on in certain of his nerve cells, and those that went on in certain of his muscle cells) must surely be counted as parts of the act that consisted in his raising of his arm just now. But they are not themselves acts of his. So I shall suppose that acts of mine may have events that are not acts of mine as parts—and in particular, that my cleaning of the floor (and thus my cleaning of the house) has an event among its parts (viz., Stuff's dissolving the dirt) that is not itself an act of mine.

But then if you are a strict speaker, who refuses to allow that I spoke truly when I said to you on the telephone "I'm cleaning the house", you cannot take it to be a necessary condition for an event E to be part of my house-cleaning that E occur at a time throughout which I would speak truly if I said this. For Stuff's dissolving the dirt was part of it; yet it was occurring at a time when, on your view, I spoke falsely when I said this.

And a strict speaker also cannot argue that my buying a new vacuum cleaner on Thursday was not part of my house-cleaning on Friday on the ground that it would have been false to say while I was buying the vacuum cleaner "I am now cleaning the house"; and he cannot argue that my walking about the house, admiring its cleanliness, is not part of my house-cleaning on the ground that it would have been false to say while I was walking and admiring "I am now cleaning the house". For a strict speaker cannot take the truth of this to be a necessary condition for an event E to be part of my house-cleaning. But of course any speaker, however loose or strict, can certainly take the following to be a necessary condition for an event E to be part of my house-cleaning: that E not occur before my house-cleaning starts, and that my house-cleaning not occur before E starts.

On Some Parts of Some Events

This suffices to make the vacuum-cleaner-buying on the one hand, and the admiring walk on the other, not parts of my house-cleaning.

And any speaker, however loose or strict, can certainly take the following to be both necessary and sufficient for an event E to be part of my house-cleaning: that E play a part in my getting the house clean, that E be on my route to a clean house. What precisely does this come to? My own inclination is to think that it has to do with causality; in any case, I shall try to give an account of what it comes to in terms of the causal relations that E and my house-cleaning do or do not have to other events. But it is a complicated business: it will take us the next three chapters to get the matter fully spelled out.

2. Meanwhile, however, it will pay us to take a closer look at one of the parts of that house-cleaning, viz., the event that was my vacuuming of the carpets. Now the carpets in my house do not all run into one another; there is a carpet in the living room, a carpet in the hall, another in the dining room, and so on—all separated by blank spaces of floor. And in fact I do not, when I clean, do all the dusting first, then all the vacuuming, then . . . ; I clean one room at a time. So the event that was my vacuuming of the carpets had a part (viz., my vacuuming of the living room carpet) that occurred from 10:30 to 10:48, then a part (viz., my vacuuming of the hall carpet) that occurred from 11:12 to 11:29, then a part. . . . Now at 11:02 exactly, I was dusting the banisters; and not even as loose a speaker as I am would allow that it would have been true to say *then* "I am vacuuming the carpets."

And, as I think, no part of the event that was my vacuuming of the carpets was occurring at exactly 11:02, for no event that was occurring then played a part in my getting the carpets vacuumed.

My vacuuming of the carpets was a 'temporally discontinuous' event: there are times t and t' such that part of my vacuuming of the carpets was occurring at t, and part of my vacuuming of the carpets was occurring at t', and there are times t^*, between t and t', such that no part of my vacuuming of the carpets was occurring at t^*.

Was there really, then, such an event as my vacuuming of the carpets? That is, *can* there be temporally discontinuous events? I cannot imagine why not. Indeed, a good many perfectly respectable events turn out on a close look to be temporally discontinuous. Consider, for example, the event that was my typing of the preceding sentence. I paused a long time after typing "many" and before typing "perfectly": so there were times t and t' such that part of my typing of the sentence was occurring at t, and part of my typing of the sentence was occurring at t', and there was a time t^*, between t and t' (any time during my pause, in fact) such that no part of my typing of the sentence was occurring at t^*. If Sirhan paused between aiming his gun and firing it, then Sirhan's killing of Kennedy too was a temporally discontinuous event.

But we have to remember that the fact that a person pauses before going on does not itself make the event he is involved in temporally discontinuous. After pouring Stuff on the kitchen floor, I paused (and then talked for a bit on the telephone), but an event *was* occurring throughout that time that was part of my cleaning of the house: viz., Stuff's dissolving the dirt on the kitchen floor. So not just any old pause shows a temporal discontinuity.

Another example is this. I began vacuuming by pressing a button on the vacuum cleaner, which closed an electrical circuit, which started the motor, which caused air to be sucked up through the hose. We might picture this sequence of events as in the diagram below.

air's starting to be sucked up through the hose

$\uparrow$

motor's starting

$\uparrow$

electrical circuit's closing

$\uparrow$

my pressing the button

(The arrows indicate direction of causality.) Directly after this sequence of events, I started pushing the nozzle about on the carpet. But although the sequence went very quickly, there was a pause: I paused briefly between pressing the button and pushing the nozzle about. But during that pause events were occurring that were parts of my vacuuming of the carpets, viz., the electrical circuit's closing, the motor's starting, and air's starting to be sucked up through the hose. For these events certainly played a part in my getting the carpets vacuumed. So while my vacuuming of the carpets was, as I said, a temporally discontinuous event, it is not *this* pause that shows it so.

The possibility of pauses without discontinuity is, of course, due to its being the case that an act of A's may have, among its parts, events that are not themselves acts of A's. Stuff's dissolving the dirt was part of the floor-cleaning, but is not an act of mine; the electrical circuit's closing was part of my vacuuming of the carpets, but is not an act of mine.

But of course there are pauses that do mark discontinuities. During my pause in typing, nothing at all was occurring that was part of the typing of that sentence; during Sirhan's pause before firing (if he paused before firing), nothing at all was occurring that was part of his killing of Kennedy.

And there may be discontinuity without anything that would count as a pause: even if I did not pause for a single moment between 10:48 and 11:12 (in that I was dusting banisters throughout the whole of that time), that was, nevertheless, a time during which no part of my vacuuming of the carpets was occurring.

3. Suppose that I cleaned the kitchen floor last; having cleaned the kitchen floor, I had cleaned the house. I cleaned the kitchen floor, you will remember, by pouring Stuff on it. Suppose I poured the Stuff on it at T. I have marked T in the following diagram as a rectangle rather than a point, making T a time-stretch rather than a time-point, for pouring things *takes* time. And suppose also that Stuff went about its work throughout the time between T and T'—at T', the last of it evaporated. At T'', shortly after T', I swept up the dust (again a rectangle rather than a point), and thereby finished cleaning the kitchen floor, and thereby finished cleaning the house.

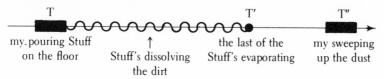

T		T'	T''
my pouring Stuff on the floor	↑ Stuff's dissolving the dirt	the last of the Stuff's evaporating	my sweeping up the dust

Stuff's dissolving the dirt was, as I said, part of my cleaning of the kitchen floor, and thus part of my cleaning of the house. So also was my sweeping up the dust which Stuff leaves behind after it evaporates, for that too played a part in my getting the kitchen floor clean. So if I am asked when my cleaning of the house occurred, any answer I give will be true only if the time-stretch I give includes not merely T, not merely T', but also T''. So, for example, if I started cleaning the house Friday morning, and T'' is 5 P.M. Friday, I would speak truly if I answered "My cleaning of the house occurred on Friday", or "My cleaning of the house occurred last week", or "My cleaning of the house occurred in early December", or "My cleaning of the house occurred in 1974", and so on; but I would speak falsely if I answered, for example, "My cleaning of the house occurred last Friday morning". For it did not: it *was occurring* on Friday morning, but since it took the whole day, it did not *occur* Friday morning.

Now consider my neighbor. She uses a newer product, Super-Stuff—Super-Stuff does not only dissolve dirt, it disintegrates it, so that nothing at all is left to be swept up. And suppose that her pouring Super-Stuff on her kitchen floor occurred at T; and suppose that Super-Stuff went about its work throughout the time between T and T'—at T', the last of it evaporated.

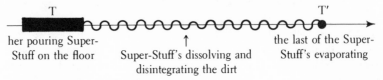

T		T'
her pouring Super-Stuff on the floor	↑ Super-Stuff's dissolving and disintegrating the dirt	the last of the Super-Stuff's evaporating

Is Super-Stuff's dissolving and disintegrating her dirt part of her cleaning of her kitchen floor, and thus part of her cleaning of her house? I should imagine that the only reason for distinguishing, for saying that while Stuff's dissolving my dirt is part of my cleaning of my kitchen, Super-Stuff's dissolving and disintegrating her dirt is *not* part of her cleaning of her kitchen, is this: Stuff leaves dust, which I have to sweep up, Super-Stuff leaves no dust, and she needs to do nothing at all. If I die after pouring out Stuff, the kitchen will not become clean (unless somebody else sweeps up the dust); if she dies after pouring out Super-Stuff, her kitchen will become clean anyway.

But it is a very poor reason for distinguishing. Stuff's dissolving my dirt is part of my cleaning of my kitchen floor since it plays a part in my getting my kitchen floor clean. Super-Stuff's dissolving and disintegrating her dirt plays a part in her getting her kitchen floor clean. Indeed, it plays a *larger* part in her getting her kitchen floor clean than Stuff's dissolving my dirt plays in my getting my kitchen floor clean—for it leaves her with nothing at all more to do, whereas Stuff's dissolving my dirt leaves me with some sweeping to do.

Plainly, anyway, just as my cleaning of my kitchen floor is not over until Stuff has dissolved my dirt *and* I have swept up the dust it leaves,

On Some Parts of Some Events

so also is her cleaning of her kitchen floor not over until Super-Stuff has dissolved and disintegrated her dirt. For a cleaning of the kitchen floor is not over until the floor is *clean*.

Strict speakers, of course, may insist that while she is standing about, waiting for the floor to be finally clean, she speaks falsely if she says "I am cleaning the kitchen floor"; but as we saw, that does not matter, for they cannot take its being true to be a necessary condition for an event occurring then to be part of her cleaning of her kitchen floor.

So if she is asked when her cleaning of the house occurred, any answer she gives will be true only if the time-stretch she gives includes, not merely T, but also T'.

4. The bearing of this on the case we began with is obvious. We are supposing that Sirhan's shooting of Kennedy caused the onset of a hemorrhage, which caused Kennedy's death. The event that was the onset of that hemorrhage surely played a part in Sirhan's getting Kennedy to be dead. It was an event Sirhan caused, by shooting Kennedy; admittedly, Sirhan might not have caused that event in order to get Kennedy to be dead—he might have had no thought at all about *how* his shooting of Kennedy should kill him—but that event caused Kennedy's death, and it was by causing that event that Sirhan got Kennedy to be dead. So it seems right to say that that event was part of Sirhan's killing of Kennedy.

No doubt there was nothing Sirhan had to do after the occurrence of that event in order, finally, to get Kennedy to be dead—just as there was nothing my neighbor had to do after the occurrence of the event that was Super-Stuff's dissolving and disintegrating the dirt on her floor in order, finally, to get her floor to be clean. But this only shows that the occurrence of the event played a very large role in Sirhan's getting Kennedy to be dead.

Would it have been true for him to say, while that event was taking place, "I am killing Kennedy"? Certainly, strict speakers would say that if Sirhan is sitting, brooding, in his cell while the onset of hemorrhage takes place, and if he then says "I am killing Kennedy", he speaks falsely—"Well, strictly speaking, he's not killing Kennedy *now*; he's sitting, brooding, in his cell". But as we saw, that does not matter, for they cannot take its being true to be a necessary condition for an event occurring then to be part of Sirhan's killing of Kennedy.

Now it seems to me as plausible as anything in this area can be, that if an event x is part an event y, y does not cause x. So if the onset of a hemorrhage was part of Sirhan's killing of Kennedy, then

> Sirhan's killing of Kennedy caused the onset of that hemorrhage

is not merely odd or misleading, but *false*. Since, by hypothesis,

> Sirhan's shooting of Kennedy caused the onset of that hemorrhage

is true, it follows that

> Sirhan's shooting of Kennedy is Sirhan's killing of Kennedy

is false too. The shooting, though part of the killing, is not identical with it.

Not only was there nothing Sirhan had to do after the occurrence of the event that was the onset of a hemorrhage in order, finally, to get Kennedy to be dead; there was nothing he had to do after the occurrence of the event that was his shooting of Kennedy in order, finally, to get Kennedy to be dead. The shooting itself was enough; after the shooting, Sirhan himself could have done anything or nothing, and all the same, his killing of Kennedy would have occurred anyway. It was this fact, as we saw, that leads people to want to identify the shooting with the killing. But it is easy enough to account for this fact *without* identifying the shooting with the killing. For Sirhan's shooting of Kennedy itself killed Kennedy. And, as we saw in Chapter I, from the fact that Sirhan's shooting of Kennedy killed Kennedy, it follows that Sirhan killed Kennedy. *That* is why shooting Kennedy was enough: whatever Sirhan may have done or not done after having shot Kennedy, if his shooting of Kennedy kills Kennedy, Sirhan kills him.

It is, then, possible that your killing of a man, or your cleaning of a kitchen floor, may still be occurring after your death. This is, of course, due to its being the case that an act of yours may have among its parts events that are not themselves acts of yours. Events that are not acts, and a fortiori not your acts, and that occur after your death, may nevertheless be parts of some act of yours. Indeed, such events *are* parts of some killing, or floor-cleaning, of yours if they play a part in your getting your victim to be dead, or your floor to be clean.

As for the time of a killing, it seems plain it should be dealt with in the same way as the time of a house-cleaning. By hypothesis,

> Sirhan's shooting of Kennedy occurred at T

is true. But

On Some Parts of Some Events

Sirhan's killing of Kennedy occurred at T

is false, for a part of the killing—viz., the event that consisted in the onset of a hemorrhage—occurred after T. No doubt the killing *was occurring* at T, for the shooting, after all, was part of the killing; but since the killing was still occurring after T, it did not *occur* at T.

When did the killing occur? Any answer we give will be true only if the time-stretch we give includes T; but I think it will be true only if it also includes all of the time between T and T'. For it is not just the event that consisted in the onset of a hemorrhage that occurred after T and yet was part of the killing: *every* event that played a part in the killing is part of the killing, and I should imagine that that includes events occurring right up to T' itself. Plainly, anyway, just as a cleaning of a kitchen floor is not over until the floor is clean, so also is a killing of a man not over until the man is dead. So while we can, truly, say that Sirhan's killing of Kennedy occurred in June 1968, and we can, truly, say that it occurred in 1968, we speak falsely—and not merely misleadingly—if we say it occurred at t, where t does not include both T and T'.

If you shoot a man, is your aiming of your gun before firing it part of your shooting of him? I think so. (It certainly seems as if your aiming your gun at your victim plays a part in your getting him shot.) Now suppose that Sirhan did pause between aiming and firing; this would mean, as we saw, that his shooting of Kennedy was a discontinuous event, for there was no part of the shooting that was occurring at any time during that pause. So if Sirhan did pause between aiming and firing, I was wrong to blacken in the whole of the time-stretch T in the diagram on page 48 above: there should have been a blank space in the middle to represent a time during which no part of the shooting was occurring. There being such a time would not make it false to say that the killing occurred at t, where t includes the whole of the time-stretch T—as we know, we can truly say that Sirhan's killing of Kennedy occurred in June 1968, and there are a great many times in June 1968 during which the killing was not occurring. Deficiency of time makes for falsity, not excess. But if anyone does want to fix on the smallest time-stretch t such that it can truly be said that the killing occurred at t, then he must subtract the times of discontinuities. I do not remember the times or dates in the case of Sirhan's killing of Kennedy, but it might be that for a given killing, the smallest t such that it could be truly said that the killing occurred at t was this: the time-stretch that includes all and only times between 10:02 A.M. and 10:08 A.M. Friday the thirteenth, and 10:11 A.M. and 11:59 P.M. Friday the thirteenth. For most ordinary purposes, however, "Friday the thirteenth" suits us well enough: for most ordinary purposes, we have no use for the smallest t such that it can truly be said that the killing occurred at t.

5. It does seem intuitively right to say that an event x is part of an event y if and only if x plays a part in y. What we must now do is to replace that locution with something more precise.

V

Parts of Events (I)

It will be necessary to make certain assumptions.

I shall assume, first,

(I)   Causality is transitive.

Is (I) true? Some people think it obviously true; others think it obviously false. My own view is that it is true. People say, "You surely
don't think that the loss of a nail could have caused the loss of a country, do you?" No doubt it does not often happen that the loss of a nail
causes the loss of a country. But it might happen that the loss of a nail
causes the loss of a shoe, which causes the loss of a rider, which
causes . . . the loss of a country. And if this did happen, I should
think it eminently right to say that the loss of the nail caused the loss
of a country *by* causing the loss of a shoe, which caused the loss of a
rider, which caused. . . . And if the loss of the nail caused the loss of
a country *by* causing the loss of . . . , then it surely follows that the
loss of the nail caused the loss of a country. (Compare the fact that
"Sirhan killed Kennedy by shooting him" entails "Sirhan killed Kennedy".)

H. L. A. Hart and A. M. Honoré say: "The cause of a fire may be
lightning, but it would be rare to cite the cause of the lightning (the
state of electric charges in the atmosphere) as the cause of the fire:
similarly the cause of the motor accident may be the icy condition of

the road, but it would be odd to cite the cold as the cause of the accident".[1] They may well be right. On the other hand, would it be *false* to say of the cause of the lightning that it was the cause of the fire? Would it be *false* to say that the cold was the cause of the accident?

Of course, if "was the cause of" meant "was the sole thing which caused", then the relation attributed to the icy condition of the road and the accident by

(1)   The icy condition of the road was the cause of the accident
would plainly be intransitive. But this is of no interest. For if "was the cause of" meant "was the sole thing which caused", "was the cause of" would not mean "caused"—since "caused" does not mean "was the sole thing which caused". (I take it to be plain enough that "caused" does not mean "was the sole thing which caused": as I said, on page 21 above, it just is not the case that we can truly say of at most one thing that it caused this or that.) So even if "was the cause of" meant "was the sole thing which caused", and the relation attributed by (1) was therefore intransitive, it would not follow that the relation attributed by

(2)   The icy condition of the road caused the accident
was intransitive.

And in any case, "was the cause of" surely does not mean "was the sole thing which caused". What "was the cause of" means seems to me a very puzzling question. That it just means "caused" seems to me a plausible idea. Zeno Vendler says it does.[2] (Hart and Honoré wobble: some passages suggest they think it does, others suggest they think it instead means "was the sole thing which caused".) If Vendler is right, then (as I said) my own view is that the relation attributed by both (1) and (2) is transitive. But it does not seem to me obvious that he is right. For this reason I avoid "was the cause of" and use only "caused": the only occurrences of "the cause" in this book are in this and the preceding two paragraphs, and in the index.

But I should stress that I do not think of myself as having produced an *argument* for the truth of (I). I hope only to have made (I) seem more plausible to those who think it false.

I take it to be obvious, and in need of no argument, that no event

[1] *Causation in the Law* (Oxford: Clarendon Press, 1959), p. 40.
[2] See his "Effects, Results, and Consequences," *Linguistics in Philosophy* (Ithaca, N.Y.: Cornell University Press, 1967).

causes itself. I take it to be just as obvious that no event causes any part of itself and that no event is caused by any part of itself. Since I shall use "part" in such a way that "Every event is part of itself" is true, we may write the conjunction of these theses as follows:

(II)   No event causes any of its parts; no event is caused by any of its parts.

A number of variables will be used in Chapters V through VII (*x*, *y*, *C*, *E*, *d*, and so on). Unless otherwise indicated, they are to be taken to range over, and only over, events. So, for example, I shall take it that we may say—(II) being true—that

(NC$_1$)   If *x* is part of *y*, then $-(y$ causes $x)$.

Assumption

(III)   *C* causes *y* if and only if *C* causes all of *y*'s parts

is probably not obviously acceptable. We are not accustomed to talk of parts of events, and have not asked ourselves what causal relations we should take the parts of an event *y* to have to the events that cause *y*. Once we do, however, it seems to me we find (III) very plausible. For how could an event *C* cause an event *y* without causing everything that *y* consists of? And if an event *C* causes everything that an event *y* consists of, surely it causes *y*. I take it, then, that we can say

(NC$_2$)   If *x* is part of *y*, then (C) $(C$ causes $y \supset C$ causes $x)$.

Assumption (III) says something about what causes an event *y*; what of what an event *y* causes? We might initially be inclined to think the matter symmetrical: i.e., that just as *C* causes *y* if and only if *C* causes all of *y*'s parts, so also *y* causes *E* if and only if all of *y*'s parts cause *E*. But only initially. Take Sirhan's shooting of Kennedy, for example. That caused Kennedy's death. Yet it had parts that did not. Sirhan's retracting of the trigger of his gun the first one-hundredth of an inch did not cause Kennedy's death; yet it was part of Sirhan's pulling of the trigger of his gun, and hence part of Sirhan's shooting of Kennedy.

Nor can we say that *y* causes *E* if and only if *some* part of *y* causes *E*. For one part of *y* might cause a further part of *y*; and if we require that *y* cause every event that any of its parts cause, we shall be committed to the possibility that *y* causes some of its own parts, which is ruled out by (II).

Suppose that *x* is part of *y*, and that *x* causes *E*. As we just saw, *y* does not cause *E* if

(i)   *E* is part of *y*.

But *y* also does not cause *E* if

(ii)   part of E is part of y:

if y causes E, then, by (III), y causes every part of E, so if part of E is part of y, y causes part of itself, which is ruled out by (II). Moreover, suppose that

(iii) E causes part of y;

here too it cannot be the case that y causes E, else, by (I), y would cause part of itself, which is ruled out by (II). And lastly, suppose that

(iv)   part of E causes part of y;

here too it cannot be the case that y causes E: for if y causes E, then, by (III), it causes every part of E, and y therefore, by (I), would cause part of itself, which is ruled out by (II).

But now let us ask: what if (i) through (iv) are all false? That is, suppose that x is part of y, and that x causes E. But suppose also that no part of E is part of, or causes part of, y. Does y cause E? I am inclined to think it does.

There is one and (I think) only one kind of case that might seem to make trouble for the idea that it does. Suppose I bang on a door, and then bang on it, and then . . . six times. Suppose that my first banging on the door causes Alfred's death, Alfred being a rather nervous man. Consider now the event—I'll call it 'six'—which consists of my six bangings on that door. Did six cause Alfred's death? It cannot be said that six did not cause Alfred's death on the ground that Alfred's death occurred while six was occurring. We are all, I hope, familiar with the fact that an event C may cause an event that occurs while C is occurring. Moreover, it should not be said that six did not cause Alfred's death on the ground that, not merely did Alfred's death occur while six was occurring, but Alfred's death occurred before six had ended. Surely an event C may cause something that is over before C is over. Suppose that I raise my hand from the floor to the top of my head. And suppose that near floor level is a small table, and that as my hand moves up from the floor, it topples over the table. My raising of my hand from floor to head-top caused the toppling over of that table—even though my raising of my hand was not over until after the table had toppled. I should stress that I am not saying that an event C may cause something that begins *before* C begins; I am saying only that an event C may cause something (that begins when or after C begins, but) that is over before C is over.

There is room, I suppose, to insist that while part of my hand-

Parts of Events (I)

raising—viz., that part which ended when the table started to topple—caused the table-toppling, the hand-raising itself did not cause the table-toppling. And similarly for six and Alfred's death. Now I have no doubt that part of my hand-raising did cause the table-toppling; but I find it very hard to see why anyone would say that the hand-raising itself did not. Of course if it were a general truth that an event y causes an event E only if every part of y causes E, then it would be plain that the hand-raising itself did not cause the table-toppling: for while the hand-raising had a part that caused the table-toppling (the part that ended when the table began to topple) it had parts that did not cause the table-toppling (all parts that began after the table began to topple). But as we saw, this is *not* a general truth. Sirhan's shooting of Kennedy had parts that did not cause Kennedy's death; yet Sirhan's shooting of Kennedy did cause Kennedy's death.

I am inclined to think, in fact, that if an event C causes an event E, then if we combine C with C' to form a compound event, then—if no part of E is part of, or causes part of, the compound event—the compound event also causes E. In particular, that the event consisting of the first bit of the hand-raising and the remainder of the hand-raising caused the table-toppling; that the event consisting of Sirhan's retracting the trigger the first one-hundredth of an inch and the rest of his shooting of Kennedy caused Kennedy's death; that the event consisting of the first banging on the door and the five later bangings on the door caused Alfred's death. You surely cannot (in general) construct an inefficacious event by simply adding an inefficacious event to an efficacious one.

I shall have nothing whatever to say in what follows as to how causality should be analyzed. But it is worth noting here that anyone who is sympathetic to the most common account, which appeals to generalizations, should be prepared to agree with me. Thus, if every event that is a first banging on a door causes a nervous man's death, then surely every event that is a compound of a first banging on a door and five further bangings on that door causes a nervous man's death.

As I said, then, effects are not symmetrical with causes: we cannot say that just as an event C causes an event y if and only if C causes all of y's parts, so also does an event y cause an event E if and only if all of y's parts cause E. But something *like* (III)—containing the exceptions I indicated—does seem to me to be a truth, namely

(IV)   E is caused by y if and only if there is an x such that x is part
of y, and x causes E, and no part of E is part of y, and no
part of E causes part of y.

If I am right, a rather nice little result comes out straightway. Let us
say that x and y are 'discrete' just in case they have no part in common; and let us say that x and y are 'causally independent' just in case
no part of x causes any part of y and no part of y causes any part of x.
The nice little result is this: if x and y are caused by events, and are
discrete and causally independent, then x and y do not have exactly
the same causes. Suppose that x and y are caused by events, and that
they are discrete and causally independent; suppose also that they have
exactly the same causes. By hypothesis, y is caused by an event. Let us
take α to be an event that causes y. Then α also causes x. We may
depict x, y, and α as in the diagram below.

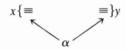

(Here, as throughout in these diagrams, the arrows indicate direction
of causality.) Consider, now, the event that consists of α and x—let us
call it β. We know, by (II), that β does not cause x. But we also know,
by (IV), that β causes y (for α causes y, and x and y are by hypothesis
both discrete and causally independent). So there is an event that
causes y and does not cause x; so x and y do not have exactly the same
causes, and our assumption that they do is contradicted.

An assumption I made in the course of this little proof is not jus-
tified by anything so far said, viz., the assumption that there *is* such an
event as β. That there is is a consequence of a principle we shall be
looking at in the following chapter. For the moment, I ask you only to
go along with the assumption that there is—I find it hard, in any case,
to see why we should say there is not.

Let us say that x and y 'overlap' just in case they are not discrete
(i.e., just in case they have a part in common). A very much nicer
result—less elegant, but in the long run more useful—that also comes
out is:

(V)   If x and y are caused by events and (C) (C causes y ⊃ C
causes x), then *either* x and y overlap, *or* y causes x, *or* part
of y causes x and part of x causes part of y.

Since we shall make much use of this result, I give it a label; and to avoid the clutter of different styles of label, the label I give it is a roman numeral. This may make it appear a further assumption. But it is not: it follows from assumptions (I) through (IV). I do not think that the details of the proof are themselves of interest, and the proof itself is rather long. Readers who prefer to skip it are invited to turn to page 68 below, where the proof ends.

First we prove a little lemma, viz., that if x and y are caused by events, and are discrete, and if also (C) (C causes $y \supset$ C causes x), then part of y causes part of x. Suppose that x and y are caused by events, and are discrete, and that (C) (C causes $y \supset$ C causes x). By hypothesis, y is caused by an event. Let us take α to be an event that causes y. Then α also causes x. We may again depict x, y, and α as in the diagram above. Consider, now, the event that consists of α and x—let us call it β. We know, by (IV), that β causes y if no part of y is part of β, and no part of y causes part of β. But we also know that β *does not* cause y—for, by (II), β does not cause x, and, by hypothesis, (C) (C causes $y \supset$ C causes x). It follows that either part of y is part of β, or part of y causes part of β. But no part of y is part of β: for by hypothesis, x and y are discrete, so that no part of y is part of x; and by (III), α causes every part of y, so that by (II) no part of y is part of α. It follows that part of y causes part of β. Plainly, however, no part of y causes part of α. It follows that part of y causes part of x.

A second lemma is this: if x and y are caused by events, and are discrete, and if also (C) (C causes $y \supset$ C causes x), then part of y causes x. Suppose that x and y are caused by events, and are discrete, and that (C) (C causes $y \supset$ C causes x). By our first lemma, it follows that part of y causes part of x. Suppose, however, that it is not the case that any part of y causes the whole of x. Let γ consist of all of the parts of x that are caused by any part of y; then there must be an event—let us call it δ—that is part of x but wholly discrete from γ, if it is to be the case that no part of y causes the whole of x. Then δ is caused by no part of y, and no part of δ is caused by any part of y.

Now by hypothesis, y is caused by an event. Since δ is part of x, and x is (by hypothesis) caused by an event, it follows, by (III), that δ is caused by an event. So y and δ are caused by events. Moreover, y and δ are discrete (since, by hypothesis, x and y are discrete, and δ is part of x). Lastly, (C) (C causes $y \supset$ C causes δ): for, by hypothesis, (C) (C causes $y \supset$ C causes x), and δ is part of x. By our first lemma, it follows that part of y causes part of δ. Since we had earlier shown that no part of δ is caused by any part of y, our supposition has led to a contradiction.

Here again I made an assumption, vix., that there *is* such an event as γ. (And β too.) That there is is a consequence of the principle I mentioned, which we shall be looking at in the following chapter. For the moment, I ask you only to go along with the supposition that there is—I find it hard, in any case, to see why we should say there is not.

Suppose, now, that x and y are caused by events, and that (C) (C causes y ⊃ C causes x). One thing that is obvious is that either

(i) x and y overlap,

or

(ii) x and y are discrete.

Let us concentrate on (ii). If x and y are caused by events, and (C)(C causes y ⊃ C causes x), and if also x and y are discrete, then by our second lemma, part of y causes x.

We know, by (IV), that if part of y causes x, then *either* y causes x, *or* part of x is part of y, *or* part of x causes part of y. It follows that if part of y causes x, then *either* y causes x, *or* part of x is part of y, *or* part of y causes x and part of x causes part of y.

So we can conclude that if x and y are caused by events, and (C)(C causes y ⊃ C causes x), and if also x and y are discrete, then *either* y causes x, *or* part of x is part of y, *or* part of y causes x and part of x causes part of y. Since if the antecedent is true, the second disjunct of the consequent is false, we may say: if x and y are caused by events, and (C)(C causes y ⊃ C causes x), and if also x and y are discrete, then *either* y causes x, *or* part of y causes x and part of x causes part of y.

It is plain, as I said, that if x and y are caused by events, and (C)(C causes y ⊃ C causes x), then either

(i) x and y overlap,

or

(ii) x and y are discrete.

We are in a position to conclude, therefore, that

(V)   If x and y are caused by events and (C)(C causes y ⊃ C causes x), then *either* x and y overlap, *or* y causes x, *or* part of y causes x and part of x causes part of y.

It is perhaps worth drawing attention to the fact that the disjuncts in the consequent of (V) are not exclusive. If x and y are depictable as in the diagram, then *both* x and y overlap, *and* part of y causes x and part of x causes part of y:

Parts of Events (I)

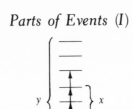

It is probably not at all obvious why it was worth proving (V) from (I) through (IV). I promise that it was. As we shall see, there is a very interesting kind of event—I shall call them the 'complete' events—of which something stronger than (V) is true.

Consider again the event that consisted in my vacuuming of the carpets last Friday. I suggested in the preceding chapter that it included, among other events, the sequence of events that may be depicted as in the diagram below.

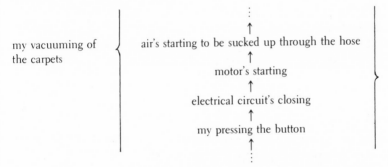

Now consider another event, namely the event such that x is part of it just in case x is an event that is both part of my vacuuming of the carpets and discrete from the electrical circuit's closing. I shall call this event Alpha, and depict part of it in the diagram below.

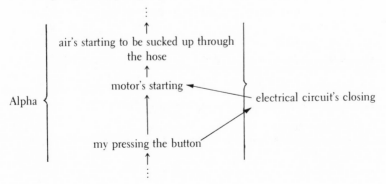

I am not asking you to imagine that the electrical circuit's closing did not happen, or that it did not stand in the causal relations in which it in fact did stand; I am asking you only to attend to an event, Alpha, which does not contain it.

I said I was asking you to attend to Alpha, plainly taking it that there is such an event as Alpha. Is there such an event? I find it hard to see why we should say there is not.

Alpha is discrete from the electrical circuit's closing and hence is not identical with my vacuuming of those carpets. Yet I should imagine that Alpha and my vacuuming of the carpets have exactly the same causes, and exactly the same effects. They plainly have the same causes. And they have the same effects if it can be supposed that not only does the electrical circuit's closing cause something in Alpha, but so also does every event that is part of the circuit's closing cause something in Alpha—if every part of it causes something in Alpha, then, by (IV), Alpha causes no part of it. Since this does seem to be a plausible supposition—causality being transitive—*one* account of what it is for events x and y to be identical is incorrect. What I have in mind is the proposal that we should say an event x is identical with an event y just in case x and y have the same causes and the same effects.[3] It is, at first glance, a highly plausible suggestion; but the fact that there are—and I think there is no good reason not to allow that there are—events such as Alpha shows it to be false.

What are the events 'such as' Alpha? I shall call an event IC an 'incomplete' event just in case there is an event E such that E is caused by part of IE, and E causes part of IE, but E is discrete from IE. A complete event, then, is an event CE such that there is *no* event E such that part of CE causes E and E causes part of CE, and E is discrete from CE. ("Complete" because it is in an obvious sense 'causally complete'.) By hypothesis, Alpha is an incomplete event; my vacuuming of the carpets, I think, is a complete event.

As I said earlier, we are not accustomed to talk of parts of events, and have not asked ourselves just which events we should regard as parts of them and which not. But I think that once we do ask this, it is plausible to take the nominalizations that standardly appear in writings on action, at any rate, to refer to complete events. Take my vacuuming of those carpets. Take, next, anything one is inclined to think

[3] See Donald Davidson, "The Individuation of Events," in *Essays in Honor of Carl G. Hempel*, ed. Nicholas Rescher et al. (Dordrecht, Holland: D. Reidel, 1970).

Parts of Events (I)

must surely turn out to be part of it; if that part causes something, E, which causes something else that one is inclined to think must surely turn out to be part of the carpet-vacuuming, it will seem natural to take E to be part of it too. The electrical circuit's closing was surely a part; so was the motor's starting; but so also, then, were all the changes in the state of the motor that were caused by the electrical circuit's closing, and that caused the motor's starting. Those changes played a part in the vacuum-cleaning; and whatever plays a part in that is part of it.

I do not say that if CE is a complete event then every event E that is caused by part of CE, and that causes part of CE, is itself *part* of CE: I say only that E is not discrete from CE. Suppose that that electrical circuit's closing caused somebody's death. And now consider the event—I'll call it Beta—such that x is part of it just in case x is identical with the electrical circuit's closing, or x is identical with the death, or x has no parts discrete from both the electrical circuit's closing and the death. (Thus, e.g., if the death has parts not identical with itself, then all parts of the death, as well as the death itself, are parts of Beta.) We may depict Beta as in the diagram below.

$$\text{Beta}\begin{cases} & \text{the death} & \\ & \uparrow & \\ \text{electrical circuit's closing} & \end{cases}$$

Is there such an event as Beta? I find it hard to see why we should say there is not. Now in virtue of (I) and (III), my pressing of the button caused Beta; so part of my vacuuming of the carpets caused Beta. Since the electrical circuit's closing caused the motor's starting, Beta caused the motor's starting—cf. (IV); so Beta caused part of my vacuuming of the carpets. But Beta is not *part* of my vacuuming of the carpets: for the death is not part of it, but is instead caused by it. On the other hand, Beta is not discrete from it, for Beta and my vacuuming of the carpets share the electrical circuit's closing.

In passing, I should imagine that Beta is an incomplete event, for I should imagine that the circuit's closing caused the death only via causing an event E that caused the death—an event E that is discrete from both the circuit's closing and the death, and that is therefore discrete from Beta. If we suppose that there was a temporal gap between the circuit's closing and the death, Beta is temporally discontinuous. But not every temporally discontinuous event is incomplete. Let

Gamma be the event such that x is part of it just in case x is identical with Caesar's crossing of the Rubicon, or x is identical with my grating pepper onto an egg just now, or x has no parts discrete from both the Rubicon-crossing and the pepper-grating just now. Is there such an event as Gamma? I find it hard to see why we should say there is not. Gamma, then, is like Beta in being temporally discontinuous; but on the (surely plausible) assumption that the crossing caused nothing that caused any part of the pepper-grating, Gamma is a complete event. Indeed, my vacuuming of the carpets is, as we saw, temporally discontinuous, for there were temporal gaps between my vacuuming of the living room carpet and my vacuuming of the dining room carpet and my . . . ; and yet it too is surely complete.

Moreover, not every incomplete event is temporally discontinuous. Suppose that in my hand is a cup, and in the cup is an egg; and suppose I raise my hand, thereby raising the cup, thereby raising the egg. I take it that the event that is the rising of my hand causes the event that is the rising of the cup, which causes the event that is the rising of the egg. Now it seems to me that there is an event such that x is part of it just in case x is identical with the rising of my hand, or x is identical with the rising of the egg, or x has no parts discrete from both the rising of the hand and the rising of the egg. This event is plainly incomplete; but it is not temporally discontinuous—there is no temporal gap between the rising of the hand and the rising of the egg.

To go back, then. If y is a complete event, then if part of y causes x, and x causes part of y, x is not discrete from y. Similarly, if y is a complete event, then if part of y causes x, and *part* of x causes part of y, x is not discrete from y—for if part of y causes x, then by (III), it causes every part of x, including that part that causes part of y, from which it follows (if y is complete) that that part of x, and therefore x itself, is not discrete from y. If x is not discrete from y, x and y overlap. So if y is a complete event, then something stronger than (V) is true of it: i.e., we may say

(VI)   If x and y are caused by events and (C)(C causes $y \supset$ C causes x) and y is complete, then *either* x and y overlap, *or* y causes x.

That is, if y is complete, the third disjunct of the consequent of (V) collapses into the first.

With (VI) in hand, it is easy enough to say under what conditions a complete event that is caused by an event is part of a complete event that is caused by an event.

(VI) says that if x and y are caused by events and y is complete, and if also

(OC)   (C)(C causes y ⊃ C causes x) & $-$ (y causes x)

is true, then x and y overlap. [Hence "(OC)": it is short for "overlap-condition".] Let us suppose that a given x and y are caused by events and that *both* x and y are complete, and also that (OC) is true of them; it follows that x and y overlap. But let us suppose that x is not part of y—i.e., let us suppose that there is an event that is part of x but discrete from y—and let us give the name Delta to it. From the fact that Delta is part of x we can draw a conclusion about it, viz.,

(C)(C causes x ⊃ C causes Delta) & $-$ (x causes Delta).

[Cf. (NC$_1$) and (NC$_2$).] We were given that (OC) is true of x and y, so

(C)(C causes y ⊃ C causes x)

is true, and we can therefore conclude that

(C)(C causes y ⊃ C causes Delta).

Now we know, from (VI), that

If Delta and y are caused by events and (C)(C causes y ⊃ C causes Delta) and y is complete, then *either* Delta and y overlap, or y causes Delta.

By hypothesis, y is caused by events. Since, by hypothesis, x is too, Delta, being part of x, is also caused by events: cf. (III). By hypothesis, moreover, y is complete, and Delta is discrete from y. It follows that y causes Delta. It follows also that if there is such an event as Delta was said to be, there is an event d such that

(C)(C causes x ⊃ C causes d) & $-$ (x causes d) & y causes d.

And now if we want to have it turn out that x and y do not merely overlap, but more, that x is part of y, we need only require that x and y satisfy, not merely (OC), but also

(NDC) $-$ (∃d) [(C)(C causes x ⊃ C causes d) & $-$ (x causes d) & y causes d].

["(NDC)" is short for "no-Delta-condition".] For if x and y satisfy (NDC) as well as (OC), there is no such event as Delta was said to be, and x is therefore part of y.

I think it is easy enough to see also that if x and y are caused by events and both x and y are complete, and if also x is part of y, then both (OC) and (NDC) are true of them. Suppose the antecedent is true of x and y. Since, by hypothesis, x is part of y, they satisfy (OC): cf. (NC$_1$) and (NC$_2$). What of (NDC)? Suppose that (NDC) is false, i.e., that for some d,

> (C)(C causes x $\supset$ C causes d) & $-$(x causes d) & y causes d.

We know, from (VI), that

> If d and x are caused by events and (C)(C causes x $\supset$ C causes d) and x is complete, then *either* d and x overlap, *or* x causes d.

By hypothesis, x is caused by events; since (C)(C causes x $\supset$ C causes d), d is also caused by events. By hypothesis, x is complete. Since $-$(x causes d), d and x overlap. By hypothesis, x is part of y; so part of d is part of y. But then, by (II), it follows that y *does not* cause d. And our supposition has led to a contradiction.

We are in a position, then, to say that a complete event x that is caused by events is part of a complete event y that is caused by events just in case Part (x, y), where

(D$_{5a}$)   Part (x, y) just in case

> (C)(C causes y $\supset$ C causes x) & $-$(y causes x) &   (OC
> $-$($\exists d$) [(C)(C causes x $\supset$ C causes d) & $-$(x causes d)
> & y causes d].   (NDC

VI

Parts of Events (II)

Are there any events that are *not* caused by events? Well, consider the event—I shall call it Ay—such that x is part of it just in case x occurred prior to midnight last night. If there is such an event as Ay, there is at least one event not caused by any event. For suppose an event z caused Ay. It is plausible to assume, and I shall assume it throughout, that

(VII)   No event causes an event which wholly precedes it;

so it must be that z has a part, viz., z', which occurred prior to midnight last night. It follows that z' is part of Ay. By hypothesis, z caused Ay. It follows, by

(III)   C causes y if and only if C causes all of y's parts,

that z caused z'. But

(II)   No event causes any of its parts; no event is caused by any of its parts

rules out that any event should cause part of itself.

Again, consider my sneezing just now. I assume there was at least one event that caused it. Consider, then, the event—I shall call it Bee—such that x is part of it just in case x caused the sneezing, or x has no parts discrete from all y such that y caused the sneezing. If there is such an event as Bee, there is a second event not caused by any event. For suppose an event z caused Bee. Let x be an event that caused the sneezing. It follows that x is part of Bee. By hypothesis, z caused Bee. It follows, by (III), that z caused x. It follows, by

(I)   Causality is transitive,

that z caused the sneezing. It follows that z is part of Bee. But (II) rules out that any event should be caused by part of itself.

I am strongly inclined to think that if a thing is not caused by an event, it is not caused by anything at all, and thus that Ay and Bee are caused by nothing. (See pages 149ff. below.) It is not necessary, however, that this point be granted now. What we need now is only that Ay and Bee—if there are such events as Ay and Bee—are events that are caused by no event.

Bee may perhaps initially strike one as a less peculiar candidate event than Ay is, and it is worth bringing out in passing that it is, in its own way, at least as peculiar as Ay. Caesar's crossing of the Rubicon, for example, is part of Bee. For suppose that that sneezing just now was caused by the event that was my grating pepper onto an egg just before the sneezing. Now Gamma, you may remember, was the event such that x is part of it just in case x is identical with Caesar's crossing of the Rubicon, or x is identical with my grating pepper onto an egg just now, or x has no parts discrete from both the Rubicon-crossing and the pepper-grating. We know, by

(IV) E is caused by y if and only if there is an x such that x is part of y, and x causes E, and no part of E is part of y, and no part of E causes part of y,

that the sneezing is caused by Gamma if and only if there is an x such that x is part of Gamma, and x causes the sneezing, and no part of the sneezing is part of Gamma, and no part of the sneezing causes part of Gamma. Well, there is an x such that x is part of Gamma, and x causes the sneezing: the pepper-grating is such an x. Moreover, Gamma wholly precedes the sneezing, so no part of the sneezing is part of Gamma, and no part of the sneezing causes part of Gamma. So Gamma caused the sneezing. It follows that Gamma is part of Bee. But then, by what is surely an unquestionable assumption,

(VIII)   If x is part of y, every part of x is part of y—

it is an assumption I have relied on in a number of places already— Caesar's crossing of the Rubicon is part of Bee.

If Ay and Bee are events, they are complete events. Consider Cee, however: Cee is the event such that x is part of it just in case x is identical with Ay, or x is identical with my sneezing just now, or x has no parts discrete from both Ay and the sneezing. Let us suppose that there was an event that occurred prior to midnight last night that caused an event E after midnight, and that E caused my sneezing just now; if there is such an event E, Cee is an incomplete event. So if there are such events as Ay and Bee on the one hand, and Cee on the other, there are events caused by no event that are complete and events caused by no event that are incomplete.

Ay, Bee, and Cee are very peculiar events, if they are events. So is Gamma a peculiar event, if there is such an event as Gamma. So also are some of the other events we looked at in the preceding chapter and about which I said: I find it hard to see why we should say there is no such event. Alpha, for example. And Beta too. But of course it is hardly an argument to the effect that they are not events that they would be very peculiar events if they were events.

These peculiar candidate events were in a certain sense 'constructed', and by a very simple procedure at that. I took a property that is possessed by at least one event; and I then invited you to attend to a (peculiar) event such that x is part of it just in case either x has that property or x has no parts discrete from all y such that y has that property. Take Gamma again, for example. There are two events that have

the property 'is identical with Caesar's crossing of the Rubicon or is identical with my grating pepper onto an egg just now',

viz., Caesar's crossing of the Rubicon, and my grating pepper onto that egg. Gamma, then, is the event such that x is part of it just in case either x has this property or x has no parts discrete from all y such that y has it. Take Bee. There are, I should imagine, a great many events which have

the property 'caused my sneezing just now'.

My grating pepper onto that egg, for example, has it. Bee, then, is the event such that x is part of it just in case either x has this property or x has no parts discrete from all y such that y has it. My grating pepper onto the egg has the property, so it is part of Bee. But then, as we saw, Gamma also has the property, so Gamma too is part of Bee. Now Caesar's crossing of the Rubicon does not have the property; but it is, as we saw, part of Bee, for it is not discrete from all y such that y has the property—indeed, it is part of an event (viz., Gamma) that has it. Lastly, take Ay. There are a great many events that have

the property 'occurred prior to midnight last night'.

Ay, then, is the event such that x is part of it just in case either x has this property or x has no parts discrete from all y such that y has it. Since every event that has no parts discrete from all y such that y has it is itself an event that has it, it was possible to abbreviate here, and to say, more briefly, that Ay is the event such that x is part of it just in case x has it.

Now it seems to me that we should accept that the peculiar candidate events constructed in this way really are *bona fide* events. It seems to me, that is, that we should accept the following principle:

> For any property F, if there is an x which has F, then there is a unique entity E such that for all x, x is part of E just in case either x has F or x has no parts discrete from all y such that y has F, and such that E is an event.

(Notice that while "x" and "y" still range over events, "F" ranges over properties, and "E" ranges over entities generally.) If we allow ourselves a useful piece of terminology, we can abbreviate this principle in a perspicuous way. What

> x is part of E just in case either x has F or x has no parts discrete from all y such that y has F

says is that E has a certain relation to the events that have F. Let us say it says that E is a 'fusion' of them. If there is a unique entity E which is a fusion of them, E is *the* fusion of them. Then we can abbreviate the principle as follows:

> For any property F, if there is an x which has F, then there is a unique entity E such that E is the fusion of all x that have F, and such that E is an event.

What if F is a property that no events have? For example, it seems plain enough that there is no event x that has the property 'is a prime number'. Now every event x has at least one part, viz., itself; so whatever event x you choose, x has parts discrete from all events y such that y is a prime number. So if we are to suppose about E that

> x is part of E just in case either x is a prime number or x has no parts discrete from all y such that y is a prime number,

then no event is part of E. But every event has at least one part, viz., itself. So there is no event E that is the fusion of all x that are prime numbers. So I shall take it that if the principle is itself plausible, so also is

(IX)   For any property F, if (and only if) there is an x that has F, then there is a unique entity E such that E is the fusion of all x that have F, and such that E is an event.

I shall call (IX) the Principle of Event-Fusion.[1] And I shall call Ay, for example, the fusion of all events that occurred prior to midnight last night; and I shall call Gamma, for example, the fusion of all events that are identical with Caesar's crossing of the Rubicon or identical with my grating pepper onto that egg—more briefly, the fusion of Caesar's crossing of the Rubicon and my grating pepper onto the egg.

I do not have any argument for the truth of the Principle of Event-Fusion. Is the weaker thesis

(i)   If there is an event that has F, then there is a unique entity E such that E is the fusion of all events that have F

true for all F? It seems to me that it is—just as it seems to me that the following are true for all F:

If there is a material object that has F, then there is a unique entity E such that E is the fusion of all material objects that have F,

If there is a shoe that has F, then there is a unique entity E such that E is the fusion of all shoes that have F,

and so on. But I have no argument to the effect that any of these is true. On the other hand, I find it very hard to see what sort of argument could be produced to the effect that they are not true. I cannot, in fact, imagine what a dispute as to their truth or falsity would look like.

Supposing (i) is true, is

(ii) E is an event

true? Here it seems to me there is room, if not for dispute, then anyway for discussion. Supposing there is a unique E, which is the fusion of all events that have F, is E an *event*? It seems to me plain that, supposing there is a unique E that is the fusion of all material objects that have F, E is a material object. But surely E might be the fusion of all shoes that have F and not itself be a shoe. If there is one shoe that is in the closet, then the fusion of all shoes in the closet is a shoe; but if there are nine shoes in the closet, then the fusion of all shoes in the

[1] The notion 'fusion' comes from Henry S. Leonard and Nelson Goodman, "The Calculus of Individuals and Its Uses," *The Journal of Symbolic Logic*, 5 (1940), 45–55. (See also page 96 below.) In naming the principle as I did, I imitate Richard Cartwright's "Fusion Principle" for material objects; see his "Scattered Objects," in *Analysis and Metaphysics*, ed. Keith Lehrer (Dordrecht, Holland: D. Reidel, 1975).

closet, while (as I should suppose) a perfectly respectable material object, is not a *shoe*. And why should we take events to be like material objects in this respect rather than like shoes?

If, as I should suppose, the question whether or not an entity is a material object has to do only with the question whether or not the entity is 'made of material', then it would be no surprise that—if there is a material object that has F, and therefore an entity that is the fusion of all material objects that have F—

> The fusion of all material objects that have F is a material object

is true. For conjoining things 'made of material' yields something that is, itself, 'made of material'. (Conjoining things made of wool yields something that is itself made of wool. And so on.) But of course the question whether or not an entity is a shoe is a question not of what it is made of, but of what its shape is. So it is no surprise that—even if there is a shoe that has F, and therefore an entity that is the fusion of all shoes that have F—

> The fusion of all shoes that have F is a shoe

may be false, and that the question whether it is true or false turns on what F is. One shoe is of course of the right shape to be a shoe; but conjoining several shoes is (at least) likely to result in an entity of the wrong shape to be a shoe.

Now consider the question whether or not an entity is an event. What has that question to do with? We shall be looking more closely in Chapter VIII at the question what an event is. For the moment, however, let us notice that it is in an important respect different from the question whether or not an entity is a shoe. It might be said, for example, that a shoe has a space-shape, whereas an event has a time-shape. Thus, for example, John's running in the Boston Common this morning had the following time-shape: forty minutes continuous. Again, John's running in the Boston Common yesterday morning had the following time-shape: twenty minutes continuous, then a ten-minute gap, then twenty minutes continuous. (He broke for a ten-minute rest yesterday.) But though it might be said that every event has some time-shape or other, there is no time-shape that every event has, nor are there even any rough limits as to the possible time-shapes events may have. By contrast, there are at least rough limits as to the possible space-shapes shoes may have.

Whatever else an event may be, it is a happening, an occurrence.

Parts of Events (II)

And isn't the result of conjoining any two happenings itself a happening? Of course, if the two conjoined events occur at separated times, then the result of conjoining them is temporally discontinuous; but, as we know, this is no barrier to its being an event—my vacuuming of the carpets, after all, was temporally discontinuous and was nevertheless a quite respectable event. Again, we may have to invent a name for the result of conjoining the two events, there being none naturally available for it (for example, no nominalization); but it plainly cannot be said that where there is no naturally available name, there is no entity, so why should it be said that where there is no naturally available name, there is no event?

However I do not really think of the rhetorical question "And isn't the result of conjoining any two happenings itself a happening?" as an *argument* for the thesis that events are like material objects in this respect rather than like shoes, i.e., as an argument for the following thesis:

> If there is an event that has F and therefore an entity that is the fusion of all events that have F, then the fusion of all events that have F is an event.

I hope merely to have made it appear less strange.

If that thesis is true, then so also is

> If there is an event that has F and is caused by C and therefore an entity that is the fusion of all events that have F and are caused by C, then the fusion of all events that have F and are caused by C is an event.

And I think that a stronger thesis than this is true, viz.,

> If there is an event that has F and is caused by C and therefore an entity that is the fusion of all events that have F and are caused by C, then the fusion of all events that have F and are caused by C is an event *that is caused by* C,

or, more simply,

> If there is an event that has F and is caused by C, then the fusion of all events that have F and are caused by C is an event that is caused by C.

A certain consequence of this thesis, viz.,

> If there is an event that has F, and if also all events that have F are caused by C, then the fusion of all events that have F is caused by C,

is of interest. Notice that it bears a close relation to assumption

(III)   C causes y if and only if C causes all of y's parts

of the preceding chapter. Assumption (III) seems to me as plausible as anything in this area can be. Let us notice, now, that one of (III)'s conjuncts is trivially true. That is, (III) is the conjunction of

(III.a)   If C causes y, then C causes all of y's parts,

and

(III.b)   If C causes all of y's parts, then C causes y.

(III.b) is trivially true: since, as I said, I am so using "part" that an event is part of itself, C cannot cause all of y's parts unless it does cause y itself. [(III.a) is not trivially true; hence the usefulness of (III).] Now what I am going to call (III.b*), viz.,

(III.b*)   If there is a y such that y has F, and if also C causes all y such that y has F, then the fusion of all y that have F is caused by C

is obviously stronger than (III.b); yet it seems to me that if the Principle of Event-Fusion is true, then (III.b*) is fully as plausible as (III) is. For notice that if an event that has F is caused by C, then by (III), every part of it is caused by C; so if every event that has F is caused by C, every event that is part of any event that has F is caused by C. According to the Principle of Event-Fusion, if there is an event that has F, there is an event that is the fusion of all events that have F; and it seems entirely plausible to take it that that event too is caused by C.

Now, as I said, I have no argument *for* the Principle of Event-Fusion. But it seems to me that there is no argument against it either. So far as I can see, we would have reason to reject it only if we could not give the peculiar event-fusions it commits us to a place among events: i.e., only if we could not give a plausible account of (i) what their temporal relations are to other events, (ii) what their causal relations are to other events, and (iii) what other events they have as parts and are parts of. But we can.

Take Ay, for example. When did Ay occur? At T—where T is any time-stretch that includes all those times up to midnight last night at which events were occurring. My sneezing, however, occurred at 2:18 this afternoon. Now it seems right to say that an event x precedes an event y just in case there are times t and t' such that x occurs at t and y at t', and t precedes t'. So then Ay preceded my sneezing just now. Take Gamma, for example. When did Gamma occur? At T—where T is any time-stretch that includes 44 B.C. and 2:17 this afternoon (for that was then the pepper-grating occurred). So Ay did not precede Gamma, but rather temporally overlapped it. Like Ay, however,

Parts of Events (II)

Gamma preceded the sneezing. These results are as they should be.

Assumptions (I), (II), (III), and (IV) yield conclusions about what causal relations the peculiar event-fusions have to other events. Take Ay, for example. What causal relations does Ay have to your getting out of bed yesterday morning? Well, that was part of Ay, so it follows, by (II), that Ay did not cause it. It also follows, by (III), that whatever causes Ay causes your getting out of bed yesterday morning—though this is not a very interesting piece of information, for as we know, no event causes Ay. And it also follows, by (IV), that Ay causes every event that your getting out of bed causes, except such events as share parts with Ay, or have parts that cause parts of Ay. Take Gamma, for example. (II) yields the conclusion that Gamma did not cause Caesar's crossing of the Rubicon, and did not cause my grating pepper onto that egg, for they are parts of Gamma. (III) yields that every event that caused Gamma caused both the Rubicon-crossing and the pepper-grating—not an uninteresting piece of information, for it is plausible to suppose that Gamma is caused by events. And (IV) yields that Gamma causes every event the Rubicon-crossing causes and every event the pepper-grating causes, except such events as either of these cause that share parts with Gamma, or have parts that cause parts of Gamma.

If we allow ourselves (III.b*) as well—and I suggest we do—further causal conclusions follow. Take Gamma, for example. Gamma is the fusion of all events that are identical with Caesar's crossing of the Rubicon or with my grating pepper onto the egg. Now the Rubicon-crossing and the pepper-grating are the only events that are identical with Caesar's crossing of the Rubicon or with the pepper-grating. So it follows, by (III.b*), that every event that caused both the Rubicon-crossing and the pepper-grating caused Gamma. All these conclusions look entirely plausible.

And what about the parts of these peculiar event-fusions, and the events that they are parts of?

We can easily enough say what are the complete parts of any of the peculiar event-fusions that are complete and caused by events—such as Gamma, for example. In the preceding chapter, we saw that if x and y are complete and caused by events, then x is part of y just in case Part (x, y), where

(D_{5a})   Part (x, y) just in case

$(C)(C$ causes $y \supset C$ causes $x) \ \& \ -(y$ causes $x) \ \&$ (OC)

$-(\exists d)[(C)$ causes $x \supset C$ causes $d) \ \& \ -(x$ causes $d) \ \& \ y$

causes $d]$.   (NDC)

Now Gamma is complete and caused by events. So every complete part of Gamma is complete and caused by events—by (III). So we can say that a complete event x is part of Gamma just in case Part $(x,$ Gamma); and if I was right in Chapter V, this assigns to Gamma just those complete parts that it should.

We shall postpone discussion of incomplete events until the following chapter. Thus, we shall postpone in particular the question under what conditions an incomplete event x is part of Gamma.

What events is Gamma part of? We can easily enough say what complete events that are caused by events Gamma is part of: if y is complete and caused by events, then Gamma is part of y just in case Part (Gamma, y). And again, if I was right in Chapter V, this assigns Gamma, as part, to just those complete events that are caused by events that it should. Since we are postponing discussion of incomplete events, we are postponing the question under what conditions Gamma is part of an incomplete event y.

But we have now to ask under what conditions Gamma is part of a complete event that is *not* caused by events. Under what conditions is a complete event that is caused by events part of a complete event that is not?

Moreover, we shall have to make a place among events for peculiar event-fusions such as Ay and Bee. Under what conditions is a complete event that is not caused by events part of a complete event that is not caused by events?

In order to answer these questions, we have first to ask just what events that are not caused by events there *are.* I have suggested that a great many ordinary events—such as my sneezing just now, and Caesar's crossing of the Rubicon—are caused by events. The event-fusions Ay and Bee are not caused by events; what other events are not caused by events?

Some philosophers of science used to say that certain submicroscopic events have no causes at all, and so certainly are not caused by events. I have no very clear idea which submicroscopic events they meant, or what made them say this of them. I gather that no one says this nowadays—which is *very* fortunate for my purposes, since I am about to invite you to assume something I am sure is incompatible with what they had in mind.[2]

[2] If they said, not merely

(i)   Submicroscopic events of kind K have no causes,

Parts of Events (II)

Let us begin by noticing that accepting the Principle of Event-Fusion commits us to accepting

> (X) There is at least one complete event that is caused by no event and causes no event.

For there presumably is such a property as the property 'is self-identical'; so that if

> For any property F, if (and only if) there is an x that has F, then there is a unique entity E such that E is the fusion of all x that have F, and such that E is an event

is true, then so also is

> If there is an x that is self-identical, then there is a unique entity E, such that E is the fusion of all x that are self-identical, and such that E is an event.

Now the antecedent of this conditional is true: my sneezing this afternoon, for example, is an event that is self-identical. So there is a unique entity E that is the fusion of all events that are self-identical. But surely every event is self-identical; so E is the fusion of *all* events. And E is an event. This event E, which is the fusion of all events, I shall call S-E (short for "the Super-Event"). Since S-E contains all events, there is no event outside it for it to cause, and there is no event outside it that might cause it; so S-E is caused by no event and causes no event. Moreover, S-E is complete: for since it contains all events, there is no event that is discrete from it. So (X) is true.

What we are not committed to by accepting the Principle of Event-Fusion, but which I suggest we now assume, is

> (XI)   There is at most one complete event that is caused by no event and causes no event.[3]

From (X) and (XI) it follows that there is exactly one complete event that is caused by no event and causes no event—it is S-E, of course.

---

but also
(ii)   Every event has at least one submicroscopic event of kind K among its parts,
and
(iii)   Some events are caused by events,
then I have *already* invited you to assume something which is incompatible with what they had in mind, for the conjunction of (i), (ii), and (III) entails that (iii) is false.

[3] I drew attention on page 70 above to the fact that incomplete events make trouble for the idea that events x and y are identical just in case x and y have the same causes and the same effects. Notice now that if what is caused by no event and causes no event is causeless and effectless, then if (XI) is false, there are complete events that also make trouble for it: for if x and y are causeless and effectless, x and y have the same causes and effects.

Acts and Other Events

An interesting consequence of (XI) comes out as follows. Let us say that an event E is 'temporally left-bounded' just in case there is a time t such that for all times prior to t, E is not yet occurring. (I say 'left-bounded' because I am now thinking of the time-line as drawn from left to right.) Then it follows from (XI) that

(XII)   If x is temporally left-bounded, and if also there is an event which occurs prior to x, then x is caused by an event.

For suppose x is temporally left-bounded; and suppose also that there is an event—let it be y—which occurs prior to x. Let z be the fusion of all events that are identical with x or caused by any part of x. Then z causes no event (for no part of z causes any event discrete from z.) Moreover, z is complete (same reason). If z is also caused by no event, then, by (XI), z is identical with S-E. But z is *not* identical with S-E, for y is an event that is discrete from x (since it occurs prior to x), and discrete from every event caused by x—cf. (VII)—and y is therefore discrete from z. It follows that z is not caused by no event; i.e., it follows that z is caused by an event. It follows, by (III), that x is caused by an event.

If (XI) is true, and therefore (XII) is, then *all* of the events I earlier (loosely) called ordinary events are events caused by events. I said that a great many of them—such as my sneezing just now, and Caesar's crossing of the Rubicon—seem to me to be events caused by events; if (XII) is true, then all are. In particular, every human act is—for I should imagine that every human act is temporally left-bounded and preceded by some event or other.

Moreover, I should imagine that those who said that certain submicroscopic events have no causes thought that among them are submicroscopic events that are temporally left-bounded and preceded by other events. It is therefore fortunate that what is said nowadays is, not that those events have no causes, but rather that they are not 'determined'.

Why should we accept (XI)? It has to be confessed that my reason is no better than this: if we do accept it, it is easy to give an account of the part-whole relationships among events that are caused by no event, and I have found no way (hard or easy) of doing so without accepting it.

On the other hand, while I have no good reason for asking that (XI) be accepted, it is not plain what argument may be brought forth against it. That human beings sometimes act freely? Surely human freedom had better be compatible with causality!

More interesting, while people may say "Why shouldn't there be more than one complete event that is caused by no event and causes no event?", I doubt that anyone is going to be able to produce an example of an event that is complete and caused by no event and a cause of no event *and* that is not identical with S-E. Perhaps it will be thought we can produce one by subtracting an event from S-E? Which event should we subtract? An ordinary event, such as my sneezing just now? Let E be the fusion of all events that are parts of S-E but discrete from my sneezing just now. Unfortunately, E is incomplete: for my sneezing just now was caused by an event outside it and caused an event inside it. And I should imagine that every ordinary event is caused by an event outside it and causes an event outside it; so subtracting an ordinary event will always result in an incomplete event. Moreover, subtracting an event-fusion such as Gamma will also result in an incomplete event. Subtracting a 'temporally right-bounded' event-fusion such as Ay results in a temporally left-bounded event that is complete and causes no event; on the other hand, every such event appears to be caused by an event. If E, for example, is the result of subtracting Ay from S-E, then if every ordinary event in E is caused by an event, E surely is. [Notice that if every ordinary event in E is caused by Ay, and E is the fusion of ordinary events in E, then it follows, by (III.b*), that E is caused by Ay.]

So I shall simply go ahead and assume that (XI) is true. With (XI) in hand, it is, as I said, easy to give an account of the part-whole relationships among events that are caused by no event—a plausible one, I think.

Let us, for simplicity, first draw one further conclusion, viz.,

(XIII)   If x is complete and caused by no event, then x causes every event discrete from itself.

(XIII) follows easily enough from (XI). Suppose that x is complete and caused by no event. Then either (i) x causes no event, or (ii) x causes events. If (i), then x is complete, caused by no event, and causes no event, and is therefore, by (XI), identical with S-E. Since there is no event discrete from S-E, every event discrete from S-E is caused by S-E. So every event discrete from x is caused by x. If (ii), then let y be the fusion of all events that are caused by x; x, then, causes every part

87

of y. The fusion of all events that are parts of x or parts of y is complete, caused by no event, and causes no event, and is therefore, by (XI), identical with S-E. It follows that every event discrete from x is in y, and therefore that x causes every event discrete from itself.

We know that if x *and y are complete and caused by events*, then x is part of y just in case Part (x, y), where

(D_{5a})   Part (x, y) just in case

   (C) (C causes y ⊃ C causes x) & −(y causes x) &   (O⊄

   −(∃d)[(C)(C causes x ⊃ C causes d) & −(x causes d)

   & y causes d].   (ND⊄

Suppose that x *and y are complete and caused by no event*. Notice that if x and y are caused by no event, then (OC) is trivially true, and (NDC) is true just in case

   −(∃d)[−(x causes d) & y causes d];

i:e., if x and y are caused by no event, then Part (x,y) just in case

   x causes every event y causes.

So if x and y are complete and caused by no event, then Part (x, y) just in case x causes every event y causes.

Now it comes out as follows that if x and y are complete and caused by no event, then x is part of y just in case x causes every event y causes. Suppose, (i), that x and y are complete and caused by no event, and that x is part of y. Since x is complete and caused by no event, it follows, by (XIII), that x causes every event discrete from itself. By (II), y causes an event only if it is discrete from y. Since x is part of y, every event discrete from y is discrete from x. So whatever events y causes, x causes too. Suppose (ii), that x and y are complete and caused by no event, and that x causes every event y causes. By (XIII), y causes every event discrete from itself. It follows that x causes every event discrete from y. It follows, by (II), that no part of x is discrete from y, and x is therefore part of y.

And we can, therefore, conclude that if x and y are complete and caused by no event, then x is part of y just in case Part (x, y).

Is this plausible? If (XI) is true it is. Ay, for example, is the fusion of all events that occurred prior to midnight last night. Let Ay' be the fusion of all events that occurred prior to midnight the night before last. Ay' should turn out to be part of Ay, and Ay should turn out to not be part of Ay'. And they do. Ay' is complete and caused by no event, so by (XIII), Ay' causes every event discrete from itself; so it causes every event discrete from Ay, and therefore causes every event

Parts of Events (II)

Ay causes. But there are events that Ay' causes that Ay does not (viz., every event that occurred yesterday); so it is not the case that Ay causes every event that Ay' causes.

If x *is caused by no event and* y *is caused by events*, then by (III), x must not be part of y. Notice, however, that here too we can say that x is part of y just in case Part (x, y): for if x is caused by no event and y is caused by events, (OC) is false.

Lastly, suppose x *and* y *are complete and* x *is caused by events and* y *is caused by no event*. Here too we can say that x is part of y just in case Part (x, y). For notice that if x is caused by events and y is caused by no event, then Part (x, y) just in case

$-$(y causes x) &
$-(\exists d)[(C)(C$ causes $x \supset C$ causes $d)$ & $-(x$ causes $d)$ & y causes $d]$,

the second conjunct of which is (NDC) itself. So if x and y are complete, and x is caused by events and y is caused by no event, then Part (x, y) just in case this conjunction is true.

Now it comes out as follows that if x and y are complete and x is caused by events and y is caused by no event, then x is part of y just in case this conjunction is true. Suppose, (i), that x and y are complete and x is caused by events and y is caused by no event, and that the conjunction is true. Since y is complete and caused by no event, it follows, by (XIII), that y causes every event discrete from itself. Since, by hypothesis, $-$(y causes x), we can conclude that x is not discrete from y. It follows that x and y overlap. Then if x is not part of y, there is a part of x—call it d—that is discrete from y. If d is part of x, then, by (III), (C)(C causes $x \supset C$ causes d), and, by (II), $-(x$ causes d). If d is discrete from y, then y causes d. But by hypothesis, (NDC) is true, so there is no such d. It follows that x is part of y. Suppose, (ii), that x and y are complete and x is caused by events and y is caused by no event, and that x is part of y. Since x is part of y, it follows, by (II), that $-$(y causes x). Next, suppose that (NDC) is false. Then for some d,

(C)(C causes $x \supset C$ causes d) & $-(x$ causes d) & y causes d.

We know—from assumption (VI) of the preceding chapter—that

If d and x are caused by events and (C)(C causes $x \supset C$ causes d) and x is complete, then *either* d and x overlap, *or* x causes d.

By hypothesis, x is caused by events; since (C)(C causes $x \supset C$ causes

Acts and Other Events

d), d is also caused by events. By hypothesis, x is complete. Since $-(x$ causes d), d and x overlap. By hypothesis, x is part of y; so part of d is part of y. But then, by (II), it follows that y *does not* cause d. And our supposition has led to a contradiction.

We can, therefore, conclude that if x and y are complete and x is caused by events and y is caused by no event, then x is part of y just in case Part (x, y).

Is this plausible? Yes. Caesar's crossing of the Rubicon, for example, is complete and caused by events, whereas Ay is complete and caused by no event. Caesar's crossing of the Rubicon should turn out to be part of Ay; and it does. For

$\quad$ (C)(C causes Ay $\supset$ C causes the Rubicon-crossing) & $-$(Ay
$\quad$ causes the Rubicon-crossing)

is obviously true; and

$\quad$ $-(\exists d)[(C)(C$ causes the Rubicon-crossing $\supset$ C causes d) &
$\quad$ $-$(the Rubicon-crossing causes d) & Ay causes $d]$

is false only if there is an event which overlaps the Rubicon-crossing and is caused by Ay, and we know, from (II), that there is no such event.

Having covered the possibilities, we are in a position, then, to say that a complete event x is part of a complete event y just in case Part (x, y), where

(D$_{5a}$)$\quad$ Part (x, y) just in case
$\quad$ (C)(C causes $y \supset$C causes x) & $-(y$ causes x)& $\qquad$ (OC
$\quad$ $-(\exists d)[(C)(C$ causes $x \supset$ C causes d) & $-(x$ causes d) &
$\quad$ y causes $d]$. $\qquad\qquad$ (NDC

VII

Parts of Events (III)

Consider again my vacuuming of the carpets and Alpha, parts of which I depicted in the diagrams on page 69 above. Alpha is the fusion of all events that are parts of the carpet-vacuuming and discrete from the electrical circuit's closing. So Alpha is an incomplete event, for there is an event (viz., the electrical circuit's closing) that is caused by part of Alpha, and causes part of Alpha, but which is discrete from Alpha.

It can be shown that

Part (Alpha, my carpet-vacuuming),

and I shall not take space to show it. Unfortunately, it can also be shown that

Part (my carpet-vacuuming, Alpha).

For obviously

$(C)(C$ causes Alpha $\supset C$ causes my carpet-vacuuming) $\&$
$-($Alpha causes my carpet-vacuuming),

so that (OC) is true of my carpet-vacuuming and Alpha. Moreover, suppose that (NDC) is false of my carpet-vacuuming and Alpha; i.e., suppose that for some d,

$(C)(C$ causes my carpet-vacuuming $\supset C$ causes $d) \& -($my carpet-vacuuming causes $d) \&$ Alpha causes d.

Acts and Other Events

We know—from assumption (VI) of Chapter V—that

> If *d* and my carpet-vacuuming are caused by events and
> (C)(C causes my carpet-vacuuming ⊃ C causes *d*) and my
> carpet-vacuuming is complete, then *either d* and my carpet-
> vacuuming overlap, *or* my carpet-vacuuming causes *d*.

My carpet-vacuuming is caused by events. Since (C)(C causes my
carpet-vacuuming ⊃C causes *d*), *d* is too. My carpet-vacuuming is
complete. Since −(my carpet-vacuuming causes *d*), *d* and my carpet-
vacuuming overlap. Since Alpha causes *d*, we can conclude that *d* is
discrete from Alpha. Now every event that overlaps my carpet-
vacuuming and is discrete from Alpha contains a part of the electrical
circuit's closing. Since Alpha causes *d*, we can conclude, by

(III)   C causes *y* if and only if C causes all of *y*'s parts,

that Alpha causes part of the electrical circuit's closing. But (as I said I
would assume, on page 70 above) every part of the electrical circuit's
closing causes part of Alpha. It follows, by

(I)   Causality is transitive,

that Alpha causes part of Alpha—which is ruled out by

(II)   No event causes any of its parts; no event is caused by any of
       its parts.

Now, in light of my use of the term "part", we must surely allow
ourselves to assume about events that

(XIV)   *x* is identical with *y* just in case *x* is part of *y* and
        y is part of *x*.

I take this to be wholly obvious, and in need of no argument.

We therefore know that we cannot say, quite generally, that an
event *x* is part of an event *y* just in case Part (*x*, *y*): for

> Part (Alpha, my carpet-vacuuming) & Part (my carpet-
> vacuuming, Alpha)

is true, yet Alpha is plainly not identical with my carpet-vacuuming.

Let us take a closer look at incomplete events. Alpha is the fusion of
all events that are parts of my carpet-vacuuming and discrete from the
electrical circuit's closing; so it is the result of subtracting a complete
event (the circuit-closing) from a complete event (my carpet-vacuuming). Let Alpha' be the fusion of all events that are parts of my carpet-
vacuuming and discrete from both the circuit-closing and air's starting
to be sucked up through the hose, and depict part of it as in the
diagram below.

Parts of Events (III)

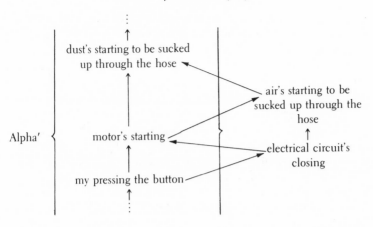

Since the fusion of the circuit-closing and the air-start is an incomplete event, Alpha' is the result of subtracting an incomplete event (the fusion of the circuit-closing and the air-start) from a complete event (my carpet-vacuuming).

It seems highly plausible that

(XV)   Every incomplete event is a fusion of complete events, and I suggest we assume it is true. Then in particular, the incomplete event that Alpha' is the result of subtracting from my carpet-vacuuming is a fusion of complete events—it is the fusion, in fact, of the complete event that is the circuit-closing and the complete event that is the air-start. So we can say that while Alpha is the result of subtracting a complete event from a complete event, Alpha' is the result of subtracting *two* complete events from a complete event. And, indeed, we can say that every incomplete event is the result of subtracting one or more complete events from a complete event.

Let us say that z_1 and z_2 and . . . 'complete' y just in case y is incomplete, and z_1 and z_2 and . . . are complete, and the fusion of y and z_1 and z_2 and . . . is complete, and the fusion of y and z_1 and z_2 and . . . is part of every complete event that y is part of.

Let us say that z_1 and z_2 and . . . 'minimally complete' y just in case z_1 and z_2 and . . . complete y, and there are no z'_1, z'_2, . . . such that z'_1 and z'_2 and . . . complete y and the fusion of z'_1 and z'_2 and . . . is part of, but not identical with, the fusion of z_1 and z_2 and.

Acts and Other Events

. . . Thus, for example, the circuit-closing and my pressing the button complete Alpha; but they do not minimally complete Alpha, since the circuit-closing also completes Alpha, and the fusion of the circuit-closing (which just is the circuit-closing) is part of, but not identical with, the fusion of the circuit-closing and my pressing the button. By contrast, the circuit-closing does not merely complete Alpha, it minimally completes Alpha.

I take it to be entirely acceptable to assume, also, that

(XVI)   If y is incomplete, then there are a z_1, z_2, . . . such that z_1 and z_2 and . . . minimally complete y.

With assumptions (XV) and (XVI) in hand, we are able to give a plausible account of the part-whole relations among incomplete events, and thus a plausible account of the part-whole relations among events generally.

There are four alternatives for a pair of events x and y.

(i) x *is complete and* y *is complete.* Here all is well: we know that x is part of y just in case Part (x, y).

(ii) x *is incomplete and* y *is complete.* It is easily seen that here too we can say that x is part of y just in case Part (x, y). Trouble arose for Alpha, for example, not because it did not turn out that Part (Alpha, my carpet-vacuuming), but rather because it did turn out that Part (my carpet-vacuuming, Alpha).

So let us define a new predicate as follows:

  $PART_1$ (x, y) just in case y is complete and Part (x, y),
where "Part (x, y)" is defined as in (D_{5a}). Then we can say that if y is complete, x is part of y just in case $PART_1$ (x, y).

(iii) x *is complete and* y *is incomplete.* Intuitively, x is part of y just in case x is part of every complete event that y is part of *and* x is discrete from z_1, z_2, . . . where z_1 and z_2 and . . . minimally complete y. Every complete event that y is part of is a complete event α such that $PART_1$ (y, α). So we can say that it is a necessary condition for x to be part of y that

  (α) $[PART_1$ $(y, \alpha) \supset PART_1$ $(x, \alpha)]$.

By (XVI), and y being incomplete, we know that there are a z_1, z_2, . . . such that z_1 and z_2 and . . . minimally complete y, and we need only now express the requirement that x be discrete from z_1 and z_2 and. . . . By definition, events E and E' are discrete if and only if they have no part in common. So we can say that it is a necessary condition for x to be part of y that

$(\exists z_1, z_2, \ldots .)[z_1$ and z_2 and . . . minimally complete y &
$-(\exists \beta)\{\text{PART}_1 \ (\beta, x)$ & $[\text{PART}_1 \ (\beta, z_1)$ or
$\text{PART}_1 \ (\beta, z_2)$ or . . .$]\}]$.

And I suggest that if we define a new predicate as follows,

$\text{PART}_2 \ (x, y)$ just in case x is complete and y is incomplete
&
$(\alpha)[\text{PART}_1 \ (y, \alpha) \supset \text{PART}_1 \ (x, \alpha)]$ &
$(\exists z_1, z_2, \ldots .)[z_1$ and z_2 and . . . minimally complete y &
$-(\exists \beta)\{\text{PART}_1 \ (\beta, x)$ & $[\text{PART}_1 \ (\beta, z_1)$ or
$\text{PART}_1 \ (\beta, z_2)$ or . . .$]\}]$,

we can say that if x is complete and y is incomplete, x is part of y just
in case $\text{PART}_2 \ (x, y)$.

I take this to be eminently plausible. It takes mere industry to
become clear, for example, that

PART_2 (my pressing the button, Alpha)

and

PART_2 (my pressing the button, Alpha$'$).

(iv) x *is incomplete and* y *is incomplete.* In light of (XV), we can say
that x is part of y just in case every complete part of x is a complete
part of y. So if we define a new predicate as follows,

$\text{PART}_3 \ (x, y)$ just in case x is incomplete and y is incomplete
& $(\alpha)[\text{PART}_2 \ (\alpha, x) \supset \text{PART}_2 \ (\alpha, y)]$,

we can say that if x is incomplete and y is incomplete, then x is part of
y just in case $\text{PART}_3 \ (x, y)$. And this too is eminently plausible: it takes
mere industry to become clear, for example, that

PART_3 (Alpha$'$, Alpha),

but not

PART_3 (Alpha, Alpha$'$).

If this is right, we have what we want: we can say that an event x is
part of an event y just in case *PART* (x, y), where

(D_{5b})   *PART* (x, y) just in case $\text{PART}_1 \ (x, y)$ or $\text{PART}_2 \ (x, y)$ or
$\text{PART}_3 \ (x, y)$.

A number of comments are called for.

1. I have not, of course, *defined* ". . . is part of ——" for events:
construed as a definition, my account would be circular. For the
terms "complete" and "incomplete" appear in the definientia of
"$\text{PART}_1 \ (x, y)$", "$\text{PART}_2 \ (x, y)$", and "$\text{PART}_3 \ (x, y)$"; and it will be
remembered that I defined those terms as follows:

I shall call an event *IE* an 'incomplete' event just in case there is an event *E* such that *E* is caused by part of *IE*, and *E* causes part of *IE*, but *E* is discrete from *IE*. A complete event, then, is an event *CE* such that there is *no* event *E* such that part of *CE* causes *E* and *E* causes part of *CE*, and *E* is discrete from *CE*.

That is, I defined them by use of ". . . is part of ——". (And the role of ". . . is part of ——" in the definition of ". . . minimally completes ——" can hardly have been overlooked.)

The circle could be made a little larger. For example, I think it will be plain that we can define "complete" and "incomplete" as follows:

> *y* is complete just in case *y* is the fusion of all *x* such that Part (*x*, *y*);
>
> *y* is incomplete just in case *y* is not complete.

But this only makes the circle larger. For it will be remembered (from page 78 above) that the term "fusion" was introduced as follows: we are permitted to rewrite

> *x* is part of *E* just in case either *x* has *F* or *x* has no parts discrete from all *y* such that *y* has *F*

as

> *E* is a fusion of all *x* which have *F*.

And I know of no way of defining "complete" and "incomplete" which does not ultimately involve use of the term ". . . is part of ——".

Nevertheless, something *has* been gained. If I am right in thinking that an event *x* is part of an event *y* just in case *PART* (*x*, *y*)—however peculiar x and y may be, whether temporally continuous or discontinuous, caused by events or not caused by events, complete or incomplete—then it appears that we really may have it that the Principle of Event-Fusion is true. That is, we can give the peculiar event-fusions which that principle commits us to a place among events, for we can give a plausible account of, not merely what temporal relations they have to other events, not merely what causal relations they have to other events, but also what events they have as parts and are parts of. (Cf. page 82.)

Moreover, we are able to say that events, together with the relation of discreteness (among events), form a model of the Leonard-Goodman 'Calculus of Individuals' [1]: i.e., when we take the variables of that

---

[1] See footnote 1, Ch. VI, for the reference.

Parts of Events (III)

calculus to range over events, and assign that relation to the primitive predicate, ". . . is discrete from ____", the axioms of that calculus are true.

2. If an event x is part of an event y just in case $PART$ (x, y), then—in light of assumption

(XIV) x is identical with y just in case x is part of y and y is part of x—

we have in hand an obvious criterion for event-identity:

   x is identical with y just in case $PART$ (x, y) & $PART$ (y, x).

It is worth noting that if every event were complete, then that very much simpler criterion for event-identity which I mentioned on page 70 above would also have been true: i.e., it would have been true to say that

   x is identical with y just in case x and y have the same causes and same effects.

For suppose, (i), that x and y are complete, and that x and y are identical. Since x and y are identical, they have the same causes and same effects. Suppose, instead, (ii), that x and y are complete, and that x and y have the same causes and same effects. Since x and y have the same causes,

(OC) $(C)(C$ causes $y \supset C$ causes $x)$ & $-(y$ causes $x)$

is true of them; since x and y have the same effects, there is no event which y causes and x does not, so

(NDC) $-(\exists d)[(C)(C$ causes $x \supset C$ causes $d)$ & $-(x$ causes $d)$ & y causes $d]$

is also true of them. It follows that

   Part (x, y).

By hypothesis, y is complete; so it follows that

   $PART_1$ (x, y),

and therefore that

   $PART$ (x, y).

Analogous reasoning yields

   $PART$ (y, x).

And it follows that x is identical with y.

Alas, not every event is complete. But what this shows is that when we are dealing with events which are complete, appeal to the simpler criterion suffices.

97

Acts and Other Events

3. What is commonly called 'The Identity Thesis' is a thesis which contains as one conjunct the following:

Every mental event is identical with some physical event.

(The thesis is commonly taken to have other conjuncts, viz., conjuncts identifying mental states and states of affairs with physical states and states of affairs, mental facts with physical facts, mental properties with physical properties.) Now it is often said that this thesis—at any rate, this conjunct of the thesis—may plausibly be maintained only by one who has in hand a criterion of event-identity. It has never been plain to me why this should be said. Perhaps some people say it because the logical form of the conjunct is

$$(x)[Mx \supset (\exists y)(Py \ \& \ x = y)].$$

But this would be a poor reason for saying it. After all, we may easily restate the conjunct as follows,

Everything which is a mental event is a physical event,

the logical form of which is

$$(x)[Mx \supset Px].$$

But in any case, it does not matter, for we now do have in hand a criterion for event-identity. I do not for a moment argue that this conjunct of the Identity Thesis is true; I only offer the criterion for event-identity which it has been said we must have if we are so much as to take the thesis seriously.

VIII

Events, States of Affairs, and Activities

What are events? One answer is this:

(D₆ₐ)   Event (y) just in case there is an entity e such that $PART$ (e, y).

This answer is true. For we know, by (D₅ᵦ), that $PART$ (e, y) just in case

$$PART_1 \ (e, y) \text{ or } PART_2 \ (e, y) \text{ or } PART_3 \ (e, y).$$

We know, also, that the definiens of "$PART_1 \ (x, y)$" contains, as a conjunct, "y is complete," and that the definientia of "$PART_2 \ (x, y)$" and "$PART_3 \ (x, y)$" contain, as a conjunct, "y is incomplete." So we know that "$PART \ (e, y)$" entails

y is complete or y is incomplete.

Now "complete" and "incomplete" are mere shorthand for "complete event" and "incomplete event"; so what entails this plainly entails that y is an event. So if there is an entity e such that $PART$ (e, y), then y is an event. Moreover, if y is an event, then there is an entity e—if only y itself—such that $PART$ (e, y). So the answer I just gave is true.

But I doubt that anyone who wonders what an event is will be satisfied by this answer. For if you do not know what an event is, you can hardly be supposed to know what a complete event or an incomplete event is.

Acts and Other Events

For analogous reasons, I doubt that anyone will be satisfied by the answer—also true—that

(D$_{6b}$)   Event (x) just in case there is an entity e such that $PART$ (x, e).

Let us look at some other answers.

1. A number of people have been attracted to the view that an event is a something's-having-a-property.[1] Thus suppose that John is now running, so that an event is now occurring that consists in John's running. According to this view, this event is John's possessing a certain property—thus, I suppose,

the property 'is running.'

Again, suppose Jim is now doing some shopping, so that an event is now occurring that consists in Jim's shopping. According to this view, this event is Jim's possessing a certain property—thus, I suppose,

the property 'is shopping.'

I do not believe that any of the people who have been attracted by this view would be prepared to say, in all seriousness, that

(D$_{6c}$)   Event (x) just in case for some y, and some property, x is y's possessing that property.

I do think they would be prepared to say, in all seriousness, that

(S$_1$)   If Event (x) then for some y, and some property, x is y's possessing that property;

but I think that they would agree that

(S$_2$)   If for some y, and some property, x is y's possessing that property, then Event (x)

cannot be taken seriously. Consider, for example, the entity x that is my left thumb's possessing

the property 'is dirty.'

I suppose there is such an entity as x, for my left thumb *is* dirty. But this entity—if there really is, as I suppose, such an entity—is surely no event. If anything at all is certain about events, it is that they are happenings, occurrences; and while there was a happening, an occurrence, and thus an event, which was my left thumb's becoming dirty, and while there will be a happening, an occurrence, and thus an event, which will be my left thumb's ceasing to be dirty, there is no happening, or occurrence, which is its *being* dirty. If, as I think, there

---

[1] See, e.g., Jaegwon Kim, "On the Psycho-Physical Identity Theory," *American Philosophical Quarterly*, 3 (1966), 227–235.

Events, States of Affairs, Activities

is such an entity as my left thumb's being dirty, it is surely a *state of affairs* and not an event.

Those who put forward the view of events that we are looking at do not tell us how to single out those entities x that are a y's possessing a property and that are events from those entities x that are a y's possessing a property and that are not events. For their purposes, they say,[2] it is not necessary to distinguish between events and states of affairs: it is enough for their purposes if (S_1) is true. They may be right. In any case, I think we should not bother to press them on it. For it seems to me not only that there are entities x that are a y's possessing a property and that are not events, but also that there are events that are not a y's possessing a property. (S_1), in other words, must be given up along with (S_2).

My first ground for rejecting (S_1) comes out as follows. I asked a moment ago that you suppose that John was then running; suppose there not only was then but still is occurring an event that consists in John's running. Let us suppose that he is running in the Boston Common, and indeed that he has been running there and will continue to run there throughout his running; I should imagine, then, that just as an event is occurring that is

(a)   John's running,

so also an event is occurring that is

(b)   John's running in the Boston Common.

If (S_1) is true, then—I suppose—so also are

(i)   event (a) is John's possessing the property 'is running,'

and

(ii)   event (b) is John's possessing the property 'is running in the Boston Common.'

Now it is plausible to suppose—and it is supposed by those who put forward this view of events—that

(S_3) y's possessing the property F is identical with z's possessing the property G just in case y is identical with z and the property F is identical with the property G.

It is also plausible to suppose—and it is supposed by just about everybody—that

(S_4) the property F is not identical with the property G if it is possible that a man should possess the property F and not possess the property G.

[2] See *ibid.*, pp. 231–232.

Acts and Other Events

It is plainly possible that a man should possess the property 'is running' and not possess the property 'is running in the Boston Common'—I am sure there in fact is a man who is now running and is not running in the Boston Common, since he is running elsewhere. It follows, by (S_4), that these properties are not identical. It follows, by (S_3), that if (i) and (ii) are true, then event (a) is not identical with event (b).

Those who put forward the view of events we are looking at would cheerfully accept this conclusion: event (a), they would say, while concurrent with event (b), is not identical with it.

I think they are wrong to accept this conclusion. It seems to me plain that (a) *is* identical with (b). For these events are, as I take it, both complete; and it seems to me plain that everything that causes the one causes 'the other,' and that everything the one causes, 'the other' causes.

Indeed, there is independent reason to think (a) is identical with (b). (b)—i.e., John's running in the Boston Common—surely has the property 'is a running,' and therefore is a running. If it is a running, it surely is a running by John. If so, it is identical with an entity that is a running by John. We surely ought to be able to conclude that it is identical with an entity that is one of John's runnings. If it is, it surely is identical with (a). Else there would be *two* events, which go on throughout the same place and throughout the same time, and each of which is one of John's runnings.

If you agree with me that (a) is identical with (b), then you must give up (S_4) or (S_3) or give up either (i) or (ii) or both. But we really, after all, had better keep (S_4). And (S_3) really does seem plausible for these entities: if there are such entities as a something's-having-a-property, then surely (S_3) does give their identity-conditions. So if I am right that event (a) is identical with event (b), it is one or both of (i) and (ii) that must be given up.

Of course it would still be possible to retain (S_1). It could be said that while (i) is true, (ii) is not: that (ii) must be replaced by

(ii′)   event (b) is identical with John's possessing the property 'is running.'

Alternatively, it could be said that while (ii) is true, (i) is not: that (i) must be replaced by

(i′)   event (a) is identical with John's possessing the property 'is running in the Boston Common.'

102

Or it could be said that both (i) and (ii) are false: that (i) must be replaced by

(i″)   event (a) is identical with John's possessing the property 'is running in the Boston Common while wearing gym shoes,'

and (ii) must be replaced by

(ii″)   event (b) is identical with John's possessing the property 'is running in the Boston Common while wearing gym shoes,'

because John is running while wearing gym shoes. Thus it could be said that while every event *is* a something's-having-a-property, it is not always possible to detect which property from the words used in referring to the event. Proponents of this view would in any case want to say that it was not always possible to detect which property from the words used to refer to the event. Consider, for example, the event Mary was just now describing to Sam; one could not tell from *these* words what property was such that the event was a something's-having-it.

On the other hand, is it to be the case that one can never detect which property from the words used to refer to the event? And if ever, then why not in the case of the words I used to refer to events (a) and (b)?

So I think we really should suppose that if (S_1) is true, then (i) and (ii) are. Since it seems to me plain, as I said, that event (a) is identical with event (b), it seems to me that (i) and (ii) are not both true, and therefore that (S_1) is not true.

But while this seems to me a good reason to reject (S_1), I do not for a moment take it to be a conclusive one. For, as I said, the proponents of (S_1) would cheerfully accept the conclusion that event (a) is not identical with event (b), and I have in hand no proof that they are wrong to do so—for I have in hand no proof that (a) and (b) have the same causes and same effects.

There is, however, a second reason to reject (S_1), and this second reason is a conclusive one.

Let us take a closer look at the properties that have been mentioned so far. I shall give the name "(1)" to some words, viz., the words

(1)   the property 'is running';

and the name "(2)" to the words

(2)   John possesses the property 'is running.'

I asked a few moments ago that you suppose that John was then running; let us suppose he is still running. So John possesses the property 'is running.' The words (2)—which I just now wrote in writing the preceding sentence—contain the words (1); to what property did I refer by (1) when I wrote (2) then? I am using the words (1) in such a way that the property I referred to when I wrote (2) then was the property that a thing has just in case it was then running. I.e., it is the property to which I would have been referring by the words

(3)   the property 'is now running,'

had I written, instead, the sentence "So John possesses the property 'is now running.' "

Suppose that the time at which I wrote the sentence "So John possesses the property 'is running' " was 10:07 A.M., February 8, 1975. John was running at that time. So John possesses the property 'was then running.' And the property I referred to by (1) at 10:07 A.M. is the very same property as that to which I just now—at 10:13 A.M.—referred by the words

(4)   the property 'was then running,'

when I wrote—as I did at 10:13 A.M.—the sentence "So John possesses the property 'was then running.' "

Again, this property is the very same property as that to which I would be referring by the words

(5)   the property 'was running at 10:07 A.M., February 8, 1975,'

if I said, or wrote, at any time in the future the sentence "John possesses the property 'was running at 10:07 A.M., February 8, 1975' "; and it is the same as the property to which I would be referring by the words

(6)   the property 'is (tenselessly) running at 10:07 A.M., February
           8, 1975,'

if I said, or wrote, at any time at all the sentence "John possesses the property 'is (tenselessly) running at 10:07 A.M., February 8, 1975.' " More briefly, the property I referred to by (1) at 10:07 A.M., which is the same as the property I referred to by (4) at 10:13 A.M., is the property to which (5) now and in future refers, and is also the property to which (6) at any time refers.

Notice that (S_4) makes no trouble for this claim. It is not possible that a man should possess the property to which I referred by (1) at 10:07 A.M. and not possess the property to which (5) and (6) refer. A man could not have the property a thing has just in case it was then running without also having the property a thing has just in case it was running at 10:07 A.M., and the property a thing has just in case it is (tenselessly) running at 10:07 A.M.: for the time then *was* 10:07 A.M.

Now the property to which (5) and (6) refer—and therefore the property to which I referred by (1) at 10:07 A.M.—is a property such that if you have it at any time, then you have it at every time. It cannot be that you possess the property to which (5) and (6) refer on a Saturday morning but not on the Saturday afternoon. If it is true to say of you at 10:07 A.M., February 8, 1975, that you possess that property, then it is true to say of you at any time that you possess that property.

Now we are not told so, explicitly, by the proponents of the view of events we are looking at, but it seems to me entirely plausible to attribute to them—to some of them, at any rate—the view that

(S₅)   *y*'s possessing the property *F* exists at, and only at, such times as *y* possesses the property *F*.

I should, myself, think this a plausible view to take of the existence-conditions of those entities *x* that are a something's-having-a-property: if there are such things at all, they exist so long, and only so long, as the something has the property.

If (S₅) is true, the event that consists in John's running cannot be John's possessing the property to which I referred by (1) at 10:07 A.M. For John possesses that property at all times; so, by (S₅), his possessing that property exists at all times. But the event that consists in his running does not exist at all times. John sometimes sleeps, after all.

Indeed, there is no property to which I might at any time refer by (1) that is such that the event which consists in John's running is John's possessing it.

The proponents of the view of events we are looking at may be expected to say that I have been grossly unfair to them: i.e. that the properties *they* have in mind are very different from the ones I have been drawing attention to. The properties *we* have in mind (they may be expected to say) are, as it were, 'undated properties,' i.e., properties such that a man may have them at one time and not at another. We allow (I take it they will allow this) that the property to which we refer by the words

(7)   the property 'is red'

when we say, as we now do, i.e., at 10:25 A.M., February 8, 1975, that John's chameleon possesses the property 'is red,' is the same as the property to which

(8)   the property 'is (tenselessly) red at 10:25 A.M., February 8,

1975,'

refers, and thus is a property such that if a thing has it at any time, the thing has it at every time. But now consider a different property, viz., the property to which

(9)   the property 'red,'

and

(10)   the property 'being red'

refer. This is not the same as the property to which we referred by (7) at 10:25 A.M.; it is a property John's chameleon possessed at 10:25 A.M., but then ceased to possess at 10:28 A.M., and now does not possess. Now the property such that the event that consists in John's running—the event we have been talking about—is John's possessing it, is like the property to which (9) and (10) refer: it is the property to which

(11)   the property 'running'

and

(12)   the property 'being running'

refer. *That* is a property a man has only while he runs. So, by (S_5), John's possessing it does *not* exist at all times—for John, after all, does not run at all times.

But this really will not help. Let us suppose that John runs in the Boston Common every Saturday morning. So John does not only possess this morning the property to which (12) refers, he possessed the property to which (12) refers last Saturday morning too, and the Saturday morning before that, and so on. By (S_5), the entity that is John's possessing that property existed then, too. I.e., the very same entity that exists this morning existed on all Saturday mornings past also.

Let us suppose, moreover, that John never runs except on Saturday mornings, and then only in the Boston Common. By (S_5), the entity that is John's possessing the property to which (12) refers went out of existence when John stopped running last Saturday and came back into existence when John started running again this morning. Some people would say this is impossible: they would say that if an entity goes out of existence, then it cannot itself—the very same entity— come back into existence.

Well, perhaps the thesis that if an entity goes out of existence it cannot come back into existence is a mere prejudice. (It is, in fact, very hard to find any other ground for this thesis than what issues from verificationism.)

But that does not matter: there is a second difficulty. It is perfectly possible that an event consisting in a man's running should cause a later event consisting in hís running. Thus we might suppose that the event that occurred last Saturday and that consisted in John's running caused the event that is occurring this morning and that consists in John's running. Imagine whatever causal route you like (e.g., imagine that his running last Saturday did such wonders for his heart that his doctor coerced him into doing the same again this morning). Now if the event that occurred last Saturday and that consisted in John's running is John's possessing the property to which (12) refers; and if, also, the event that is occurring this morning and that consists in John's running is John's possessing the property to which (12) refers; then what we here suppose is that an event causes itself. But assumption

(II)   No event causes any of its parts; no event is caused by any of its parts

of the preceding chapters is surely *not* a mere prejudice—surely an event *cannot* cause itself.

The arguments I have produced against the view of events we are looking at turn on the supposition that (S_5) does indeed give the existence-conditions of entities that are a something's-having-a-property. I did say above that I took this to be a plausible view of their existence-conditions; I said also that it seems to me plausible to attribute (S_5) to some of those who hold the view of events we are looking at. Some, but *not* all. Chisholm, for example, rejects (S_5); and we ought to attend to what he proposes we replace it with.

Chisholm's account of events is motivated by the need to explain what he calls "the fact of *recurrence*"—i.e., "the fact that there are some things that recur, or happen more than once."[3] John's running, for example; Chisholm thinks that can recur—indeed, that it can happen every Saturday morning. For Chisholm invites us to remember that we do say such things as "John is running again this morning, in fact, the same thing has been happening every Saturday morning for the last six months," and that they are often true. Chisholm proposes that we take such things literally: to say (sometimes truly) that there is an event happening now, which has also happened on a number of occasions in the past.

But because Chisholm holds that if an entity goes out of existence it cannot come back into existence, he does not opt for (S_5). He proposes that we distinguish between an event's existing on the one hand and its

[3] See Roderick Chisholm, "Events and Propositions," *Nous*, 4 (1970), 15–24.

occurring or taking place on the other hand. When John stopped running last Saturday at noon, the event that consisted in his running did not go out of existence, it only stopped occurring; and when John started running this morning, the event that consists in his running did not come into existence again, it only started occurring again. The event exists at all times, whether John is running or not; it is occurring at and only at such times as John is running. Thus we are to replace (S₅) with something more complicated, viz.,

(S₅') y's possessing the property F exists at all times, but y's possessing the property F is occurring at, and only at, such times as y possesses the property F.

It should be stressed that on Chisholm's view a man's possessing the property F exists at all times even if he never possesses the property; but of course if he never possesses the property, then his possessing of it—though it exists—never occurs. For an event to recur, then, is not for it to come back into existence after having gone out of existence; it is, rather, for it, simply, to re-occur.

And how shall we make room for the fact—let us suppose it a fact—that the event that occurred last Saturday morning consisting in John's running caused the event that is occurring this morning consisting in John's running? More generally, what on a view such as this can it come to for one event to cause another? I am inclined to think that one who holds a view such as this must take sentences of the form

Event C causes event E

to have the logical form

That event C occurs causes that event E occurs—

it not being events (which exist all the time) that cause and get caused, but rather their occurring. (And it could, of course, be insisted that expressions of the form "that event x occurs" do not refer to events but instead to facts, or perhaps better, to no entity at all.) In any case, I take it we would be urged to describe what we are supposing to be a fact as follows: that John's running occurred last Saturday caused that John's running is occurring this morning. Now I am inclined to think that

(II')   The occurring of an event does not cause any later occurring of that same event

is fully as plausible as assumption (II); but we will be told that this is a mere prejudice, issuing from the assumption that events cannot re-occur, and that once one gives up this prejudice surely one will have to allow that the occurring of one event at one time can perfectly well cause the re-occurring of that same event at a later time. So Chisholm does not merely avoid a conflict with our metaphysical prejudice that if an entity goes out of existence it cannot come back into existence; he is also able to make room for the causal fact I proposed we take to be a fact.

But there is yet another difficulty, which does face Chisholm's view, and does seem to me conclusive against it.

Let us suppose that this morning John ran first north across the Boston Common and then back south across it. Suppose also that John is lazy, so that is all the running he did this morning, viz., first north, then south, across the Common. I am inclined to think that the event that occurred this morning and that consisted in John's running north across the Common was part of the event that occurred this morning and that consisted in his running. Chisholm, however, cannot agree. For let us suppose that John has never run north across the Common before: whenever he ran in the past, it was always either east or west across the Common. On Chisholm's view, the event that consists in John's running has occurred, and recurred, many times in the past; but the event that consists in John's running north across the Common occurred for the first time only this morning. Now it seems unquestionable that

> If an event has occurred many times in the past, then every part of it has occurred many times in the past.

It follows on Chisholm's view that the event that occurred this morning and that consisted in John's running north across the Common is not part of the event that occurred this morning and that consisted in John's running.

We have not yet reached what seems to me the conclusive objection to Chisholm's view. I noted above that although it seems to *me* plain that the event that occurred this morning consisting in John's running is identical with the event that occurred this morning consisting in John's running in the Boston Common, I cannot prove it, since I cannot prove that everything that causes the one causes 'the other,' and that everything the one causes 'the other' causes. Similarly, though it seems to *me* plain that the event that occurred this morning consisting in John's running north across the Common is part of the event that occurred this morning consisting in John's running, I cannot prove it, since I cannot prove that

PART (John's running north across the Common, John's running).

Nevertheless, this does remind us that an account of what events are must make room for parts of events—as I take it, an account of what events are that does not contain, or at any rate leave room for, an account of what it is for an event to have this or that event as part is by virtue of that an incorrect account of what events are.

Chisholm's account of events has room for an account of what it is for an event to have this or that event as part. But I think the only tool available to him to construct such an account is the entailment-relation. For it seems to me that appeals to causality will yield a criterion for part-hood according to which the event that occurred this morning and that consisted in John's running north across the Common *is* part of the event that occurred this morning and that consisted in John's running.

I do not, of course, propose that he opt for the following thesis-schema,

y's verb-phrase$_1$ing is part of z's verb-phrase$_2$ing just in case "y verb-phrase$_1$s" entails "z verb-phrase$_2$s":

for plainly

John runs north across the Common

entails

John runs,

yet, as we saw, Chisholm's view of events rules out that the event that consists in John's running north across the Common is part of the event that consists in John's running. Rather I propose he opt for—indeed, I think it the only account available to him—the thesis-schema

y's verb-phrase$_1$ing is part of z's verb-phrase$_2$ing just in case "z verb-phrase$_2$s" entails "y verb-phrase$_1$s".

It would follow that the event that consists in John's running is part of the event that consists in John's running north across the Common; and I think that Chisholm—more generally, anyone for whom an event is a something's-having-a-property—would be glad to accept this conclusion.

More generally, it would be possible to extend the view to allow for 'molecular' as well as 'atomic' events. Thus it could be said that atomic events are a something's-having-a-property, but that molecular events are more complex. Consider, for example, the event that occurred this morning and that consisted in John's running *and* John's chewing gum. (I am supposing that John chewed gum this morning, too.) That event could be said to be molecular: it could be said to have, as parts, John's running and John's chewing gum, in that

John runs and John chews gum

entails

John runs

and

John chews gum.

This particular kind of molecular event could be called a 'conjunctive molecular event'. [4]

Indeed, room could be made for (at least some of) the peculiar events that we looked at in preceding chapters. Take Gamma, for example. Gamma, you may remember, was the fusion of Caesar's crossing of the Rubicon and my grating pepper onto an egg. It could be said that this is a perfectly respectable event, though it is a conjunctive molecular event; and that it has, as parts, Caesar's crossing of the Rubicon and my grating pepper onto an egg, since

Caesar crosses the Rubicon and JT grates pepper onto an egg

entails both

Caesar crosses the Rubicon

and

JT grates pepper onto an egg.

Of course, if you are Chisholm, you will think these events different in an important respect. Let us suppose that John chews gum every morning on which he runs; then the event that consists in John's running and John's chewing gum has recurred many times in the past—it occurs every Saturday morning, in fact, since we are supposing he runs every Saturday morning. But Caesar crossed the Rubicon only once and never will again; so the event that consists in Caesar's crossing of the Rubicon and my grating pepper onto an egg occurs only once—however often I grate pepper onto an egg. I.e., a part of the

[4] What Chisholm calls 'conjunctive events' are different from what I here propose (for him) calling 'conjunctive molecular events'. Chisholm would not call John's running *and* John's chewing gum a conjunctive event; what he would call a conjunctive event is, for example, John's running *while* he chews gum. See *ibid.*

conjunctive molecular event (viz., my grating pepper onto an egg) may recur over and over again; but the conjunctive molecular event does not—on the supposition, surely unquestionable, that

> An event occurs many times only if every part of it occurs many times.[5]

So it looks as if this account of the matter has a future. Alas, it is a short one. For just as

> John runs north across the Common

entails

> John runs,

so also does

> John runs south across the Common

entail

> John runs.

So the event that consists in John's running would then be part of both the event that consists in John's running north across the Common and the event that consists in John's running south across the Common. These two events would literally share a part. But it surely is unquestionable that

> If an event x and an event y have a part in common, then (if they occur) there is a time at which both are occurring— i.e., such a time as their common part is occurring.

(I insert the parenthetical clause because, it will be remembered, Chisholm distinguishes between the existence and the occurring of events.) But we may surely take it that there is never a time at which John is running north acros the Common and at which, also, John is running south across the Common. I take this to be conclusive against this account of the parts of events.

I have, of course, no proof that this is the *only* way of accounting for what it is for an event to have this or that event as part which is available to Chisholm. Nevertheless, I believe we can say: it seems likely that this is the only one available to him, and in the absence of anything more plausible as replacement for it, there is conclusive reason to reject his account of what events are.

---

[5] It should be stressed: the event that consists of Caesar's crossing of the Rubicon and my grating pepper onto an egg is not, for Chisholm, a conjunctive event. It is not identical with what is, for Chisholm, a conjunctive event, viz., Caesar's crossing of the Rubicon *while* I grate pepper onto an egg. The latter event has never occurred; the former event has.

2. A rather more obscure proposal is that an event is a something's-having-a-property-at-a-time.[6] On this view, the event that occurred this morning and that consisted in John's running is John's possessing the property to which

(1)   the property 'being running'

refers at the time at which he ran—i.e., throughout the time from 9:48 A.M. to 10:47 A.M., February 8, 1975, which, let us suppose, is the time throughout which he ran this morning.

Now what makes me call this proposal obscure is this. I am inclined to think that if the following two expressions, viz.,

(2)   John's possessing the property 'being running' throughout 9:48 A.M. to 10:47 A.M., February 8, 1975,

and

(3)   John's possessing the property 'is (tenselessly) running throughout 9:48 A.M. to 10:47 A.M., February 8, 1975',

refer to anything at all, then it is to one and the same thing that they refer. After all, surely what

the chameleon's possessing the property 'being red' throughout 9:48 A.M. to 10:47 A¡M., February 8, 1975,

refers to is what

the chameleon's being red throughout 9:48 A.M. to 10:47 A.M., February 8, 1975;

refers to; and surely what that refers to is what

the chameleon's possessing the property 'being red throughout 9:48 A.M. to 10:47 A.M., February 8, 1975',

refers to; and surely what that refers to is what

the chameleon's possessing the property 'is (tenselessly) red throughout 9:48 A.M. to 10:47 A.M., February 8, 1975',

refers to. The property to which

the property 'is (teselessly) running throughout 9:48 A¡M. to 10:47 A.M., February 8, 1975',

[6] See, e.g., Alvin I. Goldman, *A Theory of Human Action*, (Englewood Cliffs, N.J.: Prentice-Hall, 1970). (Strictly speaking, Goldman says only that acts are a something's-having-an-act-property-at-a-time; and he draws attention to difficulties that arise even for this more restricted thesis. I ignore the qualifications and difficulties.) It seems to me possible that Kim, in "On the Psycho-Physical Identity Theory," really means to be opting for this rather more obscure proposal too: his account of events there is preceded by the words "Suppressing reference to time. . . ." In any case, Kim says in a later paper that an event is "a concrete object (or *n*-tuple of objects) exemplifying a property (or *n*-adic relation) at a time"—see his "Causation, Nomic Subsumption, and the Concept of Event," *Journal of Philosophy*, 70 (1973), 217–236.

refers, however, is a property such that if John has it at one time, he has it at all times. So if

(S₅)   y's possessing the property F exists at, and only at, such times as y possesses the property F

tells us the existence-conditions of a something's-having-a-property, then the entity to which (3) refers, and therefore the entity to which (2) refers, exists at all times. If you are not Chisholm, you will take it to follow that the entity to which (3) refers, and therefore the entity to which (2) refers, is occurring at all times. If you are Chisholm, then you reject (S₅) in favor of

(S₅')   y's possessing the property F exists at all times, but y's possessing the property F is occurring at, and only at, such times as y possesses the property F.

But in that case also, the entity to which (3) refers, and therefore the entity to which (2) refers, is occurring at all times. But I cannot imagine that the proponents of the view of events being considered mean that the event that occurred this morning and that consisted in John's running is an entity that is occurring at all times. I therefore take it they must mean for (2) to refer to something *other* than what (3) refers to. I therefore called this proposal an obscure one: it just is not plain what, on this view, an event is supposed to be.

3. What seems to me a more interesting proposal than any we have looked at is suggested by some remarks of Nicholas Wolterstorff's.[7]

Let us go back for a minute. I earlier imagined someone to say that the property that on his view a certain event is a something's-possessing is the property to which

(1)   the property 'running'

and

(2)   the property 'being running'

refer. Now I am happy to allow that (2) refers to a property. But (1) surely does not. *Running* surely is not a property; running, after all, is

---

[7] See his *On Universals* (Chicago and London: University of Chicago Press, 1970). I say only that the view of events that I shall sketch is suggested by his remarks, rather than that it is his view, partly because he says nothing about events generally (he speaks only of acts), partly because his remarks (about acts) are very brief, and I have added what I regard as flesh but he may regard as fat, and partly because there are places at which the view I lay out conflicts with remarks he does explicitly make—I shall note, below, two particularly important conflicts. (It is not important, but perhaps just worth mentioning, that what he calls "actions" I call "activities".)

good exercise, but no property is good exercise. If there is such an entity as running, it is, I should imagine, an *activity*, not a property.

Are there such things as activities? Is there, in particular, such a thing as the activity 'running'? It is of great interest to notice that if we grant that there are activities, we are able to give a simple account of yet another use—a *very* common use—of the verb "do".

I drew attention in Chapter II to three uses of the verb "do": first, as an auxiliary, as in

John did wax my dining room floor;

second, as a pro-verb, as in

John did my dining room floor;

third, as a relational predicate, as in one reading of

John did his shopping—

i.e., the reading under which it says that John carried out a certain job or task, viz., the job or task that was his shopping. Let us ask, now, what the role of "do" is in

(3)   John did some shopping.

I suppose there is *a* reading of (3) under which "do" functions as a pro-verb. But there is another reading, under which its truth does not require that John did anything to or with or on or in respect of an entity that was some shopping; what I have in mind is a reading under which its truth requires only that John shopped for a while, more briefly, that John shopped. This is the use of "do" we want to look at now.

It is, as I said, very common. And its commonness contributes, I am sure, to the inclination to take "do" to stand for the 'agent-relation' and to take acts to be 'things done'. (See Chapter II, section 4.) But if I was right in Chapter II, then if "some shopping" in (3) is taken to refer to an event, the "do" in it must be a pro-verb and hence is not functioning in the way that interests us now.

What I suggest is that if we allow that there are activities, we may take what (3) says—under the reading in which "do" is not a pro-verb—to be that John stands in a certain relation to an activity, the activity 'shopping'. What relation? Well, we could call it the 'engages-in-relation'. Or the 'indulges-in-relation'. Or the 'commits-relation' (compare committing murder, bigamy, suicide . . .). I shall call it the 'does-some-relation': it is the relation x has to y just in case y is an activity and x engages in y. If we ignore its tense, we may then rewrite (3) as

(3.1)   Does-some (John, shopping).

We are in this way able to handle an otherwise very puzzling group of sentences. Consider, for example,

(4)   John did something.

(4) has a pro-verb reading, of course. ("I don't know which floor he did this morning, but I know he did something—I heard the buffer going.") But it also has a non-pro-verb reading. Compare

(5)   John did something, and Mary did the same thing.

There is a reading of (5) under which it may, ignoring tense, be rewritten as

(5.1) $\exists x)$ [Does-some (John, x) & Does-some (Mary, x)];

there is a reading of (4) under which it is entailed by this, and under which, therefore, it may be rewritten as

(4.1) $(\exists x)$ Does-some (John, x).

Consider also the question "What are you doing?" This too has a pro-verb reading; but it also has a reading under which it may be rewritten, ignoring tense, as "For which x is it the case that Does-some (you, x)?"

Tense may be introduced easily enough. Let us say that the 'does-some-at-relation' is the relation x, y, and t have just in case y is an activity, and t is a time, and x engages in y at t. Then (3) may, *not* ignoring tense, be rewritten as

(3.2) $(\exists t)$ [Does-some-at (John, shopping, t) & Before (t, Now)].

With tense in hand, there is an easy way of expressing *one* kind of recurrence. I.e., consider

(6)   John did something, and then he later did the same thing again.

This may be rewritten as

(6.2) $(\exists x)(\exists t)(\exists t')(\exists t'')$ [Does-some-at (John, x, t) &—Does-some-at (John, x, t') & Does-some-at (John, x, t'') & Before (t, t') & Before (t', t'') & Before (t'', Now)].

Consider, moreover,

(7)   John did some shooting at 10 A.M., with a rifle, behind the barn.

We may rewrite this as

(7.2)   Does-some-at-with-behind (John, shooting, 10 A.M., a rifle, the barn) & Before (10 A.M., Now).

We shall, of course, want (7) to entail such sentences as

John did some shooting at 10 A.M., with a rifle

and
>John did some shooting at 10 A.M. behind the barn;

but this is easily enough secured by allowing ourselves 'meaning-rules' such as

(8)   If   Does-some-. . .-behind-. . .   (. . .)   then   Does-
>some-. . .(. . .)
>If   Does-some-. . .-with-. . .   (. . .)   then   Does-
>some-. . .(. . .)

.
.

It would be no surprise if a further possibility occurred to us. I earlier characterized the reading of

(3)   John did some shopping

that occupies us here as follows: it is a reading under which (3) requires for its truth only that John shopped for a while, more briefly, that John shopped. Why not take

>John shopped

itself to be rewritable as (3.2)? Then we shall be able to account for the fact that

>John shopped and Mary shopped

entails

>There is something John and Mary both did;

more important, we are able to account for the fact that

>John shot a man at 10 A.M. with a rifle behind the barn

entails

>John shot a man:

we need only take the former to be rewritable as

>Does-some-to-at-with-behind (John, shooting, a man, 10
>A.M., a rifle, the barn) & Before (10 A.M., Now),

and the latter to be rewritable as

>($\exists t$) [Does-some-to-at (John, shooting, a man, t) & Before
>(t, Now)],

and appeal to meaning-rules such as those in (8) to justify the inference.

It should be stressed that although the account of the entailment-relations among 'action-sentences', which I point to here, requires appeal to meaning-rules, it does *not* require the assumption of a battery of meaning-rules for each verb. I.e., we do not need one meaning-rule allowing us to delete the with-clause from a sentence whose main verb is "shoot", and another allowing us to delete the with-clause from a sentence whose main verb is "kill", and so on; we need assume only the one meaning-rule, which allows deletion of the with-clause. In other words, on this account it is no accident that the same word, "with", introduces the clause in all of these sentences, and we are able to say that it plays the same role in all of them.

I leave open whether or not this account of the entailment-relations among 'action-sentences' has any future. As I said at the outset, I am not concerned here with the logical form of any sentence. For the moment, in fact, only two things interest me. *If* there are activities, then on the one hand it does no harm to suppose that (3) is rewritable as (3.2), and on the other hand we are able to characterize this fourth use of "do" as follows: it when standing alone (as in "What are you doing?"), and the result of following it by "some" (as in "John did some shopping"), are relational predicates, which stand for the 'does-some-relation'.

Worth noticing is that whether or not there are activities there had better, it seems, be jobs or tasks. I think that

(3)   John did some shopping

means the same as

John shopped;

and *perhaps* all of these 'fourth-use' uses of "do" are eliminable in a similar way (if only at the cost of a flat denial that such sentences as (4) have non-pro-verb readings). But I am inclined to think that 'third-use' uses of "do", as in

(9)   John did his shopping,

are not eliminable. (Compare, also,

John did his job,

John did his homework,

and

John did the work he was paid to do.)

One is perhaps at a first glance inclined to think that (9) is paraphrasable as

John needed to shop and he shopped.

But a second glance makes plain it is not. For in the first place, John might have needed to shop for certain things (e.g., groceries), but have shopped for something else (e.g., a stereo set); if so, I take it that although he needed to shop, and did shop, he did not do his shopping.

More important, second, a man might have needed to shop and have shopped, but not have done *all* of his shopping—he might have done only part of his shopping, and someone else have done the rest of it for him; in that case, it would be false to say that he had done his shopping. It really does seem as if jobs and tasks should paraphrase out. Consider

> John did his shopping himself last week, and Mary did it for him this week.

Does this say there is one job, which John did last week and Mary did this week? Or does it say there were two jobs, one that John did last week, the other that Mary did this week, though the two jobs are very, very similar? Or is John's shopping a fusion of shoppings? Does the sentence say that John did a part of the fusion last week and Mary did another part this week? There is an absurdity in this: one feels it is a mere accident that the language allows what appears to be reference to such entities. We should surely be able to take the "did" in such a sentence to be, as it were, a *trompe l'oeil* relation-term, just as "There was a . . ." in

> There was a shortage of beef recently

is a *trompe l'oeil* quantifier. But unfortunately while the apparent quantifier in this sentence is eliminable—i.e., the sentence is paraphrasable as

> Recently people wanted more beef than was available—

the apparent relation-term in (9) is not.

For completeness, the fifth, and as I think, sole remaining, use of "do" ought to be mentioned here. What I have in mind is its use as an intransitive verb, as in

> That won't do,

in which I think it means "work" or "serve" or "suffice". (But whether this is the sole remaining use of "do" turns on whether it is acceptable to take the "do" in "We did without food for three days" to be a pro-verb, and the "do" in "I did him an injustice" as a 'fourth-use' use of "do", and so on. It's an amusing game.)

Let us in any case suppose that there are activities. The thesis about events suggested by Wolterstorff's remarks is this: an event is a something's-engaging-in-an-activity. So, for example, the event that occurred this morning consisting in John's running is John's engaging in the activity 'running'.

It must not be stressed that the event is *not*, on this view, John's

Acts and Other Events

having the 'does-some-relation' to the activity 'running': it is, instead, his engaging in (his 'doing some') running. There are two important differences between these. In the first place, it seems to me that there is a principle for relations analogous to

(S₅) y's possessing the property F exists at, and only at, such times as y posseses the property F,

viz.,

(S₅*) y's having the relation R to α exists at, and only at, such times as y has the relation R to α;

if so, the entity (assuming there is one) that is John's having the 'does-some-relation' to the activity 'running' exists at, and only at, such times as John runs. In which case we are committed to the supposition that this entity comes into existence every Saturday morning and goes out of existence roughly an hour later. Of course, if you are Chisholm, you will think that the right principle for properties was

(S₅′) y's possessing the property F exists at all times, but y's possessing the property F is occurring at, and only at, such times as y possesses the property F,

and that its analogue for relations is

(S₅′*) y's having the relation R to α exists at all times, but y's having the relation R to α is occurring at, and only at, such times as y has the relation R to α.

In which case we are committed to the supposition that John's having the 'does-some-relation' to the activity 'running' does not come into and go out of existence, but is occurring every Saturday morning and only on a Saturday morning. But there is no reason at all to suppose that a man's *engaging in* an activity exists or occurs whenever he engages in that same activity: we may perfectly well take it that although you engage in that same activity again and again, every week, the entity that was your engaging in it last week is not identical with the entity that was your engaging in it the week before, or the week following.[8]

This was what I had in mind when I spoke earlier of *one* kind of recurrence. On this view of events, sentences like

[8] Here is the first conflict with what Wolterstorff says. Wolterstorff says that "Mary's coughing is taking place at a certain time if and only if Mary is coughing at that time" (*ibid.*, p. 132); thus Wolterstorff thinks an event may take place again and again. He does not, however, commit himself on the question whether Mary's coughing exists during the times at which it is not taking place: he says only that it *may* be that it does (*ibid.*, p. 133).

Events, States of Affairs, Activities

(6)   John did something, and then he later did the same thing again

are often true, and what they say is: a certain activity 'recurred' in the sense that it was engaged in more than once. But on this view there is no second kind of recurrence: the event that consists in a man's engaging in an activity does not recur. But on this view, also, there is no need to make room for a second kind of recurrence: anyone who says "The same thing has been happening every Saturday morning for the last six months" may well be taken to be saying that the same thing has (or—depending on how relaxed your use of this sentence is—that the same thing has or different things have) been engaging in the same activity every Saturday morning for the last six months.

Second, it seems to me that there is a principle for relations analogous to

(S_3) y's possessing the property F is identical with z's possessing the property G just in case y is identical with z and the property F is identical with the property G,

viz.,

$(S_3{}^*)$ y's having the relation R to α is identical with z's having the relation S to β just in case y is identical with z and α is identical with β and the relation R is identical with the relation S;

and that there is a principle for activities analogous to

(S_4) the property F is not identical with the property G if it is possible that a man should possess the property F and not possess the property G,

viz.,

$(S_4{}^*)$ the activity A is not identical with the activity B if it is possible that a man should engage in the activity A and not engage in the activity B.

If so, the entity (assuming there is one) that is John's having the 'does-some-relation' to the activity 'running' is not identical with the entity (assuming again there is one) that is John's having the 'does-some-relation' to the activity 'running in the Boston Common'—for it is possible that a man should engage in the activity 'running' and not engage in the activity 'running in the Boston Common'. But there is no reason at all why a man's *engaging in* the activity 'running' should not be identical with his *engaging in* the activity 'running in the Boston Common': indeed, I should have thought your engaging

121

in the one *is* identical with your engaging in the other if it is in the Boston Common that you do your running.[9]

So the event that occurred this morning and that consisted in John's running is *not* John's having the 'does-some-relation' to the activity 'running': it is, instead, his engaging in (his 'doing some') running.

Moreover, since it was in the Boston Common that John did all his running this morning, the event that occurred this morning and that consisted in John's running is identical with the event that occurred this morning and that consisted in John's running in the Boston Common.

Further, we may have it that the event that occurred this morning and that consisted in John's running north across the Common is part of the event that occurred this morning and that consisted in John's running. So also for the event that occurred this morning and that consisted in John's running south across the Common. More generally, we may have it that an event x is part of an event y just in case PART (x, y).

It will have been noticed that while I earlier gave as examples of activities the activity 'running' and the activity 'shopping', I here give as examples such activities as the activity 'running in the Boston Common' and the activity 'running north across the Common'. If there are activities at all, then I should imagine these are activities too. But of course one who wants to explain the entailment of

John ran

by

John ran in the Boston Common

along the lines I indicated above will rewrite the latter, not as

Does-some (John, running in the Boston Common),

but rather as

Does-some-in (John, running, the Boston Common)—

just as one who wants to explain the entailment of

---

[9] Here is the second conflict with what Wolterstorff says. On Wolterstorff's view, the event that consists in John's running is a 'case' of the predicable universal 'running'; presumably the event that consists in John's running in the Boston Common is a case of the predicable universal 'running in the Boston Common'. Now he says (*ibid.*, p. 134) that if x and y are cases, then "x is identical with y only if x and y are cases of the same predicable"; and he also says (p. 177) that "one and the same thing can never be a case of two different predicable universals". It follows that the event that consists in John's running is *not* identical with the event that consists in John's running in the Boston Common.

Events, States of Affairs, Activities

> John is taller than Jim

by

> John is taller than Jim and Jack

will rewrite the latter, not as

> Taller-than-Jim-and-Jack (John),

but rather as

> Taller-than (John, Jim) & Taller-than (John, Jack).

I rather like this account of events. Or rather, this sketch of an account of events, for it plainly is no more than that. Activities certainly call for discussion. In the first place, there are important differences among activities, which require looking into and explaining. There are, for example, what we might call 'mass-activities', such as 'running', 'shopping', 'running in the Boston Common'—one can do a little or a lot of running, shopping, running in the Boston Common. And on the other hand there are what we might call 'count-activities', such as 'killing', 'killing Kennedy', 'eating an apple'—I suppose it could be said that a man had done a little or a lot of killing (though not a little or a lot of killing Kennedy or eating an apple), but only in the sense that he has killed few or killed many. Second, and at least as pressing, is the question what activities there are, and why. Why are there no such activities as 'knowing' and 'hating Jones'? The verbs "know" and "hate" are commonly called 'state' verbs, and have no present progressive; can we say that if a verb has no present progressive its gerund does not stand for an activity? And if so, why? Moreover, my examples have all been of activities that people engage in, a man's engaging in one or another of them being an act of his. But what about the event that occurred yesterday and that consisted in the fall of a certain tree? Are we to say that that was the tree's engaging in the activity 'falling'? Can we say that if a verb has a present progressive its gerund does stand for an activity? And if so, why?

In addition, engagings-in-activities call for more discussion than I have given them. I said that entities which are a something's-engaging-in-an-activity differ from entities which are a something's-having-the-'does-some-relation'-to-an-activity in both existence-conditions and identity-conditions, and this tells us something about what they are by way of pointing to how they differ from some entities it is easy to confuse them with. But there are other entities it is easy to confuse them with, so this is obviously not the end of the matter.

I cannot now provide these discussions I say are called for. That fact does not incline me to reject the thesis that an event is a something's-engaging-in-an-activity; indeed, I think these discussions called for only because, as I said, I rather like that thesis.

Others may feel differently. Anyone who does is invited to withhold judgment: nothing important in what follows will turn on accepting the thesis.

But it is important that the following thesis be accepted: an event is a happening, an occurrence, a something that takes place. If you do not accept *this* thesis, you and I are not talking about the same entities when we use the term "events". Perhaps one who wonders what an event is would not be any more satisfied if he was told that an event is a happening, an occurrence, a something that takes place than he would be if he was told that

(D_{6a})   Event (y) just in case there is an entity e such that
        PART (e, y).

But if this thesis is not particularly enlightening, it has, in my view, at least the virtue of being obviously true.

4. I shall assume that events do not recur. (Though a man may do the same thing again, it is not the case that the same event may happen again.) Therefore there is no need to distinguish, as Chisholm does, between an event's existing and an event's occurring; and I shall assume that for an event to exist is for it to occur.

I am happy to grant that there are such entities as a something's-having-a-property and a something's-having-a-relation-to-a-something. These, however, I shall call 'states of affairs'—for example, my left thumb's possessing the property 'is dirty' or the property 'being dirty' is a state of affairs, not an event.

Consider my left thumb's possessing the property 'being dirty'; and suppose that my left thumb only intermittently possesses this property. Does the entity that consists in my left thumb's possessing that property come into and go out of existence? Anyone who feels committed to the metaphysical thesis that if an entity goes out of existence it cannot come back into existence will insist that the entity that consists in my left thumb's possessing the property 'being dirty' does no such thing. He will insist that we distinguish between the existing and the what? the *obtaining?* of a state of affairs. Others may be content to say that states of affairs are a special kind of entity (though, after all, what isn't?), and that the metaphysical thesis is not true of them. It does not in the least matter for my purposes which is said. But some policy must be adopted; and I shall speak of a state of affairs as obtaining or not obtaining when I mean what the latter group would express by speaking of it as existing or not existing, and simply leave open what is the case between successive obtainings.

What I do think worth stressing, however, is that states of affairs do not have parts that temporally succeed one another. (So it was no wonder that those who identified events with a something's-having-a-property had trouble making room for parts of events.) If my thumb is dirty from 9:48 A.M. to 10:47 A.M., then its possessing the property 'being dirty' obtains from 9:48 to 10:47; and there is no part of it that does not obtain throughout the whole of that time. By contrast, if an event that consists in John's running starts to occur at 9:48 A.M. and ends at 10:47 A.M., then, though the event is occurring at every time during that time, for every time within that time there is a part of the event that is not occurring at that time. E.g., if John is running north across the Common at 10 A.M., then there is a part of his running— viz., his running south across the Common—that is not occurring at 10 A.M., and that will begin to occur only at (say) 10:16 A.M.

Events, in fact, are in one respect very like what some people have said physical objects are. It will be remembered that according to some people a physical object is a four-dimensional object: a tennis ball, for example, is a longer or shorter (depending on how long it lasts) four-dimensional cylindrical object, more or less curled in shape (depending on how curly a path is followed by what—speaking with the vulgar—is called 'the tennis ball'). On this view of a tennis ball, the ball (like an event) has parts that temporally succeed others of its parts: as later parts of it come into existence, earlier parts of it go out of existence. I do not find it plain that this is an intelligible view to take of physical objects; our present interest in it is only that it makes of physical objects things very like events—in just that respect in which events differ from states of affairs.

I hasten to say that if there are such four-dimensional cylindrical curls as a tennis ball is said to be, events are not to be identified with them. Suppose John's running is identified with a certain curl. Suppose also that John sweats all over throughout the time he runs; there seems no option but to identify his sweating with the same curl. But plainly the event that consists in his running is not identical with the event that consists in his sweating.

It should be noted, however, that not all events have parts that temporally succeed others of their parts. I should imagine that there are point-events, which occur at a time-point and only at that time-point. If there are such events, then while they may have parts that are not identical with themselves, there is no part of such an event that comes into existence after another part has gone out of existence. Are there point-events? Well, perhaps one object's coming into contact with another is such an event. Perhaps also the death of a man is another such event. Such events as these—if they are point-events—have no temporally successive parts.

Are there events with *no* parts not identical with themselves? If there are point-objects participating in point-events, I suppose there are, e.g., a point-object's coming into contact with another point-object (if their coming into contact is a point-event). Are there such things? I make a gift of the question to anyone who feels competent to answer it.

IX

Causal Verbs

Sirhan's killing of Kennedy, then, is an event, i.e., a happening, an occurrence, and it has for parts all and only those events x such that

PART $(x,$ Sirhan's killing of Kennedy$)$.

In particular, Sirhan's shooting of Kennedy is part of Sirhan's killing of Kennedy. And so also is the onset of hemorrhage, which event the shooting caused, and which itself caused Kennedy's death.

In virtue of what is an event a killing? Well, an event x is a killing just in case there is an event y that is a killing, and that is such that

PART $(x, y,)$ & PART (y, x).

We can do better than this, but it is a long story.

1. A great battery of verbs are similar to "kill" in a certain interesting respect. Intuitively, it seems plausible to say that to kill someone is to cause him to die. So, similarly, does it seem plausible that to melt something is to cause it to melt, to sink something is to cause it to sink, to move something is to cause it to move, to break something is to cause it to break, and so on. The verbs I draw attention to here are commonly called 'causal verbs'.

It has been said that these verbs are definable in terms of causality: more specifically, that a verb is a causal verb just in case the result of replacing the third-person singular of the verb for "verbs", and the gerund of some verb or verb-phrase for "verbing", in the following thesis-schema,

(T-S$_1$) z verbs y just in case z causes y's verbing,

is a truth. For aren't

> z kills y just in case z causes y's dying,
>
> z melts y just in case z causes y's melting,
>
> z sinks y just in case z causes y's sinking,
>
> z moves y just in case z causes y's moving,
>
> z breaks y just in case z causes y's breaking

truths?

Unfortunately they are not. Suppose I coerce Smith into shooting Jones in the head. Then I cause Smith's shooting Jones in the head. Suppose also that Smith's shooting Jones in the head causes Jones's dying. Then, causality being transitive, I cause Jones's dying. But I do not kill Jones; Smith kills him.[1] I *get* Jones killed, but getting a man killed is not killing him. (Compare also 'having a man killed'—as when you pay to have it done—and 'letting a man be killed'.)

Again, if I order my cook to melt some chocolate for me, and he therefore does, then I cause the chocolate's melting (by causing the cook to put the chocolate in a pan, on the stove, etc.), but *I* do not melt the chocolate. (Though I get it melted.) So it may be that z causes y's melting, though z does not melt y. Again, if I order my lieutenant to sink the *Titanic*, and he therefore does, then I cause its sinking, but *I* do not sink it. So it may be that z causes y's sinking though z does not sink y. If I order my butler to move the teacups, and he therefore does, then I cause the teacups' moving, but *I* do not move them. So it may be that z causes y's moving, though z does not move y. And similarly for "break".

It would be no surprise that this happened to our test for a causal verb if the account of events given in section 3 of Chapter VIII is correct. On that account, my killing (or melting, sinking, . . .) something or someone is my engaging in a certain activity—viz., the activity 'killing him' (or 'melting it', or . . .); and therefore there is such an event as my killing him if and only if I engage in that activity—thus only if *I* engage in it. My causing a man's dying by getting someone else to engage in the activity 'killing him' is not enough. *I* have to engage in it.

---

[1] One who, knowing the facts, nevertheless says that I killed Jones uses "kill" in a special way. I call it the SDS use of "kill", in honor of their chant: "LBJ, LBJ, how many kids did you kill today?"

Causal Verbs

There is here, in any case, a phenomenon that has not been sufficiently attended to. There seems to be a rule here, one so firm that we adhere to it even in the case of entirely new verbs. Take the verb "smile", for example. It is an intransitive verb. But suppose you sign on as apprentice to the chief photographer. As he is about to photograph a batch of children for their school yearbook, he notices that a child in the back row looks gloomy, this being undesirable in such photographs. "Smile that child up there in the back row," he says to you; I want to see if you can." You know perfectly well that he does not want to see merely whether you can cause the child to smile—as, e.g., by paying a more experienced apprentice to cause the child to smile. You know he wants *you* to smile the child—and while causing it to smile is necessary for that, it is not sufficient.

Or again, suppose you sign on as nurse in a new hospital, and the resident says, "Sneeze that patient every hour—we want to be sure his nasal passages are kept clear"; you may not know *how* to sneeze the patient (is pepper allowed? or is there some chemical specially prepared for the purpose?), but you know perfectly well that it is you who are to sneeze the patient—getting someone else to sneeze him may satisfy (if the resident does not really care who sneezes him), but will not count as *your* sneezing him.

The same again if you sign on as babysitter, and the mother says, as she leaves, "Sleep Albert as soon after 7:30 as you can."

We can construct transitive verbs out of adjectives, too; and the same rule still holds. If your customer says, "I like the work you do better than the work your assistants do; so would *you* red the inside of this heart they just tattooed on my arm?" you would know perfectly well that he does not merely mean that you are to cause the inside of the heart to be red—as, e.g., by getting one of your assistants to red it.

Yet surely "kill", "melt", "sink", "move", and "break"—even the newly invented transitive verbs "smile", "sleep", and "red"—should turn out to be causal verbs. Surely it is intuitively right that to kill is to cause to die, to melt is to cause to melt, to sink is to cause to sink, and so on.

Intuition, I think, is right. That is, it seems to me that to kill is to cause to die—i.e., if z kills y, then z does cause y to die, and indeed z's killing of y is z's causing of y's dying. All we need do is remember that we can say this without saying also that to cause to die is to kill: for it is (I hope) plain that z may cause the event that is y's dying without there being any such event as z's killing of y.

So I suggest that we take intuition to say only that

If x is a killing of y by z, then there is an α that is y's dying, and x is a causing of α by z,

and that we take this to be true.

Which causings of dyings are killings? What is necessary for the truth of "Alfred killed Bert" beyond the fact that Alfred caused Bert's dying? The question is one I find extremely difficult, and I have no even remotely plausible answer to propose. Fortunately our purposes do not require an answer.

Intuition, I think, is right about "melt", "sink", and the others. It seems to me that to melt is to cause to melt—i.e., if z melts y, then z does cause y to melt, and indeed z's melting of y is z's causing of y's melting. A thing can melt more than once (melt, solidify, melt, solidify, etc.) and you can melt a thing without causing all of its meltings. So I should have said, not "y's melting" (which implies uniqueness), but "one of y's meltings". (A thing can die only once, so it was permissible to speak of *the* event that is y's dying.) A thing can similarly sink more than once; and you can sink a thing without causing all of its sinkings. So what we want for "melt" and "sink" is, I think:

If x is a melting of y by z, then there is an α that is among y's meltings, and x is a causing of α by z,

and

If x is a sinking of y by z, then there is an α that is among y's sinkings, and x is a causing of α by z.

Is the verb "cause" itself a causal verb? If y is an event, then to cause y is to cause y to occur. And perhaps if an event y occurs, there is an entity that is y's occurring, viz., y itself. So perhaps we could say that if x is a causing of an event y by z, then there is an α that is y's occurring (and thus is y itself), and x is a causing of α by z. But what if y is not an event? After all, other things than events are causable. For example, a man's being grossly overweight, which is a state of affairs, might well have been caused by his overeating. (Compare causing the inside of a tattooed heart to be red.) Well, states of affairs do not occur, but they do obtain. Is it the case that if a state of affairs y obtains, there is an entity that is y's obtaining? If there is such an entity, is it y itself? And can we then say, quite generally,

If x is a causing of y by z, then there is an α that is y's occurring or obtaining, and x is a causing of α by z?

I shall leave this open. The verb "cause" is plainly very different from the causal verbs we have been looking at, but I suggest we allow it to be a causal verb all the same. Since

> If x is a causing of y by z, then there is an α that is y, and x is a causing of α by z

is true, the following is true no matter what we write in the blank:

> If x is a causing of y by z, then there is an α that is y, or is y's _____, and x is a causing of α by z.

And I suggest we say that a verb is a causal verb only if the result of replacing its gerund for "verb$_1$ing", and the gerund of some verb or verb-phrase for "verb$_2$ing", in the following thesis-schema,

(T-S$_2$) If x is a verb$_1$ing of y by z, then there is an α that is y, or is (among) y's verb$_2$ing(s), and x is a causing of α by z,

is a truth. (I put "among" in parentheses, since for some replacements for "verb$_2$ing"—e.g., "dying"—it may be omitted.) "Kill", "melt", and "sink" pass this test, as they should, and do does "cause".

I do not suppose that anyone is likely to feel satisfied with the proposal that a killing is a causing of a dying. If anyone is puzzled as to what it is in virtue of which an event is a killing of something by something, he is likely to be at least as much puzzled as to what it is in virtue of which an event is a causing of something by something— we are, after all, relatively at home with talk of killings, and relatively unfamiliar with talk of 'causings'. We shall have more to say about causings in chapters XI and XII; for the moment, all I ask is that we allow that there *are* causings, indeed, that a killing is a causing of a dying, a melting is a causing of a melting, a sinking is a causing of a sinking, and so on, my point here being only that we can say not merely "and so on", but "and so on, for all the causal verbs".

2. But it will have been noticed that I did not say that a verb is a causal verb *just in case* the result of making appropriate replacements in (T-S$_2$) is a truth: I said that a verb is a causal verb *only if* this is the case. A further condition must be met.

Let us go back for a moment. I drew attention in Chapter I to the fact that anyone who believes that "kill" is definable as "cause to die" is committed to supposing that

> Sirhan's shooting of Kennedy killed Kennedy

is a truth, for Sirhan's shooting of Kennedy certainly caused Kennedy's death. Now "kill" is not definable as "cause to die"; but still Sirhan's shooting of Kennedy did kill Kennedy.

Acts and Other Events

Again "melt", "sink", "move", and "break" are not definable as "cause to melt", "cause to sink", "cause to move", and "cause to break"; but

> The cook's heating of the chocolate melted it
> The lieutenant's torpedoing of the ship sank it
> The butler's leaning on the piano moved it
> The butler's leaning on the punchbowl broke it

may nevertheless all be true.

More generally, all of the verbs one feels inclined to call causal verbs accept expressions that refer to events as subjects. I think, in fact, it is at least in large part because the verbs one feels inclined to call causal verbs do (as I shall put it) accept events as subjects that it is so natural—at first blush—to take them to be definable in terms of causality. For whatever else events may do, they certainly anyway cause things.

Now it seems to me that there are verbs such that the results of making appropriate replacements in (T-S$_2$) are truths, but which one does not feel inclined to call causal verbs—and which do not accept events as subjects. Consider "kick", for example. I should imagine that a kicking is a causing of something: Alfred's kicking of Bert, for example, is surely a causing of a moving of a foot (or hoof or paw) into contact with Bert. No replacement for "verb$_2$ing" in

> If x is a kicking of y by z, then there is an α that is y, or is (among) y's verb$_2$ing(s), and x is a causing of α by z

comes readily to hand—contrast "kick" in this respect with "kill", "melt", etc. But let us invent a verb, viz., "VERB": one thing VERBS another just in case the first moves into contact with the second. Bert, for example, WAS VERBED BY something just in case that something moved into contact with Bert. "Bert's VERBING", then, is referentially ambiguous: it may refer to an event that is Bert's VERBING of something, or it may refer to an event that is something's VERBING of Bert. (Compare "Oswald's shooting", which may refer to either a shooting by Oswald, or a shooting of Oswald.) So let us allow ourselves a further linguistic device: Bert's (or anything else's) VERBING* is to be something's VERBING of Bert (or of whatever it is). Then I take it we can say that

> If x is a kicking of y by z, then there is an α that is y, or is among y's VERBING*S, and x is a causing of α by z.

If so, "kick" satisfies the necessary condition for being a causal verb that was laid out in the preceding section. But I think no one would

132

Causal Verbs

feel inclined to call "kick" a causal verb. And "kick", of course, does not accept events as subjects: only things with feet (or paws or hooves) can kick a thing, and no event has any.

Well, whatever anyone's inclinations on the matter may be, I propose that we define the term "causal verb" as follows: a verb is a causal verb just in case (i) the result of replacing its gerund for "verb$_1$ing", and the gerund of some verb or verb-phrase for "verb$_2$ing", in

(T-S$_2$)   If x is a verb$_1$ing of y by z, then there is an α that is y, or is (among) y's verb$_2$ing(s), and x is a causing of α by z,

is a truth, *and* (ii) it accepts events as subjects. "Kill", "melt", "sink", "move", "break", and "cause", then, are causal verbs; "kick" is not.

3. Perhaps it will be worth having a closer look at the causal verbs. There are interesting differences among them.[2]

First, a point of terminology. Take the verb "melt". There is a fact that can be expressed in two different ways. We can say, on the one hand, that although it sometimes occurs transitively (as in "John melted the ice cube"), it sometimes occurs intransitively (as in "The ice cube melted"). Or we can, on the other hand, say that, strictly speaking, there are two homographic and homophonic—or, as I shall say, *matching*—verbs "melt": one transitive and one intransitive. For my purposes, it makes no theoretical difference which way we express this fact. It will be plain that I was speaking in the first way a moment ago when I said "Take the verb 'melt' ", as if there were only one. This is, I think, the natural way to speak. But the points I wish to make are expressible less cumbersomely if we speak in the second way; and I shall accordingly say that there is a transitive verb "melt", which is matched by an intransitive verb "melt", these being different verbs.[3]

---

[2] For more detail than I shall indulge in, see Zeno Vendler, "The Structure of Efficacy," in *Contemporary Research in Philosophical Logic and Linguistic Semantics*, ed. Hockney et al. (Dordrecht, Holland: D. Reidel, 1975).

[3] I shall at a number of places below again say "Here we have two matching verbs rather than one," sometimes on syntactic grounds, sometimes on semantic grounds, sometimes on a mix of both. I shall do so for convenience only, and not with a view to making a theoretical point. In fact, I have much admired Charles J. Fillmore's "The Case for Case," in *Universals in Linguistic Theory*, ed. Emmon Bach and Robert T. Harms (New York: Holt, Rinehart and Winston, 1968), which argues that (some, though I think not all, of) the facts I shall be pointing to are best accommodated by saying, not "Here we have two verbs", not even "Here we have one verb with two meanings", but rather "Here we have one verb with noun-phrases in different case-relations to it". (I am indebted to Jerry A. Fodor for drawing my attention to this article.) It should be stressed, however, that it is not necessary for our purposes that we decide on these matters. What counts, for us, are the ontological differences that underlie the facts, however expressed.

Acts and Other Events

There are also two verbs "sink": one transitive (as in "John sank the Titanic"), the other intransitive (as in "The Titanic sank"). Indeed, there are a great many transitive verbs that are matched by intransitive verbs. For example, the transitive verb "move" (as in "John moved the piano") is matched by the intransitive verb "move" (as in "The piano moved"). So also for the following transitive verbs:

break, bend, dent, burst, stretch, crack, split, tear,
cook, simmer, boil, fry, burn, steam, bake, brown,
warm, cool, freeze,
wave, swing, spin, roll, twist, shake, turn, fold, wind,
pour, spill, fill, float, dry,
open, close, shut,
drown, hang, strangle,
ring, sound,
grow, improve, weaken, wake,
sail, fly, steer, start, stop, slow, speed;

each of them is matched by an intransitive verb.

Moreover, each of them accepts events as subjects. (Contrast the transitive verb "kick": the transitive verb "kick" is matched by an intransitive verb but does not accept events as subjects.)

I think, in fact, that every transitive verb that is matched by an intransitive verb *and* accepts events as subjects is a causal verb. All of the examples I gave above certainly seem to be causal verbs.

Moreover, they all seem to satisfy condition (i) in a particularly simple way: i.e., the result of replacing the verb's gerund for "verb$_1$ing", and the gerund of *the verb's intransitive match* for "verb$_2$ing", in

(T-S$_2$) If x is a verb$_1$ing of y by z, then there is an α that is y, or is (among) y's verb$_2$ing(s), and x is a causing of α by z

is a truth. Thus

If x is a melting of y by z, then there is an α that is y, or is among y's meltings, and x is a causing of α by z;

If x is a sinking of y by z, then there is an α that is y, or is among y's sinkings, and x is a causing of α by z;

.

.

.

If x is a slowing of y by z, then there is an α that is y, or is among y's slowings, and x is a causing of α by z;

134

Causal Verbs

      If x is a speeding of y by z, then there is an α that is y, or is
      among y's speedings, and x is a causing of α by z—

in which the first gerund is the gerund of the transitive verb, and the second gerund is the gerund of the transitive verb's intransitive match—are all true.

    Let us call causal verbs that satisfy condition (i) in that particularly simple way 'matched causal verbs'.

4. Consider the following verbs: "hide", "dress", "wash", "shave". How can I say "*the* following verbs", as if there is only one of each? We often say such things as

(1)   I hid the car keys,

"I dressed the doll", "I washed the handkerchiefs", "I shaved the man next door", which contain transitive verbs; but so also do we say such things as

(1')   I hid,

"I dressed", "I washed", "I shaved"—and don't these contain intransitive verbs? And aren't the verbs in the latter four sentences then the intransitive matches of the verbs in the former four sentences? And doesn't the way of speaking I proposed we adopt commit us to saying therefore that there are *two* verbs "hide" and *two* verbs "dress" and *two* verbs "wash" and *two* verbs "shave"?

    Let us take a closer look at (1'). It seems to me eminently plausible that (1') is equivalent to

(1'')   I hid myself.

[And similarly for the other sentences in the list headed by (1').] The verb in (1'), then, is strikingly different from what are, on any view, plainly intransitive verbs. Consider "sleep". There is no transitive verb "sleep" in English; on any view, "sleep" is plainly intransitive. And notice that

(2')   I slept

is certainly not equivalent to

(2'')   I slept myself:

there is no such sentence as (2'') in English. It makes no theoretical difference for my purposes, but some policy on the matter must be adopted. And I suggest that we take seriously the difference between the verb in (1') and the verb in (2'): that we, in fact, say that the verb in (1') is transitive.

Compare also the verb "eat". I say "*the* verb 'eat' ", although we say, not only such things as

(3)   I ate an apple,

but also such things as

(3')   I ate.

(3') is certainly not equivalent to

(3")   I ate myself.

Yet I suggest that we say that the verb in (3') too is transitive. For while (3') is not equivalent to (3"), (3') nevertheless entails

(3''')   I ate something—

whereas, by contrast, (2') certainly does not entail

(2''')   I slept something:

there is no such sentence as (2''') in English.

We can simplify if we notice that (1") entails

(1''')   I hid something,

so that if I am right in thinking that (1') is equivalent to (1"), we can also say that (1') entails (1'''). The policy I here propose we adopt, then, can be put as follows: the verb in a sentence of the form "*x* verbed" is transitive if the sentence entails the relevant sentence of the form "*x* verbed something". Under this policy the verbs in both (1') and (3') are transitive.

If the verbs in (1') and (3') are transitive, then (1') and (3') must be viewed as the products of deletion—deletion, that is, of the direct objects of the verbs. And surely that is just how we should view them. If I am right in thinking that (1') is equivalent to (1"), we should surely view (1') as the product of deleting "myself". (3') is not eqiivalent to (3"), and so is in an interesting way different from (1'); yet (3') is surely equivalent to (3'''), and should surely be viewed as the product of deleting "something".

In sum, then, I propose we opt for the policy I mentioned—under which the verbs in (1') and (3') are transitive. Under that policy the verbs in "I dressed", "I washed", and "I shaved" are also transitive. More generally, I take it that we can say that the verbs "hide", "dress", "wash", "shave", "eat" have no intransitive matches, and a fortiori are not matched causal verbs.

5. Many verbs that are not matched causal verbs nevertheless are causal verbs. "Kill", for example, is not a matched causal verb since it

has no intransitive match; yet "kill" is plainly a causal verb if any verb is.

Again, "raise" and "destroy" should turn out to be causal verbs: surely to raise a thing is to cause it to rise and to destroy a thing is to cause it to cease to exist. But like "kill", "raise" and "destroy" have no intransitive matches.

But all is well for "kill", "raise", and "destroy". For even if they do not pass the test for being a causal verb in the very simple way in which the matched causal verbs do, they do nevertheless pass it—for

If x is a killing of y by z, then there is an α that is y, or is y's dying, and x is a causing of α by z;

If x is a raising of y by z, then there is an α that is y, or is among y's risings, and x is a causing of α by z;

If x is a destroying of y by z, then there is an α that is y, or is y's ceasing to exist, and x is a causing of α by z

are all true. And "kill", "raise", and "destroy" accept events as subjects—for a man's shooting of a man might kill a man, raise some dust, and destroy the peace of a nation. I shall say, then, that "kill", "raise", and "destroy" are 'unmatched causal verbs'.

The verbs "hide" and "dress" seem also to be causal verbs— unmatched causal verbs, since they have no intransitive matches. For I take it that to hide a thing is to cause its being hidden and to dress a thing is to cause its being dressed. Now "is hidden" and "is dressed" are perfectly respectable verb-phrases; and I take it that

If x is a hiding of y and z, then there is an α that is y, or is y's being hidden, and x is a causing of α by z,

and

If x is a dressing of y by z, then there is an α that is y, or is y's being dressed, and x is a causing of α by z

are true. "Hide" and "dress", moreover, accept events as subjects: your putting a hat in a closet might hide it, and your putting clothes on a child would dress it.

It is of interest that what these say an event (which is a hiding of something or a dressing of something) is a causing of is not an event: it is, rather, a state of affairs. That is, an α such that α is, e.g., my hat's being hidden, and such that your hiding of my hat is your causing of α, is surely a state of affairs that consists in my hat's possessing the property 'hidden'. And similarly for "dress": what this says a dressing of something is a causing of is surely a state of affairs that consists in the thing's possessing the property 'dressed'. [I take it that for each y, there is only one state of affairs that is its being hidden, and only one state of affairs that is its being dressed; hence I omitted "among" in setting out the results of replacement in (T-S$_2$).] By contrast, a thing's melting, sinking, . . . slowing, speeding, dying, rising, and ceasing to exist are all, I take it, events.

A great many causal verbs are similar to "hide" and "dress" in this respect. Consider, for example, the verbs "clean" (as in "I cleaned the floor") and "dirty" (as in "I dirtied the floor"). I take these to have no intransitive matches. They are nevertheless causal verbs, in that they accept events as subjects, and the following are surely true:

> If x is a cleaning of y by z, then there is an α that is y, or is y's being clean, and x is a causing of α by z,
> If x is a dirtying of y by z, then there is an α that is y, or is y's being dirty, and x is a causing of α by z.

And a thing's being clean and a thing's being dirty are surely states of affairs rather than events. (Presumably for each y, there is only one state of affairs that is y's being clean and only one state of affairs that is y's being dirty.)

Consider also the following verbs:

frighten, surprise, alarm, amaze, shock, astonish, excite, disturb,
soothe, calm, satisfy, please,
deceive, confuse, disappoint, bore,
convince, persuade.

These are often given as examples of 'perlocutionary-act-verbs', and should—intuitively speaking—turn out to be causal verbs. None of them is matched by an intransitive verb (with the possible exception of "calm"); but the following are surely true:

> If x is a frightening of y by z, then there is an α that is y, or is y's being afraid, and x is a causing of α by z;
> If x is a surprising of y by z, then there is an α that is y, or is y's being surprised, and x is a causing of α by z;

.

.

.

> If x is a persuading of y by z, then there is an α that is y, or is y's being in agreement with z, and x is a causing of α by z;

and all of them accept events as subjects, for your saying some words

Causal Verbs

might frighten, surprise, alarm, . . . , or persuade a man. If so, then these verbs are causal verbs, unmatched causal verbs in fact. But a thing's being afraid, a thing's being surprised, . . . , a thing's being in agreement with another are surely (unique) states of affairs rather than events.

Here is an interesting case. The transitive verb "shine" (as in "I shined the silver") is matched by an intransitive verb "shine" (as in "The silver shines"). Intuitively, the transitive verb "shine" should turn out to be a causal verb. And so it does. It accepts events as subjects (my rubbing the silver with polish might have shined it); and it satisfies condition (i)—indeed, it satisfies condition (i) in the very simple way in which "melt" and "sink" do, for surely

> If x is a shining of y by z, then there is an α that is y, or is (among?) y's shining(s?), and x is a causing of α by z—

in which the first gerund is the gerund of the transitive verb, and the second is the gerund of the transitive verb's intransitive match—is a truth. But is a thing's shining an event? Is it a happening or occurrence? I suppose it is arguable that a thing's shining is the (unique) state of affairs consisting in the thing's possessing the property 'shiny'. But is that true? A thing may surely possess the property 'shiny' while it is dark (and thus the state of affairs, its possessing the property 'shiny', obtain in the dark); but does the thing's *shining* exist in the dark? Does anything shine while it is too dark for it to be seen? I should think not; but I leave it open.

It could of course be said that to cause a state of affairs just is to cause the onset of that state of affairs, its onset itself being an event. Better: that to cause a state of affairs just is to cause *an* onset of that state of affairs—to allow for the fact that some states of affairs obtain more than once. (A thing may be hidden, then found, then hidden again, then found again.) If so, then we can also say

> If x is a hiding of y by z, then there is an α that is an onset of the state of affairs that is y's being hidden, and x is a causing of α by z,

> If x is a dressing of y by z, then there is an α that is an onset of the state of affairs that is y's being dressed, and x is a causing of α by z,

.
.
.

139

If x is a persuading of y by z, then there is an α that is an onset of the state of affairs that is y's being in agreement with z, and x is a causing of α by z.

We will have a closer look at 'onsets of states of affairs' later. For the moment there is no need to attend to them. It will be remembered that I wrote "an α", rather than "an event α", in

(T-S$_2$)   If x is a verb$_1$ing of y by z, then there is an α that is y, or is (among) y's verb$_2$ing(s), and x is a causing of α by z:

I wished to allow a verb to be a causal verb even though for any y you choose, the result of making the relevant replacements in

y's verb$_2$ing

refers to a state of affairs rather than an event.

6. Since perlocutionary-act-verbs have been mentioned, we should perhaps say something about the 'illocutionary-act-verbs'. Consider, for example,

assert, declare, state, remark, predicate, deny,
criticize, praise,
admit, confess,
ask, answer,
command, order, request, demand,
promise.

Intuitively, these should all turn out to be noncausal verbs: while asserting something, declaring something, stating something, and so on, may all cause many things, there does not seem to be anything at all—event, state of affairs, what you will—such that to assert, declare, state, and so on, something *is* to cause that thing. In any case, they fail to pass our test for causal verbs, since none of them accepts events as subjects—no event ever has, or ever will, assert, declare, state, remark, . . . , request, demand, or promise anything.

   It would be tidy indeed if we could say that while all perlocutionary-act-verbs are causal, all illocutionary-act-verbs are noncausal. Unfortunately some illocutionary-act-verbs do seem to be causal. Consider, for example, "name"—as in "I hereby name this child Jonathan". "Name" is surely an illocutionary-act-verb. Yet it seems plausible to say that

If x is a naming of y by z, then there is an α that is y, or is y's having a new name, and x is a causing of α by z;

and also plausible to take it that "name" accepts events as subjects—

my making certain motions over a child, while saying the name "Jonathan", might name the child Jonathan. Other illocutionary-act-verbs that seem to me similar to "name" in this respect are "sentence", "appoint", "nominate", "promote", and "fire".

"Warn" is a particularly interesting case. Suppose I say "I warn you: there's a spy in the vicinity!" If you hear, and understand, then I have warned you that there is a spy in the vicinity. I have warned you of that even if you do not believe me, and thus even if I did not cause any belief in you. So one might be inclined to think that there is no event, state of affairs, what you will, such that to warn a man of something *is* to cause it, and that "warn" is therefore not a causal verb.

But notice that the snapping of a twig might warn a man of a spy in his vicinity, and that the snapping of that twig does warn him of a spy in the vicinity only if it causes him to believe that a spy is there. Again, an event that consists in my saying "I warn you: there's a spy in the vicinity!" might warn a man of a spy in his vicinity, but my saying those words does warn him of a spy in the vicinity only if it causes him to believe that one is there. Indeed, a bent twig, or a freshly dead agent with a bullet in his back, might warn a man that there is a spy in his vicinity; but neither does so unless it causes him to believe that there is.

It could, I suppose, be said that the verb "warn" is ambiguous. For convenience (and for convenience only—i.e., I have no view as how best to accommodate the facts I drew attention to), I suggest we say that there are two matching transitive verbs "warn". I shall say that the first verb "warn" is an illocutionary-act-verb: it is that which must be present in "I warn you: there's a spy in the vicinity!" if that sentence is to have a sense; and it is that which is present in the sentence a man utters when he says "Alfred warned Bert", and means for what he says to be compatible with Bert's not believing what Alfred warned him of. This verb "warn" does not accept events as subjects, for no event can say anything; and it is therefore noncausal. The second verb "warn" is not an illocutionary-act-verb: it is the one that must be present in "The snapping of a twig warned Bert of the presence of a spy" if that sentence is to be true, and it is the one that is present in the sentence a man utters when he says "Alfred warned Bert", and means for what he says to be incompatible with Bert's not believing what Alfred warned him of. Now this one does accept events as subjects; and since it also seems to satisfy condition (i), it is causal.

Acts and Other Events

"Tell", "assure", "inform", and "remind" seem to me similar to "warn" in these respects.

7. Let us now return briefly to a short list of verbs I gave in section 4: "hide", "dress", "wash", "shave", "eat". "Hide" and "dress" are causal. "Eat" is plainly not: no event has ever eaten anything or ever will. But what about "wash" and "shave"?

Both of them, I think, accept events as subjects. My moving a thing about in soapy water might have washed it; your scraping your customer's face with a razor might have shaved him.

But are they causal verbs? To hide a thing is to cause its being hidden and to dress a thing is to cause its being dressed. Now if you wash a thing you *may* cause it to be clean; but you *may* wash and wash and wash it and it never become clean. (Compare "polish": you may polish and polish a thing and it never shine.)[4] And "shave"? Is shaving a man causing him to be clean-shaven? Couldn't it be that, although you use a freshly sharpened blade and the best shaving cream on the market and shave your customer as carefully as you can, you take off no hair at all?

Perhaps it will be said that to wash a thing is to cause its being washed. (And that to polish a thing is to cause its being polished, to shave a thing is. . . .) I.e., that

> If x is a washing of y by z, then there is an α that is y, or is (among?) y's being washed(s?), and x is a causing of α by z

is a truth. But is it? Suppose Alfred washes his shirt; is there an α such that α is Alfred's shirt's being washed and such that Alfred's washing of his shirt is Alfred's causing of α? What would such an α *be?*

Should we take

(a)   Alfred's shirt's being washed

to refer to a state of affairs? Which?

Well, consider the property 'is (tenselessly) washed at some time or other'; should we perhaps take (a) to refer to the state of affirs that consists in Alfred's shirt's possessing that property? No. For if Alfred's shirt is ever washed, then it possesses that property at all times; the state of affairs that consists in its possessing it therefore obtains at all times; and

---

[4] Gilbert Ryle would perhaps call "wash" and "polish" 'task verbs', "clean" and "shine" 'achievement verbs'. See his *The Concept of Mind* (London: Hutchinson's University Library, 1949).

142

it seems eminently plausible to suppose that you cannot cause a state of affairs that already obtains—so Alfred cannot *now* cause the (already obtaining) state of affairs that consists in Alfred's shirt's possessing the property 'is (tenselessly) washed at some time or other'.

Similarly for the state of affairs that consists in Alfred's shirt's possessing the property 'is (tenselessly) washed at 3 P.M., January 9, 1976', which is when Alfred washed his shirt. Similarly for the state of affairs that consists in Alfred's shirt's possessing the property 'is (tenselessly) washed before 8:45 A.M., January 14, 1976', which is when I first wrote (a) above.

There is a state of affairs that consists in my hat's possessing the property 'is (tenselessly) hidden at some time or other'; and there is a second that consists in my hat's possessing the property 'is (tenselessly) hidden at 3 P.M., January 9, 1976'; and there is a third that consists in my hat's possessing the property 'is (tenselessly) hidden before 8:45 A.M., January 14, 1976'; all three are states of affairs such that if they obtain at any time they obtain at all times. But there is also a fourth state of affairs that consists in my hat's possessing the property 'hidden': this is a state of affairs obtaining at and only at such times as the hat is actually hidden. And perhaps we should take (a) to refer to an analogous state of affairs? But *is* there one? Is there a property 'washed' analogous to the property 'hidden'? Surely not. "My hat is hidden" is a perfectly respectable present tense sentence of English whose verb is "be"; but what is to be made of "Alfred's shirt is washed"? One who says it may simply not be a careful speaker: i.e., he may mean to be saying that Alfred's shirt *was* washed. (There is one sentence "Alfred's shirt was washed", and its verb is a passive of "wash". I suggest we say that there are two sentences "My hat was hidden": one whose verb is a passive of "hide", the other whose verb is "be".) Or he may be saying that Alfred's shirt is generally, or is supposed to be, washed (as opposed to being dry-cleaned). Or he may be speaking philosopher-ese, in which case the sentence he utters is tenseless, and its verb is a passive of "wash".

Compare "dead" and "killed". "Kennedy is dead" is a perfectly respectable sentence of English; "Kennedy is killed" is dreadful, and no one but a philosopher would fancy it a sentence.

Well, perhaps we should instead take (a) to refer to an event. Which? "Alfred's shirt is being washed" is elliptical for "Alfred's shirt is being washed by something", which is a passive transform of "Something is washing Alfred's shirt". So perhaps we should take (a) to refer to any event which might also be referred to by

(b)   Something's washing of Alfred's shirt.

Now I should imagine that Alfred can wash his shirt without causing any event which is his own washing of his shirt. But perhaps Alfred washes his shirt only if he causes *something's* washing of his shirt: e.g., a washing of it by his moving it about in soapy water, or a washing of it by his washing machine (if he washes it in a washing machine).

In any case, we can perhaps construct something similar to what I constructed for "kick" on page 132 above. (It is nice to remember that as you may wash and wash a thing and it never become clean, so may you kick and kick a thing and it never bruise or break or dent.) If so, then "wash" satisfies condition (i) as well as condition (ii), and therefore is causal. Perhaps "shave" (and "polish") can be shown to be so too. It is not really important. The only thing that turns on this is whether or not a relatively simple way of telling whether an event is a killing or a melting or a sinking or . . . may also be used to tell whether an event is a washing or a shaving (or a polishing).

8. Lastly, we must have a quick look at an interesting small group of verbs, about *some* of which something *like* what we said about causal verbs should be said.

Consider, for example, the verb in

(1)   John put the book on the table.

I think it satisfies condition (ii) for being a causal verb: i.e., I should imagine that my moving my hand in a certain way might have put a book on a table, and thus that the verb accepts events as subjects. But it plainly fails to satisfy condition (i) for being a causal verb: no matter what is replaced for "verb$_2$ing" in

If x is a putting of y by z, then there is an α that is y, or is (among) y's verb$_2$ing(s), and x is a causing of α by z,

the result is no truth, for its antecedent is a nonsense.

The verb in (1) is a member of a small class of verbs such that a verb is in the class just in case no expression either of the form "x verbed y," or of the form "x verbed," in which the verb is main verb, is a sentence. What I have in mind is this. The transitive verb "melt" may appear in such sentences as "John melted the chocolate on the stove", and *also* in such sentences as "John melted the chocolate"; the intransitive verb "melt" may appear in such sentences as "The chocolate melted on the stove", and *also* in such sentences as "The chocolate melted". By contrast, while there are such sentences as (1), there are no such sentences as

(1′)   John put the book

or

(1″)   John put.

For reasons I think will be obvious, I am going to call the verbs in this class "incomplete verbs".

It is because there are no such sentences as (1′) that the verb in (1) fails to satisfy condition (i). And indeed, it really does not seem intuitively right to call it a causal verb. I said it seems plausible that to kill someone is to cause him to die, to melt something is to cause it to melt, and so on; we cannot say "to put something is to cause it to . . .", for there are no such sentences as (as it might be) "John put something".

Nevertheless, putting something *on the table* surely is causing the thing to move onto the table; putting something *in a closet* surely is causing the thing to move into the closet; and so on. There is something causal here, and it would be good to be able to capture it.

Let us say that the incomplete verb in (1) may be 'completed' by a prepositional phrase; and let us say that the expression "put —— on the table" is a 'completed incomplete verb', 'completed verb' for short. (We should keep in mind, however, that while a completed verb contains a verb it is not itself a verb.) Then we could say that this expression is a *causal* completed verb, since it accepts events as subjects, and

> If x is a putting of y on the table by z, then there is an α that is y, or is among y's movings onto the table, and x is a causing of α by z

is a truth.

The verb in "John placed the letter in my Bible" is also incomplete. So too is the verb in "John slipped the letter under the door", if we can say that it is not identical with (though it matches) the verb in "John slipped". And the completed verbs "place —— in my Bible" and "slip —— under the door" could, for analogous reasons, also be called causal completed verbs.

Again, consider the main verb in "John made his mother cry"; that verb is incomplete if we can say that it is not identical with (though it matches) the verb in "John made a cake". It may be completed by a form of a verb. And the completed verb "make —— cry" could, for analogous reasons, also be called a causal completed verb. Similarly for the main verbs in "John got his mother killed", "John forced his mother to apologize", and "John coerced his mother into making a cake".

Again, consider the main verbs in the two sentences
(2)   John gave the boy the saltshaker.
I say "two sentences" to accommodate the fact that (as I shall put it) one entails that John caused the saltshaker to move toward the boy and the other entails that John caused the boy to own the saltshaker. Both verbs "give" are incomplete: there are no such sentences as "John gave the boy" or "John gave". (I assume we can say that neither is identical with the verb in a sentence such as "John gave a party".) Both may be completed by a noun-phrase; and the completed verbs "give —— the saltshaker" could, for analogous reasons, also be called causal completed verbs.

It might, then, seem a prima facie plausible idea that every completed verb is a causal completed verb. Alas for simplicity, it will not do. Consider, for example, the main verb in
(2)   John let Jim go.
There are no such sentences as
(2')   John let Jim
or
(2")   John let;
so I take it that the main verb in (2) is incomplete. But the completed verb "let —— go" is surely not causal: surely John can have let Jim go without causing Jim to go. Similarly for the completed verbs "allow —— to go" and "permit —— to go".

The main verb in (2) is surely, on any view, identical with the main verb in
(3)   I let the baby die.
Some people would say that (3) is true only if I caused the baby's dying. (I am not sure they are right, but it does not matter for present purposes.) If they are right, there are some incomplete verbs such that some completed verbs constructed from them are not causal and some completed verbs constructed from them are causal.

As I said, it would be good to be able to capture what is causal here. But I do not have in hand any feature F of which we could say that a completed verb is a causal completed verb just in case it has F. In-

Causal Verbs

deed, I do not even have in hand any feature G of which we could say that an expression is a completed verb just in case it has G—I indicated what I meant only by way of examples. Indeed, it is not even all that clear which are the incomplete verbs. Consider, for example, the main verb in

(4)   Bert refrained from waggling his thumb.

Certainly there is no such sentence as

(4')   Bert refrained his thumb;

is there such a sentence as

(4")   Bert refrained?

(4") is certainly not the nonsense that

(2")   John let

and

(1")   John put

are; yet it seems to me that the verb in (4) *ought* to be classed among the incomplete verbs—after all, although (4") is not a nonsense, it surely is elliptical. (Contrast it with "Bert slept", for example.) So perhaps we should insert "nonelliptical" in the definition I gave earlier, so that it reads: a verb is in the class just in case no expression either of the form "*x* verbed *y*", or of the form "*x* verbed," in which the verb is main verb, is a *nonelliptical* sentence. This emendation would allow us to call the verb in (4) an incomplete verb; and I shall call it an incomplete verb when it reappears later. But I am not certain that this does collect all and only those verbs that we would like included in this class. I shall therefore for the most part ignore incomplete verbs in what follows. I shall mention them occasionally, but only with a view to reminding you that there are such things.

X

Event-Ownership and the
Parts of Some Events

"Kill" is a causal verb; so we know that

      If x is a killing of y by z, then there is an α that is y, or is y's dying, and x is a causing of α by z

is a truth. [Cf. (T-S_2) in Chapter IX, section 1.] So we know that

(i)   there is an α that is y, or is y's dying, and x is a causing of α by z

is *necessary* for

(iii) x is a killing of y by z.

But (i) is plainly not *sufficient* for (iii). For (i) is true if

      there is an α that is y, and x is a causing of α by z

is true; but it by no means follows from this that (iii) is true. Suppose, for example, that

      there is an α that is my ice cube's melting, and x is a causing of α by me

is true; it by no means follows from this that

      x is a killing of my ice cube's melting by me.

As we saw, something stronger than the conditional I set out above is true, viz.,

      If x is a killing of y by z, then there is an α that is y's dying, and x is a causing of α by z.

(Cf. page 130 above.) So we know that

148

Event-Ownership and Parts of Some Events

(i')   there is an α that is y's dying, and x is a causing of α by z is necessary for (iii). If "kill" meant "cause to die", then every causing of a dying would be a killing, and (i') would also be sufficient for (iii). But alas, as we saw, "kill" does not mean "cause to die". If I coerce Smith into killing Jones, then I cause Jones's dying; but I do not kill him—though I get him killed by getting Smith to kill him. Thus while every killing is a causing of a dying, not every causing of a dying is a killing: my causing of Jones's dying is a causing of a dying, but is not itself a killing of Jones by me—since I do not kill Jones at all, there is no event that is a killing of Jones by me.

But there is a way in which we can get what we want.

1. Let us begin by asking under what conditions a person z causes an event E. It is often said that for an event C to cause an event E is for there to be a causal law linking C and E. Presumably no causal laws link *people* and events. So under what conditions does a person z cause an event E?

It seems a very plausible idea that a person z causes an event E only if there is an event C such that C causes E. Sirhan caused Kennedy's death, but so did the event that was Sirhan's shooting of Kennedy cause it; I caused the kitchen floor to become clean yesterday, and so did the event that was my scrubbing of the floor cause it. Indeed, it seems plausible, more generally, that every caused event is caused by an event, so that if anything, of any kind, whether person, event, state of affairs—whatever it is that can cause an event—causes an event E, then there is an event C that causes E.

On the other hand, the fact that an event C causes E does not make it false that a person z causes E. No doubt the event that was Sirhan's shooting of Kennedy caused Kennedy's death; but so also did *Sirhan* cause Kennedy's death. No doubt the event that was my scrubbing of the floor caused the floor to become clean; but so also did *I* cause the floor to become clean.

It plainly is not enough for a person z to cause an event E that there is an event C which causes it: Sirhan, after all, did not cause my kitchen floor to become clean, and I did not cause Kennedy's death. For a person z to cause an event E it is necessary *both* that there be an event C that causes E, *and* that C be in some sense *his*. What I suggest we want here is, simply, the relation I earlier called 'event-ownership':

Acts and Other Events

(D$_4$)   Owns (x, y) just in case y is an event, and x causes every-
          thing y causes.

And what I suggest we say is that

(T$_1$)   A person z causes an event E just in case there is an event C
          such that Owns (z, C) and C causes E.

Is (T$_1$) true? One conjunct of it, viz.,

> If there is an event C such that Owns (z, C) and C causes E,
> then z causes E,

is plainly true: for if there is an event C such that z causes everything
C causes, and C causes E, then z causes E. The other conjunct of it,
viz.,

> If z causes E then there is an event C such that Owns (z, C)
> and C causes E,

is less obvious. Must z cause *everything* C causes if it is to be true that
z causes E? I do not have any argument for the thesis that it must, but
I think the thesis plausible. If you are to cause E, I think it necessary
that there be an event C (which causes E), which you are responsible
for in some strong sense; and I take that sense to be this: you cause *everything* C causes.

There may be some who think the verb "cause" is ambiguous: that
it means something different when it has an event as subject from
what it means when it has a person as subject. I do not think "cause"
is ambiguous in this way, but does not matter for my purposes whether
or not it is. I want to make clear that (T$_1$) is not intended as a definition of a special sense of "cause" that takes people as subjects. If (T$_1$)
were so intended, it would be circular: it would define that 'personal-
causal-relation' in terms of a relation that a person can have to an
event C only if he has the 'personal-causal-relation' to everything C
causes. I want to stress that (T$_1$) is not intended as a definition of anything at all; (T$_1$) is simply a thesis—true, I hope—about the conditions
under which a person z causes an event E.

It seems to me, in fact, that not merely is (T$_1$) true, but so also,
more generally, is

(T$_2$) z causes an event E just in case there is an event C such that
          Owns (z, C) and C causes E.

If (T$_1$) is true, then presumably (T$_2$) is true for all values of z for which
z is an animate being; all animate beings surely are like persons in respect of the conditions under which they cause events. Is (T$_2$) true for
values of z such that z is an *in*animate object, e.g., a bullet or a gun?

Event-Ownership and Parts of Some Events

A certain bullet might have caused an event which consisted in a man's death, after all. But I should imagine that inanimate objects too are like persons in respect of the conditions under which they cause events. That is, if every caused event is caused by an event—and, as I said, I think this plausible—then in particular, an event E that is caused by a bullet is caused by an event C; and I should imagine that, as with people, the bullet has to 'own' such an event C in order for it to be true that the bullet causes E. And what about states of affairs, which are also inanimate, but which also may cause events? A man's being grossly overweight might have caused an event that consisted in his death, after all. But I should imagine that states of affairs too are like persons in respect of the conditions under which they cause events: I should imagine that a man's being grossly overweight has to 'own' an event C, which causes his death, if it is to be true that his being grossly overweight causes his death. Events too are inanimate, and (T_2) is trivially true for values of z such that z is an event. For every event causes everything it itself causes, so every event 'owns' itself; and plainly, then, an event z causes an event E just in case there is an event C 'owned' by z that causes E. [Note, then, that (T_2) does not entail that for every pair of events z and E such that z causes E there is an event C such that z causes C and C causes E: an event z 'owns' every event it causes, but it also 'owns' events that it does not cause—in particular, it 'owns' itself.]

More generally still, not merely does (T_2) seem true, but so does

(T_3) z causes y just in case there is an event C such that Owns (z, C) and C causes y.

That is, whatever it is that z causes—whether event, or state of affairs, or whatever is causable—z causes it just in case some event that z 'owns' causes it.

2. A thing's dying is, I should imagine, an event. So if (T_3) is true, so is

        z causes y's dying just in case there is an event C such that Owns (z, C) and C causes y's dying.

If "kill" meant "cause to die" then this would entail

(T_4) z kills y just in case there is an event C such that Owns (z, C) and C kills y.

A thing's melting is, I should imagine, an event. So if (T_3) is true, so is z causes y's melting just in case there is an event C such that Owns (z, C) and C causes y's melting.

People who hold that "kill" means "cause to die" also hold that "melt" means "cause to melt"; if they were right, then this would entail

(T₅)   z melts y just in case there is an event C such that Owns (z, C) and C melts y.

But as we saw, "kill" does not mean "cause to die". Nor does "melt" mean "cause to melt".

Moreover, not merely can we not obtain (T₄) and (T₅) from (T₃) by definition, the very same considerations that show these definitions to be false show that (T₄) and (T₅) are false. Take "kill". If I coerce Smith into killing Jones, then there is an event that kills Jones (e.g., Smith's shooting of Jones), which event I 'own': i.e., I cause everything it causes since I cause *it*, and, as we are supposing, causality is transitive. Thus

there is an event C such that Owns (I, C) and C kills Jones.

But *I* do not kill Jones. So (T₄) is false.

Nevertheless it will pay us to have theses *like* (T₄) and (T₅) available; and in any case, the difficulty is easily eliminated.

Take "kill" again. What went wrong? There was an event I 'owned', which killed Jones; but I did not kill Jones. To say I 'owned' that event is to say that I have to it the following relation:

(D₄)   Owns (x, y) just in case y is an event and x causes everything y causes.

And that relation is not sufficiently 'tight': you have to stand to an event C in some tighter relation than that of event-ownership if you are to have killed the person whom C killed.

But it is really very simple to fix the thing. Let us replace (D₄) with

(D₄ₐ)   Owns_cause (x, y) just in case y is an event and x causes everything y causes;

and let us define a new event-ownership relation as follows:

(D₄ᵦ)   Owns_kill (x, y) just in case y is an event and x kills everything y kills.

Now as we saw, it will not do to say (T₄); but I suggest that it will do—indeed, eminently well—to say

(T₄')   z kills y just in case there is an event C such that Owns_kill (z, C) and C kills y.

Let us suppose that I never, myself, kill anyone (or anything) at all. Then there is no event that kills something which is such that I kill whatever it kills; so in particular, there is no event that kills Jones which is such that I kill whatever it kills. So, by (T_4'), I do not kill Jones—which is just as it should be.

Since we have rewritten (D_4) as (D_{4a}), let us also rewrite (T_3) as

(T_3') z causes y just in case there is an event C such that Owns-$_{cause}$ (z, C) and C causes y.

I said that (T_3) seemed to me true; and to say T_3 is true is to say that (T_3') is true.

Is (T_4') true? It is not entailed by (T_3'), but it seems to me to be, independently, just as plausible as (T_3') is. One conjunct of it, viz.,

> If there is an event C such that Owns$_{kill}$ (z, C) and C kills y, then z kills y,

is plainly true: for if there is an event C such that z kills everything C kills, and C kills y, then z kills y. The other conjunct of it, viz.,

> If x kills y, then there is an event C such that Owns$_{kill}$ (z, C) and C kills y,

is less obvious. Must z kill *everything* C kills if it is to be true that z kills y? I do not have any argument for the thesis that he must, but I think the thesis plausible. If you are to kill y, I think it necessary that there be an event C (which kills y) which you are responsible for in some strong sense. We have seen that it does not suffice for you to be responsible for C in the sense that you *cause* everything C causes. (Consider, again, the case of Jones and me.) I think the wanted sense is this: that you *kill* everything it kills.

It should be stressed that (T_4') is not intended as a definition of the verb "kill". If it were so intended, it would be circular: "kill" appears in the definiens of "Own$_{kill}$ (x, y)". (T_4') is intended simply as a thesis—true, I hope—about the conditions under which an entity z kills an entity y.

I spoke of 'owns$_{kill}$' as a 'tighter' relation than 'owns$_{cause}$', but we should note that the former is not in the familiar sense stronger than the latter. As we have seen,

> Owns$_{cause}$ (x, y)

does not entail

> Owns$_{kill}$ (x, y)—

for, remember, I 'owned$_{cause}$' Smith's shooting of Jones, and therefore caused everything it caused, for I caused it; but I did not 'own$_{kill}$' Smith's shooting of Jones, for Smith's shooting of Jones killed Jones, and I did not. But we should notice also that

$$\text{Owns}_{\text{kill}}\,(x,\,y)$$
does not entail
$$\text{Owns}_{\text{cause}}\,(x,\,y)\text{—}$$
if your sneezing just now killed no one, then I killed everything it killed, and hence I 'own$_{\text{kill}}$' it; but I do not 'own$_{\text{cause}}$' it, for (I am sure) there are many things it caused which I did not. The sense in which 'owns$_{\text{kill}}$' is a 'tighter' relation that 'owns$_{\text{cause}}$' is just this: while what follows "just in case" in (T_4) is not sufficient for z kills y, what follows "just in case" in (T_4') *is* sufficient for it.

Consider, now, the battery of definitions that result from replacing a causal verb for "verb", and the third-person singular of the verb for "verbs", in the following definition-schema:

(D-S)   Owns$_{\text{verb}}\,(x,\,y)$ just in case y is an event and x verbs everything y verbs.

For example, there results, as well as (D_{4a}) and (D_{4b}),

(D_{4c}) Owns$_{\text{melt}}\,(x,\,y)$ just in case y is an event and x melts everything y melts.

I suggest that while (T_5) is false,

(T_5') z melts y just in case there is an event C such that Owns$_{\text{melt}}$ $(z,\,C)$ and C melts y

is true.

Compare also

(T_6') z sinks y just in case there is an event C such that Owns$_{\text{sink}}$ $(z,\,C)$ and C sinks y,

(T_7') z frightens y just in case there is an event C such that Owns$_{\text{frighten}}$ $(z,\,C)$ and C frightens y,

and

(T_8') z persuades y just in case there is an event C such that Owns$_{\text{persuade}}$ $(z,\,C)$ and C persuades y.

I should imagine that all of these are true.

Indeed, I propose we accept that if a verb is a causal verb then the result of replacing it for "verb", and its third-person singular for "verbs", in

(T-S$_3$) z verbs y just in case there is an event C such that Owns$_{\text{verb}}$ $(z,\,C)$ and C verbs y

is a truth.

3. To return, now, to our problem. I said at the beginning of this chapter that

(i')   there is an α that is y's dying, and x is a causing of α by z

is necessary, but not sufficient, for

(iii) x is a killing of y by z.

And what we want is something both necessary *and* sufficient for (iii).

Let us have a second look at

(T$_4$') z kills y just in case there is an event C such that Owns$_{\text{kill}}$ (z, C) and C kills y.

Sirhan, for example, killed Kennedy; and there in fact are events C such that

       Owns$_{\text{kill}}$ (Sirhan, C) and C kills Kennedy.

Consider, for example, Sirhan's shooting of Kennedy. Sirhan's shooting of Kennedy is an event, and Sirhan killed everything it killed, so it follows that

       Owns$_{\text{kill}}$ (Sirhan, Sirhan's shooting of Kennedy).

Moreover, we know that

       Sirhan's shooting of Kennedy killed Kennedy.

So Sirhan's shooting of Kennedy is an event C of the required kind.

We were supposing that Sirhan's shooting of Kennedy caused the onset of a hemorrhage, which caused Kennedy's dying. So I should imagine that the onset of that hemorrhage too is an event C of the required kind—i.e., that

       Owns$_{\text{kill}}$ (Sirhan, the onset of that hemorrhage) and the onset of that hemorrhage killed Kennedy.

But let us remind ourselves that Sirhan's shooting of Kennedy was *part* of Sirhan's killing of Kennedy, and that the onset of that hemorrhage was part of it too. We may well think, then, that a killing of y by z must have as a part some event C such that z 'owns$_{\text{kill}}$' C and C kills y—i.e., that

(ii)   there is an event C such that Owns$_{\text{kill}}$ (z, C) and C kills y and *PART* (C, x)

is necessary for (iii).

It would be beautifully tidy if we could say that (ii) was sufficient as well as necessary for (iii). But, alas, it is not. Consider the fusion of Sirhan's killing of Kennedy and your sneezing just now; let us call it (a). (a) contains parts (among others, Sirhan's shooting of Kennedy and the onset of hemorrhage) that Sirhan 'owns$_{\text{kill}}$' and that kill Kennedy, but (a) is not itself a killing of Kennedy by Sirhan—(a) includes a killing but is not itself one.

Why is (a) not itself a killing of Kennedy by Sirhan? It seems plain that the trouble issues from this: (a) has parts that are not parts of Sirhan's causing of Kennedy's dying—for your sneezing just now, which is part of (a), is no part of Sirhan's causing of Kennedy's dying.

It comes across, then, that while (ii) is not sufficient for (iii), the conjunction of (i') and (ii) is; and thus that we can say

(T_4'') x is a killing of y by z just in case

         (i')   there is an α that is y's dying, and x is a causing of α by z, and

         (ii)   there is an event C such that $Owns_{kill}$ (z, C) and C kills y and PART (C, x).

Sirhan's killing of Kennedy then turns out to be a killing; (a) does not—for (a), though it includes a causing of a dying, is not itself one.

Notice that (T_4'') may be taken as a definition of the three-place predicate 'x is a killing of y by z' in terms of the three-place predicate 'x is a causing of y by z' and the two-place predicate 'x kills y'.

4. If (T_4'') is true, so also are

(T_5'') x is a melting of y by z just in case

         (i')   there is an α that is among y's meltings, and x is a causing of α by z, and

         (ii)   there is an event C such that $Owns_{melt}$ (z, C) and C melts y and PART (C, x),

     .

     .

     .

(T_8'') x is a persuading of y by z just in case

         (i')   there is an α that is y's being in agreement with z, and x is a causing of α by z, and

         (ii)   there is an event C such that $Owns_{persuade}$ (z, C) and C persuades y and PART (C, x).

Each of these may be regarded as a definition in the same way as (T_4'') may.

It suggests itself, then, that we can say that for every causal verb, the result of replacing it for "verb", its third-person singular for "verbs", its gerund for "verb$_1$ing", and the gerund of some verb or verb-phrase for "verb$_2$ing" in

(T-S$_4$)   x is a verb$_1$ing of y by z just in case

         (i')   there is an α that is (among) y's verb$_2$ing(s), and x is a causing of α by z, and

(ii)   there is an event C such that Owns$_{verb}$ (z, C) and C verbs y and PART (C, x)

is a truth.

Unfortunately, however, there is the verb "cause" itself to worry about. I proposed earlier that we allow it to be a causal verb; but is there an expression such that if we write it in the blank in the following, the result is true:

x is a causing of y by z just in case

(i')   there is an α that is (among) y's ____(s), and x is a causing of α by z, and

(ii)   there is an event C such that Owns$_{cause}$ (z, C) and C causes y and PART (C, x)?

"Occurring or obtaining"?

Let us go back to killings again. It is plain that if

(i')   there is an α that is y's dying, and x is a causing of α by z

is true, then

(i)   there is an α that is y, or is y's dying, and x is a causing of α by z

is also true. So it is plain that if the conjunction of (i') and

(ii)   there is an event C such that Owns$_{kill}$ (z, C) and C kills y and PART (C, x)

is true, then the conjunction of (i) and (ii) is true.

Similarly, if the conjunction of (i) and (ii) is true, then the conjunction of (i') and (ii) is true. This comes out as follows. If (ii) is true, then there is an event C such that C kills y. Things of a great many different kinds can be killed (e.g., people, rats, cats, and marigolds); things of a great many different kinds can be caused (e.g., a man's dying, a man's being grossly overweight); but there is nothing that can be both killed *and* caused. So if (ii) is true, y is not caused. So if (ii) is true, there is nothing that is a causing of y. So if (ii) *and* (i) are true, there is an α that is (not y itself, but) y's dying, and x is a causing of α by z; i.e., if (ii) and (i) are true, (ii) and (i') are true.

The conjunction of (i') and (ii), then, is equivalent to the conjunction of (i) and (ii). And we can rewrite (T_4'') as follows:

(T_4'') x is a killing of y by z just in case

(i)   there is an α that is y, or is y's dying, and x is a causing of α by z, and

(ii)   there is an event C such that Owns$_{kill}$ (z, C) and C kills y and PART (C, x).

I shall pretend that this is what I originally called "(T_4'')".

Just as nothing can be both killed and caused, so nothing can be both melted and caused. Similarly, nothing can be both persuaded and caused. So we may safely rewrite (T_5'') and (T_8'') the same way—i.e., we may safely insert "is y, or" into their first conjuncts.

Moreover, there is an expression such that if we write it in the blank in the following, the result is true:

> x is a causing of y by z just in case
> - (i)   there is an α that is y, or is (among) y's ____(s), and x is a causing of α by z, and
> - (ii)   there is an event C such that $\text{Owns}_{\text{cause}}$ (z, C) and C causes y and $PART$ (C, z).

Write "dying" in the blank. If x is a causing of y by z, then it is plain that

(i)   there is an α that is y, or is y's dying, and x is a causing of α by z

and

(ii)   there is an event C such that $\text{Owns}_{\text{cause}}$ (z, C) and C causes y and $PART$ (C, z)

are true. If (ii) is true, there is an event C that causes y. Things of a great many different kinds can die (e.g., people, rats, cats, and marigolds); but there is nothing that can both die and be caused. So if (ii) is true, there is nothing that is y's dying. So if (ii) *and* (i) are true, then there is an α that is y itself, and x is a causing of α by z; i.e., if (ii) and (i) are true, x is a causing of y by z.

We can, then, rewrite $(T\text{-}S_4)$ as follows:

$(T\text{-}S_4)$ x is a verb_1ing of y by z just in case
> - (i)   there is an α that is y, or is (among) y's verb_2ings(s), and x is a causing of α by z, and
> - (ii)   there is an event C such that $\text{Owns}_{\text{verb}}$ (z, C) and C verbs y and $PART$ (C, x).

I shall pretend that this is what I originally called "$(T\text{-}S_4)$". And now we can say, quite generally, for all causal verbs—including the verb "cause" itself—that the results of making the appropriate replacements in $(T\text{-}S_4)$ are truths.

5. But this is not completely satisfactory. If we want to know what killings, meltings, etc. are, we want at least as much to know what causings are. As I said earlier, we are relatively at home with talk of

killings and relatively unfamiliar with talk of 'causings'. Yet this account of killings, meltings, etc. takes the three-term predicate 'x is a causing of y by z' as primitive.

I am inclined to think that nothing in the equipment used in this and the preceding chapter will enable us to define 'x is a causing of y by z'. I suggest that it is true to say:

(T_3'') x is a causing of y by z just in case

> (i)   there is an α that is y, or is y's dying, and x is a causing of α by z, and
>
> (ii) there is an event C such that $\text{Owns}_{\text{cause}}$ (z, C) and C causes y and $PART$ (C, z).

But as a definition of 'x is a causing of y by z', (T_3'') is plainly a nonstarter.

It is worth looking at something that leads to trouble if we try another route.

Consider again

(T_3') z causes y just in case there is an event C such that $\text{Owns}_{\text{cause}}$ (z, C) and C causes y.

Suppose I cause Jones's dying by coercing Smith into shooting him. How do I coerce Smith into shooting Jones? Suppose I tell Smith that my henchmen will kill his children (whom they hold as hostages) if he refuses. Then it seems to me that the following events,

> my threatening Smith,
>
> Smith's deciding to kill Jones,

and

> Smith's shooting of Jones,

are, each of them, events C such that

> $\text{Owns}_{\text{cause}}$ (I, C) and C causes Jones's dying.

Presumably there are others too—e.g., the onset of hemorrhage in Jones (if it was by causing that that the shooting caused the dying). The hypothesis suggests itself, then, that my causing of Jones's dying just *is* the fusion of all such events C; i.e., that we should say

(T_3''') x is a causing of y by z just in case x is the fusion of all events C such that $\text{Owns}_{\text{cause}}$ (z, C) and C causes y.

Sirhan's shooting of Kennedy was part of Sirhan's killing of Kennedy; so also was the onset of hemorrhage which was caused by the shooting, and which caused Kennedy's dying. Why not say also that

(T_4''') x is a killing of y by z just in case x is the fusion of all events C such that $\text{Owns}_{\text{kill}}$ (z, C) and C kills y?

Acts and Other Events

And indeed that for every causal verb, the result of replacing it for "verb", its third-person singular for "verbs", and its gerund for "verbing" in

(T-S₅) x is a verbing of y by z just in case x is the fusion of all events C such that Owns$_{verb}$ (z, C) and C verbs y

is a truth. Notice that (T-S₅) is *very* much simpler than (T-S₄); and that the resulting theses—if they were true—would define the three-place predicates 'x is a causing of y by z', 'x is a killing of y by z', 'x is a melting of y by z', etc., simply in terms of the two-place predicates 'z causes y', 'z kills y', 'z melts y', etc.

One reason why this will not do is the following. Suppose that having told Smith that my henchmen will kill his children (whom they hold as hostages), I sit back and start idly playing the harmonica (while I wait for Smith to kill Jones). And consider now the event—I'll call it (a)—that is the fusion of

my threatening Smith

and

my playing the harmonica.

(a) is an event that I 'own$_{cause}$', for I cause everything it causes; and by our old assumption of Chapter V,

(IV) E is caused by y if and only if there is an x such that x is part of y, and x causes E, and no part of E is part of y, and no part of E causes part of y

(in which the variables ranged over events), (a) causes Jones's dying, since my threatening Smith causes Jones's dying. But then if (T₃''') is true, (a) is part of my causing of Jones's dying. And surely it should not be: surely my playing the harmonica is not itself part of my causing of Jones's dying, but only takes place during it.

Take a more extreme example. Let (b) be the fusion of

my threatening Smith

and

my playing in my sandbox on my third birthday.

I 'own$_{cause}$' (b), since I cause everything it causes; and by (IV), (b) causes Jones's dying. But we obviously cannot have (b) be part of my causing of Jones's dying: my playing in my sandbox on my third birthday surely precedes my causing of Jones's dying.

The other results of replacement in (T-S₅) fare no better. Let (c) be the fusion of

Sirhan's shooting of Kennedy

and

> your sneezing just now.

I assume that your sneezing just now did not kill anybody; then Sirhan killed everything (c) killed, so that he 'owns$_{kill}$' (c). I should imagine that a thing kills a thing only if it causes that thing's dying, so that

(IV') z is killed by y if and only if there is an x such that x is part of y, and x kills z, and no part of z's dying is part of y, and no part of z's dying causes part of y

is just as plausible as (IV); if so, (c) killed Kennedy. But surely (c) is not—as (T$_4$''') would have it—part of Sirhan's killing of Kennedy. For your sneezing just now is no part of it.

There is room, of course, for the proposal that we just give up (IV)—and the related (IV')—in light of the lovely simplicity of (T-S$_5$). But I think that would be a most unfortunate move. A reader who feels tempted to make it is invited to go back to Chapter V for a second look at (what seem to me to be) the strong arguments for (IV).

A number of minor complications can be introduced into (T-S$_5$) to eliminate some of the difficulties. If we add, e.g., the clause ". . . and Owns$_{cause}$ (z, C)", so that (T$_4$'') becomes

> x is a killing of y by z just in case x is the fusion of all events C such that Owns$_{kill}$ (z, C) and C kills y and Owns$_{cause}$ (z, C),

then (c) does not turn out to be part of Sirhan's killing of Kennedy, there being many things your sneezing, and therefore (c), causes that Sirhan does not. If we also add ". . . and z verbs y at t and C occurs in t" to (T-S$_5$), so that (T$_3$''') becomes

> x is a causing of y by z just in case x is the fusion of all events C such that Owns$_{cause}$ (z, C) and C causes y and z causes y at t and C occurs in t,

then (b) does not turn out to be part of my causing of Jones's death, since (b) does not occur in t, having, as it does, a part that occurred on my third birthday, i.e., long before I caused Jones's death. But, so emended, (T-S$_5$) is less attractive; and in any case, I see no way at all of emending (T-S$_5$) so as to make (a) not a part of my causing of Jones's death—if we restrict ourselves to the equipment so far available.

What is wanted comes out of a further consideration of (a), which is the fusion of

> my threatening Smith

and

        my playing the harmonica.

Plainly, the first of these two events should turn out to be part of my causing of Jones's dying, and the second should turn out not to be part of it. (Hence their fusion should overlap, but not be part of, my causing of Jones's dying.) How precisely do they differ? I said that my playing the harmonica is not part of, but only takes place *during*, my causing of Jones's dying. I play the harmonica *while* I cause Jones's dying; I do not cause Jones's dying *by* playing the harmonica. By contrast, I do cause Jones's dying by threatening Smith.

Again, I cause Jones's dying by threatening Smith, but I do not cause his dying by playing in my sandbox on my third birthday.

Again, Sirhan killed Kennedy by shooting him, but Sirhan did not cause Kennedy's dying by your sneezing just now (this does not even make sense), or by causing your sneezing just now.

These are the hints we should try to exploit.

XI

Method and the Parts
of Some Events (I)

1. In the last section of the preceding chapter we looked at something that makes trouble for the following thesis:

(T_3''') x is a causing of y by z just in case x is the fusion of all events C such that $Owns_{cause}$ (z, C) and C causes y.

Suppose that having told Smith my henchmen will kill his children (whom they hold as hostages) if he does not kill Jones, I sit back and start idly playing the harmonica (while I wait for Smith to kill Jones). Let (a) be the event that is the fusion of

my threatening Smith

and

my playing the harmonica.

(a) is an event I 'own$_{cause}$', for I cause everything it causes; and (a) causes Jones's dying, since my threatening Smith causes Jones's dying. But then, if (T_3''') is true, (a) is part of my causing of Jones's dying. And while (a) should surely overlap my causing of Jones's dying, it should not be part of it—for my playing the harmonica should not be part of it.

One way of exploiting the hints I mentioned at the end of the last chapter is to add a clause to (T_3'''), requiring C to be an event such that z causes y by doing or causing C. If we do add such a clause, then

(a) is not an event that meets the conditions on C: for I do not cause Jones's dying by doing or causing (a). I cause Jones's death by threatening Smith, but I do not cause Jones's death by threatening Smith *and* playing the harmonica—my playing the harmonica plays no role in my causing of Jones's death.

Unfortunately it is not easy to see precisely what this new restriction on C is to look like. We cannot in fact add to (T_3''') the following:

> and z causes y by doing or causing C.

For let us remember that when "do" takes an event as object, it is a pro-verb (see Chapter II). Hence this clause does not offer a pair of alternative relations such that z must stand in one or the other of them to C.

On the other hand, it would not suffice to add to (T_3''')

> and z causes y by causing C.

I had imagined that Smith's shooting of Jones (which was caused by my threatening Smith) caused Jones's death by causing onset of a hemorrhage; it follows that I caused Jones's death by causing onset of that hemorrhage. So adding this further restriction on C allows us, still, to have the event that was the onset of that hemorrhage as part of my causing of Jones's death—which is as it should be. But what about the event that was my threatening Smith—did I cause Jones's death by causing it? Only if I caused it. And *did* I cause it? It seems to me perfectly possible—as I said a number of times earlier—that a person should cause some of his own acts. You might, e.g., cause your killing of a man by taking a drug, which sends you into some great new high, in the course of which, and because of which, you kill a man. But we surely do not cause *all* of our own acts, and if my threatening Smith is an event that I did not cause, then there is trouble—for surely it should turn out to be part of my causing of Jones's death.

Suppose Sirhan had been asleep when he killed Kennedy—a sleep he did not cause. Surely Sirhan's shooting of Kennedy should be part of Sirhan's causing of Kennedy's death; yet if Sirhan did not cause his shooting of Kennedy, then his shooting of Kennedy is not an event that meets this further restriction on C.

I suspect that the only available maneuver along these lines is to appeal to activities. Perhaps I did not cause my threatening Smith, but—if there are activities—then threatening Smith is surely an activity; and my threatening Smith was surely my engaging in that activity. (Perhaps Sirhan did not cause his shooting of Kennedy; but—if there are activities—then shooting Kennedy is surely an activity; and Sirhan's shooting of Kennedy was surely his engaging in that activity.) Now if there are activities, we can quantify over them: we can say, for example, that there was an activity such that I caused Jones's death by engaging in that activity. And then we can add that a certain event C was my engaging in that activity. So the best maneuver along these lines is (I suspect) to add to (T_3'''), instead, the following (or something like it):

> and (*either* z causes y by causing C, *or* there is an activity A such that z causes y by engaging in A, where C is z's engaging in A).

This would allow us to say that my threatening Smith is part of my causing of Jones's death, since that event was my engaging in the activity 'threatening Smith', and I did cause Jones's death by engaging in that activity. By contrast, although playing the harmonica is no doubt an activity, and my playing the harmonica is my engaging in it, I did not cause Jones's death by engaging in it. And although threatening Smith *and* playing the harmonica is yet another activity, and my threatening Smith and playing the harmonica was my engaging in it, I did not cause Jones's death by engaging in this, third, conjunctive activity—for my engaging in the activity 'playing the harmonica' played no role in my causing of Jones's death.

We cannot in fact make exactly this addition (T_3'''): there are difficulties of detail that make trouble for it.[1] But there is one possible objection to it which would, if correct, make it wrong in principle, and that objection seems to me worth spending some time on.

What I have in mind is that accepting

(T_3'''') x is a causing of y by z just in case x is the fusion of all events C such that $Owns_{cause}$ (z, C) and C causes y and (*either* z causes y by causing C, *or* there is an activity A such that z causes y by engaging in A, where C is z's engaging in A)

would commit us to supposing that if z causes y but does *not* cause y by causing something or engaging in some activity, then there is no

---

[1] Perhaps most striking is the following. The expression "z's engaging in A" implies uniqueness; but what if A is an activity that z has engaged in several times? The following revision suggests itself: replace "z's engaging in A" with "an engaging in A by z". But then may C be any one of z's engagings in A? Does the clause [already in (T_3''')] ". . . and C causes y" guarantee that only the right engaging(s) in A by z are among the events C that x is—according to (T_3''')—the fusion of?

event x that is z's causing of y. Causing an entity E is itself engaging in an activity (the activity of causing E), and engaging in an activity is doing something. So I shall sometimes, for brevity, put the point as follows: accepting (T_3'''') would commit us to supposing that if z causes y but does *not* cause y by doing something, then there is no event x that is z's causing of y. Now there are people who think that (i) we sometimes cause things and do not cause them by doing something; and at least some among them think that (ii) on all those occasions there nevertheless is an event that is our causing of the things. If they are right, then (T_3'''') is wrong in principle.

There is, after all, at least some reason to think (i) is true. No doubt very many of the things we cause we cause by doing something. If I cause the window to break, I presumably cause it to break by doing something, for instance, by throwing a rock at it. If you cause a ship to sink, you presumably cause it to sink by doing something, for instance, by torpedoing it. If you cause a man's death, you presumably cause his death by doing something, for instance, by shooting him.

No doubt very many of the things *in*animate objects cause they cause by doing something. If a gun or a bullet causes a man's death, it presumably causes it by doing something, such as by causing a hemorrhage. Events too. Sirhan's shooting of Kennedy caused Kennedy's death and did so (as we are supposing) by causing the onset of a hemorrhage.

But suppose I caused my arm to move. How? Well, suppose I caused my muscles to tense. How did I do that? If I caused them to tense in the ordinary way—i.e., in the way in which one does this when one moves one's arm in the ordinary way—then there does not *seem* to be any answer to the question how I caused them to tense. There does not in such a case seem to be anything I did, by doing which I caused them to tense.

There surely was a physiological occurrence O in my brain, which preceded my muscles' tensing, and indeed caused it. And some may wish to say I caused O, and that it was by causing O that I caused my muscles' tensing. Did I? And how did I cause O? Was there a still prior physiological occurrence O', such that I caused O', and caused O by causing O'? There is room to insist on my causing all of the preceding physiological events that caused the later physiological events, but it gets harder and harder to squeeze into as we go back in time.

I want to stress that I am not denying that there was a physiological occurrence in my brain that preceded my muscles' tensing and caused it. Nothing we have so far said sheds any doubt at all on the truth of

(T_3') z causes y just in case there is an event C such that $\text{Owns}_{\text{cause}}(z, C)$ and C causes y,

so I am sure that if I did cause my muscles to tense, there was at least one event C—presumably in my brain—such that I caused everything C caused, and such that C caused my muscles to tense. What is in question here is not whether there was such an event C. What is in question here is whether there was such an event C which *also* meets the further restriction on C in (T_3'''''), which requires that either I caused my muscles to tense by causing C, or C was my engaging in some activity, where I caused my muscles to tense by engaging in that activity. If there is no such event C, there is no event that is the fusion of all such events C—and therefore, if (T_3''''') is true, there is no event that is my causing of my muscles' tensing.

A more interesting sort of case, it seems to me, is this. Bee, you will remember, is the fusion of all events that caused my sneezing at a certain time last month. It comes out easily enough that Bee itself caused my sneezing then.[2] Now there is an event C such that

$\text{Owns}_{\text{cause}}(\text{Bee}, C)$ and C causes my sneezing then:

Bee itself is such an event. But is there an event C that meets the condition just laid out *and* also is such that either Bee caused my sneezing by causing C, or C was Bee's engaging in some activity, where Bee caused my sneezing by engaging in that activity? There does not seem to be any. Everything that caused the sneezing is itself *in* Bee; so how can Bee have caused the sneezing by causing C? And what activity could it be thought that Bee engaged in, such that Bee caused the sneezing by engaging in it? But if there is no such event C, there is no

---

[2] Suspicious readers may want to see a proof. We know, by assumption (IV) of Chapter V, that the sneezing is caused by Bee if and only if there is an x such that x is part of Bee, and x causes the sneezing, and no part of the sneezing is part of Bee, and no part of the sneezing causes part of Bee. Well, there is an x such that x is part of Bee, and x caused the sneezing: the pepper-grating is such an x. Moreover, (i) no part of the sneezing is part of Bee. For suppose that d is part of the sneezing. Then, by (III), d is caused by every y such that y caused the sneezing. It follows that d is discrete from every y such that y caused the sneezing. It follows that d is discrete from Bee. Moreover, (ii) no part of the sneezing causes part of Bee. For suppose that d is part of the sneezing, and that z is part of Bee, and that d causes z. Since z is part of Bee, z has a part in common with some y such that y caused the sneezing. Let z' and y' be events such that z' is part of z, and z' is part of y', and y' caused the sneezing. By hypothesis, d causes z. It follows, by (III), that d causes z'. Since d is part of the sneezing, it follows, by (III), that y' causes d. It follows, by (I), that y' causes z'—which is ruled out by (II).

event that is the fusion of all such events C—and therefore, if (T_3'''') is true, there is no event that is Bee's causing of my sneezing.

And yet, while perhaps it is not so obvious that there was such an event as Bee's causing of my sneezing, surely there was such an event as my causing of my muscles' tensing!

Three moves are available here.

2. We might say Yes: (i) we sometimes cause things and do not cause them by doing something, and (ii) on all those occasions there nevertheless is an event that is our causing of the things, and therefore (T_3'''') is wrong—wrong in principle.

Second, we might say No: (i) is true, but (ii) is false. So while (T_3'''') may well be false, this argument does not show it so.

Third, we might say No: (i) is false, so (again) while (T_3'''') may well be false, this argument does not show it so. This is the move I think we ought to make, and I shall come back to it in the following section.

Let us suppose for the remainder of this section that (i) is true. Some think that (ii) is also true. They think it happens (and indeed, often happens) that a person z causes something y and does not cause y by doing something, *and* that there always nevertheless then is an event that is z's causing of y—an event of a special kind, a 'basic act'.

I do not think it has ever been satisfactorily explained what a basic act is.[3] The term is sometimes defined as follows: an act is a basic act just in case its agent performs, or does, it, but not by doing something.[4] But this will not do at all. Suppose we fasten on "perform". Sirhan's killing of Kennedy, for example, is not performed at all, and *a fortiori* is not performed by doing something; yet Sirhan's killing of Kennedy should presumably not turn out to be a basic act. Suppose, instead, we fasten on "do". If Sirhan did Sirhan's killing of Kennedy (if, e.g., he covered it for a newspaper), then Sirhan's killing of Kennedy is a basic act, on this account of the matter, just in case Sirhan's doing of it was a doing of it but not by doing something—and the

---

[3] For critiques of some attempts, see Annette Baier, "The Search for Basic Actions," *American Philosophical Quarterly*, 8 (1971), 161–170, and "Ways and Means," *Canadian Journal of Philosophy*, 1 (1972), 275–293. (I think that what she calls "effectings" in the latter paper are what I call causings.)

[4] Cf., e.g., "[Basic acts] are actions we do but not *through* any distinct thing which we also do, . . ." Arthur C. Danto, *Analytical Philosophy of Action* (Cambridge: Cambridge University Press, 1973), p. 28.

question whether Sirhan's doing of it (the question whether, e.g., his covering it for a newspaper) was a doing of it but not by doing something ought surely to have nothing at all to do with the question whether or not the killing itself was a basic act.

My suspicion is that those who interest themselves in the notion 'basic act' would do best to give up the idea of defining the term. This need not leave them speechless as to what it means: there would still be available the option of offering us a thesis-schema, perhaps

> If x verb-phrased only once on a certain occasion, then x's verb-phrasing on that occasion was a basic act if x then verb-phrased but not by doing something,[5]

from which any number of sufficient conditions could be constructed in the obvious way—thus, e.g.,

> If I caused my muscles to tense only once on a certain occasion, then my causing my muscles to tense on that occasion was a basic act if I then caused my muscles to tense but not by doing something,

and so on.[6] I doubt that anything stronger than this is obtainable along these lines. Whether that would matter turns on the uses to which you propose to put the notion 'basic act'. I do not, myself, propose to make any use of it, so for my purposes it would not matter at all.

But the question whether anything stronger than this is obtainable is a later question. The prior question is whether or not what we have so far is itself true. For suppose I caused my muscles to tense but not by doing something; *is* there an event that was my causing my muscles to tense? Basic acts are presumably events, if they are anything at all. And if there was no event that was my causing my muscles to tense on that occasion, then my causing my muscles to tense on that occasion (if there was such an entity at all) was *not* a basic act.

Perhaps there are no basic acts. Or at any rate, perhaps there are no basic causings. The arguments to the effect that there are basic acts have at most shown that there must be occasions on which a thing z causes a thing y, and does not cause y by doing something; their authors have not only not shown, but seem not to have seen the need to

---

[5] Or perhaps better: If x verb-phrased only . . . was a basic act if it was an act and x then verb-phrased but not by doing something. For a man's sleeping for three hours should surely not turn out to be a basic act.

[6] Compare the suggestion I made to those who think that intentionality is the mark of action, Chapter III, pp. 44–45.

show, that when z causes y, and does not cause y by doing something, there nevertheless is an *event* x that is z's causing of y. And perhaps this cannot be shown; perhaps, indeed, it is false.

There is something attractive in the idea that there are no basic causings. Consider Bee again. Bee caused my sneezing. Bee contains everything that caused my sneezing. So so far as events go, aren't there just the two events, Bee (which caused the sneezing) and the sneezing (which was caused by Bee)? Where are we to find room for an event that was Bee's *causing of* the sneezing? Perhaps all there is a fact—whatever facts are—viz., the fact that Bee caused the sneezing, and no event which a report of the fact might be construed as also a report of.

We may even for a moment feel attracted to the idea that there are no causings at all, basic or otherwise. Suppose there was an event that was my grating pepper onto a certain egg; suppose that, shortly after, there was an event that was my sneezing; and suppose also that the pepper-grating caused the sneezing. No doubt there were lots of events $E_1, E_2, \ldots$, such that the pepper-grating caused the sneezing by causing E_1, which caused E_2, which . . . caused the sneezing; but is there an event which was the pepper-grating's causing of the sneezing? Wasn't there just the series of events, the pepper-grating, then E_1, then E_2, then . . . , then the sneezing, the members of which are related as follows: each causes the next following? Notice, in fact, that if asked "When did the pepper-grating occur?" an answer is forthcoming (as it might be, 3:15 P.M.), and if then asked "And when did the sneezing occur?" an answer is again forthcoming (as it might be, 3:16 P.M.), but if then asked "Ah, and now when did the pepper-grating cause the sneezing?" one would feel at a loss. What is one to answer? Perhaps that feeling of being at a loss is the sane response to a mad question—there being no event that was the pepper-grating's causing of the sneezing whose temporal location anyone could report.

But I hope that no one is for more than a moment attracted to the idea that there are no causings at all. A killing, after all, is a causing of a dying; a melting is a causing of a melting; a sinking is a causing of a sinking; and so on. If there are no causings, there are no killings, meltings, sinkings, and so on. But of course there are killings, meltings, sinkings, and so on. Sirhan's killing of Kennedy, for example, was a killing. So it was a causing. So really, after all, there *are* causings. And if we have a temporal problem about causings, well, that should be no surprise, in that we already noticed there was a temporal problem about killings (cf. Chapter IV), and killings are causings.

And I think that since we must grant that there are causings we might as well grant that there are basic causings [on the assumption, which we are making throughout this section, that (i) is true, i.e., that we sometimes cause things and do not cause them by doing something]. More generally, we might as well grant that *whenever* an entity z causes an entity y, there is an event x that is z's causing of y. There is in fact a benefit to be got from doing so.

I said in Chapter I that if there are acts there presumably are killings, for killings surely are paradigm acts. And I said that if there are killings then it may be presumed that there is a killing of B by A if and only if A kills B. So assuming there are acts (I said),

(1)   Sirhan killed Kennedy

is true if and only if there was an entity that was a killing of Kennedy by Sirhan; and that there is such an entity is precisely what

(1.1) $(\exists x)$ Kills$_3$ $(x,$ Kennedy, Sirhan$)$

says. So (I said), it seems to me it does no harm to suppose that (1) is—if you ignore its tense—rewritable as (1.1).

If (1) is rewritable as (1.1), so also must

(2)   Samuel killed Kennedy

be rewritable as

(2.1) $(\exists x)$ Kills$_3$ $(x,$ Kennedy, Samuel$)$,

whoever or whatever Samuel may be.

Suppose Samuel is the fusion of all events that killed Kennedy. Thus Sirhan's shooting of Kennedy, for example, is part of Samuel, since Sirhan's shooting of Kennedy killed Kennedy. And that being the case, it seems plain that (2) is true. [Note, in fact, that if I was right to say above that

(IV′) z is killed by y if and only if there is an x such that x is part of y, and x kills z, and no part of z's dying is part of y, and no part of z's dying causes part of y

is just as plausible as our old assumption

(IV) E is caused by y if and only if there is an x such that x is part of y, and x causes E, and no part of E is part of y, and no part of E causes part of y

is, then Samuel being what it is, the truth of (2) follows from the fact that Sirhan's shooting of Kennedy killed Kennedy.] But then so also is

(2.1) true: there really was such an event as Samuel's killing of Kennedy. Now Samuel does not seem to have killed Kennedy by doing something. (Compare: Bee does not seem to have caused my sneezing by doing something.) If it did not, then even if z kills y, but not by doing something, there is all the same an event x that is z's killing of y.

If Samuel killed Kennedy, but not by doing something, then surely Samuel caused Kennedy's dying, but not by doing something. I should imagine that if *any* entity z ever caused an entity y, but not by doing something, then Samuel caused Kennedy's dying, but not by doing something. Now Samuel's killing of Kennedy is a causing of a dying; in particular, it is Samuel's causing of Kennedy's dying. So if Samuel killed Kennedy, but not by doing something, there is at least one case in which z causes y, but not by doing something, and in which there is all the same an event x that is z's causing of y.

More generally, I should imagine that it will seem every bit as plausible to rewrite

(3)   Sirhan caused Kennedy's dying

as

(3.1) $(\exists x)$ Causes$_3$ $(x$, Kennedy's dying, Sirhan$)$

as it was to rewrite (1) as (1.1). For if there are acts, there surely are causings—for if there are acts, there are killings, and killings are causings; and if there are causings, it may be presumed that there is a causing of B by A if and only if A causes B. But then we shall have to be able, also, to rewrite

(4)   Bee caused my sneezing

as

(4.1) $(\exists x)$ Causes$_3$ $(x$, my sneezing, Bee$)$,

whoever or whatever Bee may be. Now in fact we know that Bee is the fusion of all events that caused my sneezing. And Bee, therefore, does not seem to have caused my sneezing by doing something. If it did not, then even if z causes y, but not by doing something, there is all the same an event x that is z's causing of y.

The benefit we get by saying that whenever an entity z kills an entity y there is an event x that is z's killing of y is this: we are able to rewrite (1) as (1.1). More immediately relevant for our purposes, the benefit we get by saying that whenever an entity z causes an entity y there is an event x that is z's causing of y is this: we are able to rewrite (3) as (3.1). It is highly plausible to suppose that (3) *is* rewritable as

(3.1)—just as it is highly plausible to suppose that (1) is rewritable as (1.1). And therefore what enables us to rewrite (3) and (1) in these ways is itself worth adopting. If we are thereby committed to events that are basic causings and events that are basic killings, then so be it.

3. So if (i) we sometimes cause things and do not cause them by doing something, then also (ii) on all those occasions there nevertheless is an event that is our causing of the things. But perhaps (i) is itself not true.

Let us go back. I said:

Suppose I caused my arm to move. How? Well, suppose I caused my muscles to tense. How did I do that? If I caused them to tense in the ordinary way—i.e., in the way in which one does this when one moves one's arm in the ordinary way—then there does not *seem* to be any answer to the question how I caused them to tense. There does not in such a case seem to be anything I did, by doing which I caused them to tense.

But why isn't the following a true answer to the question how I caused them to tense:

(1)   I caused them to tense by causing them to tense.

Again, why can't we say that

(2)   Bee caused my sneezing by causing my sneezing?

Now causing the tensing of some muscles is engaging in an activity, and so also is causing a sneezing. So if (1) and (2) are true, then these are not instances in which z causes y but does not cause it by doing something.

Isn't

(3)   Sirhan caused Kennedy's dying by causing Kennedy's dying

true also? More generally, isn't every sentence that results from replacing referring expressions for "x" and "y" in

If x caused y, then x caused y by causing y

true? If so, there are *no* instances in which z causes y but does not cause it by doing something.

More generally still, isn't every sentence that results from replacing referring expressions for "x" and "y", and the third-person past tense of a causal verb for "verbed" and the gerund of that same causal verb for "verbing", in

If x verbed y, then x verbed y by verbing y

true? Consider, for example,

If Sirhan killed Kennedy, then Sirhan killed Kennedy by killing Kennedy,

and what, given Sirhan killed Kennedy, is true if it is, viz.,

(4)   Sirhan killed Kennedy by killing Kennedy.

Aren't they true?

Some people seem to have strong intuitions against. It strikes them that (1) through (4) are obviously false. It strikes them, that is, that you *cannot* engage in an activity by engaging in that very same activity. Other people seem to have equally strong intuitions for. A colleague of mine said in response to the question whether or not Sirhan killed Kennedy by killing Kennedy: "Of course—how else?"

I do not, myself, have strong intuitions either way, and therefore feel free to let the matter be settled on systematic grounds.

It will in fact turn out to be neater to allow all of the sentences we are looking at to be true—i.e., not merely (1) through (4), but all that result from making appropriate replacements in the schemas.

I do not mean to deny that if asked how Sirhan caused Kennedy's dying, or killed Kennedy, it would be at best ungenerous to say (3) or (4). But that is how I am going to take these replies: as at best ungenerous—because so very *dull*—but true all the same.

Anyone who is prepared to take my word that it will be neater to allow such sentences as (1) through (4) to be true, and therefore to go along with me in stipulating that they are, will have to introduce the term "basic act" in some other way than I pointed to in the preceding section if he wishes to make serious use of the notion. For if there are any basic acts at all, my causing my muscles to tense was a basic act; yet it is not shown to be so by the sufficient condition set out above—viz.,

> If I caused my muscles to tense only once on a certain occasion, then my causing my muscles to tense on that occasion was a basic act if I then caused my muscles to tense but not by doing something—

since, if (1) is true, it is not the case that I caused them to tense but not by doing something. And it is not plain that any schema constructed along those lines will yield that my causing my muscles to tense was a basic act. Since, as I said, I do not propose to use the notion, this does not matter for my purposes. But there are those who find it of interest; so I shall come back to it again briefly in Chapter XVII below.

Meanwhile, let us look again at

(T_3'''') x is a causing of y by z just in case x is the fusion of all events C such that $Owns_{cause}\ (z, C)$ and C causes y and (*either* z causes y by causing C, *or* there is an activity A such that z causes y by engaging in A, where C is z's engaging in A).

If (i), we sometimes cause things and do not cause them by doing something, is false, the argument we have been looking at does not show that (T_3'''') is wrong in principle.

On the other hand, there are other difficulties facing (T_3''''). (See, for example, the difficulty mentioned in the first footnote in this chapter. A further difficulty will come out shortly—see the first footnote of the following chapter.) Moreover, (T_3'''') trades on there being such things as activities, and we might well want to see if we can give an account of what causings are that does not.

I think we can, though the only such account I have been able to construct is, alas, rather messy. However, some interesting issues arise along the way, and they should be looked into in any case.

XII

Method and the Parts
of Some Events (II)

1. It begins easily enough: what we do is to make use of that 'by-locu-tion' again, but in a different way.

As we saw,

(T_3''') x is a causing of y by z just in case x is the fusion of all events C such that $Owns_{cause}$ (z, C) and C causes y

took in too much. We do not want my harmonica-playing while I wait for Smith to kill Jones to turn out to be part of my causing of Jones's dying. We need to impose a further constraint on C. (Cf. page 163 above.)

We were supposing that I caused Jones's dying by causing onset of a hemorrhage in Jones. (How? By threatening Smith, which caused Smith's shooting of Jones, which caused the onset of hemorrhage.) So there was an entity α that caused Jones's dying by causing onset of that hemorrhage—e.g., me. By contrast, not only did I not cause Jones's dying by causing my harmonica-playing: *nothing* caused Jones's dying by causing my harmonica-playing, for my harmonica-playing played no role in *anything's* causing of Jones's dying. Let us then take as a preliminary proposal that what we should add to (T_3''') is the follow-ing further clause:

and there is an α that causes y by causing C.

176

Method and Parts of Some Events (II)

The onset of hemorrhage in Jones, then, is an event C such that

> Owns$_{cause}$ (I, C) and C causes Jones's dying, and there is an α that causes Jones's dying by causing C;

so there is an event that is the fusion of all such events C; thus—by the newly expanded (T$_3$′′′)—there is a causing of Jones's dying by me, and it has, among its parts, the onset of hemorrhage in Jones. By contrast, my playing the harmonica is *not* an event C that meets the indented condition, since nothing causes Jones's dying by causing it. This leaves it still open that my harmonica-playing is part of my causing of Jones's dying; but we do not at any rate have to conclude it is part from the fact that it is such an event C—there is no such fact.

My threatening Smith is another event C that meets the indented condition, so it, like the onset of hemorrhage, turns out to be part of my causing of Jones's dying. So also is Smith's shooting of Jones such an event C, and therefore part of my causing of Jones's dying. These conclusions are as they should be.

What about (a), which is the fusion of

> my threatening Smith

and

> my playing the harmonica?

(a) is *not* an event that meets the indented condition. No doubt I 'own$_{cause}$' (a)—plainly I do cause everything (a) causes. Moreover, by (IV), (a) causes Jones's dying. But neither I nor anyone else causes Jones's dying by causing (a). *I* do not cause Jones's dying by causing (a): for my playing the harmonica plays no role in my causing of Jones's dying. And nothing else causes Jones's dying by causing (a). Lots of events cause (a), and therefore—since (a) causes Jones's dying—cause Jones's dying; but none of these events causes Jones's dying *by* causing (a). Take an example. Let (b) be the fusion of

> its occurring to me that it would be a good idea to get Smith to kill Jones

and

> its occurring to me to play the harmonica while I wait for Smith to kill Jones.

And let us take it that the first of the events I mentioned in (b) caused my threatening Smith, and that the second of the events I mentioned in (b) caused my playing the harmonica. By assumption (IV), (b) caused both my threatening Smith, and my playing the harmonica. Now these and only these two events have the property

is identical with my threatening Smith or is identical with
my playing the harmonica;

so by our old assumption

(III.b*)   If there is a y such that y has F, and if also C causes all y such
that y has F, then the fusion of all y that has F is caused by C,

their fusion, (a), is caused by (b). Since (a) caused Jones's dying, (b)
caused Jones's dying. But (b) did not cause Jones's dying *by* causing
(a). (b) did cause Jones's dying by causing my threatening Smith; but it
did not cause Jones's dying by causing (a)—for my playing the harmonica not only played no role in *my* causing of Jones's dying, it also
played no role in (b)'s causing of Jones's dying.

So while, as we saw, a part of (a), viz., my threatening Smith, is an
event C that meets the indented condition, (a) itself does not. So we
do not have to conclude that my harmonica-playing is a part of my
causing of Jones's dying from the fact that it is part of (a), where (a) is
an event that meets the indented condition—there is no such fact.

It seems plausible, moreover, that there is no way at all in which
my harmonica-playing is going to turn out to be part of my causing of
Jones's dying. My harmonica-playing is not itself an event C that
meets the indented condition. And it surely is not going to turn out to
be part of any event C that meets it. Surely *nothing* causes Jones's
dying by causing anything that contains my harmonica-playing—as I
suggested (page 176), my harmonica-playing plays no role in *anything's* causing of Jones's dying. And it surely is not going to turn out
that my harmonica-playing splits into parts, each part of which is part
of some or other event C that meets the indented condition—not only
does my harmonica-playing not play a role in anything's causing of
Jones's dying, no part of my harmonica-playing plays a role in anything's causing of Jones's dying.

So far so good. It looks so far as if we get as parts, and as not parts,
of my causing of Jones's dying just what we should.

2. But that was, as I said, only a preliminary proposal. What we
should attend to now is the fact that what we have so far—viz.,

x is a causing of y by z just in case x is the fusion of all
events C such that $\text{Owns}_{cause} (z, C)$ and C causes y and
there is an α that causes y by causing C—

makes y itself be no part of z's causing of y.[1] For by our old assumption

---

[1] (T_3'''') of the preceding chapter also makes y be no part of z's causing of y.

(II)   No event causes any of its parts; no event is caused by any of
           its parts

no part of y is part of any event C that causes y, and y is therefore no part of the fusion of events that meet the conditions imposed on C.

Well, it should be remembered that you can cause states of affairs as well as events. And if y is a state of affairs it should surely be no part of the event that is your causing of y—events, that is, should have only events as parts. But what if y is itself an event?

Two considerations seem to me to count in favor of adopting the thesis that

(S_1)   If y is an event, then z's causing of y contains y;

and it seems to me that nothing counts against adopting it. Perhaps some would say, off the cuff, that

(1)   Sirhan's causing of Kennedy's dying caused Kennedy's
           dying,

for example, ought to turn out to be true; and if (S_1) is true, then (1) is false—see assumption (II). But I suspect that at least as many would say, off the cuff, that (1) ought to turn out to be false. And I suspect that at least as many would say they had no intuitions on the matter at all. I do not think we should heed anybody's preanalytic intuitions about such sentences as (1).

The first consideration in favor of (S_1) comes out as follows. The variables in our old assumption

(III) C causes y if and only if C causes all of y's parts

ranged over events only; yet surely if (III) is true, then so is it true that z—whatever z may be, event, state of affairs, person, whatever it is that can cause things—causes an event y if and only if z causes all of y's parts. If so, the following thesis is very plausible:

(S_2) z's causing of an event y is the fusion of z's causing of y_1, z's
           causing of y_2, . . . , for all events y_1, y_2, . . . that are parts
           of y.

Take Bee, for example. Bee caused a certain sneezing. (Bee was, in fact, the fusion of all events that caused that sneezing.) And let us suppose that that sneezing caused a certain carpet-vacuuming. (A man heard me sneeze, but thought I was issuing the order "Vacuum!") Bee therefore caused the carpet-vacuuming. Bee therefore also caused the fusion of the sneezing and the carpet-vacuuming. We know, from Chapter XI, that there therefore were such events as

(a)   Bee's causing of the sneezing,
(b)   Bee's causing of the carpet-vacuuming,

and

(n)   Bee's causing of the fusion of the sneezing and the carpet-vacuuming.

It is, as I said, very plausible to suppose that (a) and (b) are parts of (n). Consider, now, (b). The sneezing is surely part of (b). Notice that

Owns$_{cause}$ (Bee, the sneezing) and the sneezing causes the carpet-vacuuming and there is an α that causes the carpet-vacuuming by causing the sneezing—

Bee itself causes the carpet-vacuuming by causing the sneezing. No doubt we do not yet have a completely satisfactory account of the parts of an event that is a causing of y by z; but the sneezing is on Bee's route to the carpet-vacuuming, so surely it is part of (b).

Suppose we say that (n) does not contain either the sneezing or the carpet-vacuuming. Then (b) is not part of (n), which conflicts with (S_2).

If (S_2) is true, (n)—like (b)—must contain the sneezing. So (n) must contain at least part of what it is a causing of.

The carpet-vacuuming itself contains a great many events related as the sneezing and the carpet-vacuuming are: i.e., a great many event-pairs x and y such that x caused y, and indeed such that x is on Bee's route to y. Take any such pair, viz., E_1 and E_2, and consider, now,

(c)   Bee's causing of E_2.

E_2 is, by hypothesis, part of the carpet-vacuuming, and therefore part of the fusion of the sneezing and the carpet-vacuuming. So by (S_2), (c) is part of (n). But just as (b) contains the sneezing, so also does (c) contain E_1. So E_1 is part of (n) too. So (n) must contain yet another part of what it is a causing of.

Continuing in this way, we get as parts of (n) every event E_m such that E_m is part of the carpet-vacuuming, and for some event E_n that is part of the carpet-vacuuming, E_m is on Bee's route to E_n. Are any parts of the carpet-vacuuming not captured by this procedure? I am sure there are: the carpet-vacuuming comes to an end at some time, after all. But I have not the least idea which they are. And since nothing counts against adopting (S_1), we can allow ourselves to be moved by considerations of simplicity, which suggest we sweep them in along with those captured by the procedure just used. Thus (n) includes, not merely the sneezing, not merely the parts of the carpet-vacuuming captured by the procedure just used, but all the remaining parts of the carpet-vacuuming too.

If (n) contains what it is a causing of, so does (b) contain what it is a causing of: the fusion of the sneezing and the carpet-vacuuming is a complex event-fusion with causally related parts, but so is the carpet-vacuuming itself a complex event-fusion with causally related parts.

We now have good reason to take it that for at least some entities z, and some events y, such that z causes y, z's causing of y does contain y. As I said, nothing counts against adopting (S_1), so we can allow ourselves to be moved a second time by considerations of simplicity, which suggest we take it that for all entities z, and all events y, such that z causes y, z's causing of y contains y. Thus: (S_1).

A second consideration also counts in favor of adopting (S_1).

In Chapter IV, I said that z has killed y only if y is dead. If z killed y, there was an event that was z's killing of y; and presumably z's killing of y has occurred only if z has killed y, and thus only if y is dead. Suppose that Sirhan shot Kennedy on Saturday morning, but that it was not true to say of Kennedy that he was dead until midnight; then it is only at (and after) midnight that we may truly say that Sirhan has killed Kennedy, or that Sirhan's killing of Kennedy has occurred. If Kennedy's dying were part of Sirhan's killing of Kennedy, this would be no surprise; i.e., if the dying is part of the killing, then the killing plainly is not over until the dying is over, and if the dying ends only at midnight, it is no wonder the killing ends only at midnight. This by itself counts in favor of supposing that the dying *is* part of the killing.

Now a killing, as we know, is a causing of a dying; so if a dying is part of a killing, it is part of a causing of itself.

More generally, we cannot truly say that z caused an event y until y has occurred. (E.g., we cannot truly say "John caused the chocolate's melting" until the chocolate has melted, and thus until the chocolate's melting has occurred.) If z caused an event y, there was an event that was z's causing of y; and presumably z's causing of y has occurred only if z has caused y, and thus only if y has occurred. If y were part of z's causing of y, this would be no surprise, for plainly an event has not occurred until all its parts have occurred. This by itself counts in favor of supposing that y *is* part of z's causing of it.

I do not think it is a very powerful argument. Suppose John puts a piece of chocolate in a pot, on the stove, and turns the dial to Low. The chocolate then melts. No doubt it would not be true to say "John caused the chocolate's melting" until the chocolate has melted; no doubt John's causing of the chocolate's melting has not occurred until the chocolate has melted. But it does not follow that the chocolate's melting is part of John's causing of the chocolate's melting. The chocolate's melting may be divided into temporally successive parts: this bit of the chocolate's melting, then that bit, then that other bit. . . . In the case of each such part, there is an event that consists in the rising of the temperature of the bit to T, where a bit's rising in temperature to T causes its melting. I should imagine that whatever bit you choose, its rising in temperature to T does not merely cause the bit's melting, but is part of John's causing of the chocolate's melting: for each bit's rising in temperature to T is on John's route to liquid chocolate. I of course mean to include the last bit of the chocolate. If this is right, then we could say that John's causing of the chocolate's melting has not occurred until the chocolate's melting has occurred, and yet that the chocolate's melting is *not* part of John's causing of its melting. For even if the chocolate's melting is not part of John's causing of its melting, other parts of John's causing of the chocolate's melting are still occurring right up to the time at which the chocolate is liquid.

But perhaps a similar account will not be available in every case. (Could we find one in the case of Sirhan's causing of Kennedy's dying? I.e., if the dying is not part of the causing of the dying, then just what parts of the causing of the dying were going on up to the time at which it was true to say "Now Sirhan has caused Kennedy's dying"?) And perhaps, even if a similar account is available in every case, it does not matter: if I am right in thinking that nothing counts against adopting (S_1), we can allow ourselves to be moved yet another time by considerations of simplicity, which suggest that we not trouble ourselves to find such accounts.

I said that two considerations seem to me to count in favor of adopting (S_1). A third point is also just worth drawing attention to. Suppose z caused an event y. Then there was such an event as

(d) z's causing of y.

If y is not part of (d), then (d) surely caused y. It would follow that there was such an event as (d)'s causing of y, i.e., that there was such an event as

(e) z's causing of y's causing of y.

If y is not part of (d), it surely is not part of (e) either; and if y is not part of (e), then (e) surely caused y. It would follow that there was such an event as (e)'s causing of y, i.e., that there was such an event as

(f) z's causing of y's causing of y's causing of y.

And so on. Now, one could perfectly well respond that not all regresses are vicious, or that not all apparent regresses are real regresses; e.g., one could perfectly well argue that, Yes, there are such events as (e) and (f) and . . . , but that this is no worry, since (d) is identical with (e) and with (f) and with. . . . So I do not take the fact that we would be committed to there being such events as these to count in favor of adopting (S_1). But it is worth noticing that if we do adopt (S_1), we need not trouble ourselves about there being such events as (e) and (f) and . . . : if (S_1) is true, y is part of (d), and it follows from that— by our old assumption (II)—that (d) does not cause y, and therefore that there is no such event as (e), and therefore no such event as (f), and therefore no such event as. . . .

3. In the preceding section I drew attention to the discussion in Chapter IV of Sirhan's killing of Kennedy. I there spoke about the time of Kennedy's death. In Chapter IX, however, I said that a killing is a causing of a dying, and from Chapter IX onward have spoken only of dyings. I am inclined to think that a man's death is identical with his dying. But perhaps we ought to stop for a minute to see what might be thought to stand in the way of saying so.

We may say of a man who is now terminally ill of cancer that he is dying, and some people may conclude from this that the event that is his dying is taking place now. The event that is his death, however, is certainly not taking place now: it (let us suppose) will take place next month. If both of these claims were true, it would follow that the event that is his dying is not identical with the event that is his death. Now the second seems to me plainly true: the death is not taking place now. But it seems to me wrong to suppose that the dying is taking place now.

We cannot conclude from the fact that the result of replacing the gerund of a verb for "verbing" in

He is verbing now

is true, that there is an event taking place now, which the result of making the same replacement in

his verbing

may be used to refer to. We can in the case of some verbs. I should imagine, for example, that if

He is eating now

is true, then there is an event taking place now, and that

his eating

may be used to refer to it. But consider a man who is well ahead of all the competition; it may be true to say of him

He is winning now;

but it does not follow from this that

his winning

is taking place now. If he does indeed win the race, then there will be an event that is his winning of it; but that event is not taking place now, and will not take place until he crosses the finish line.

I am inclined to think that saying of a man that he is dying is like saying of a man that he is winning a race. It is not easy to say just what are the truth-conditions of "He is winning now." A man's being well ahead of all the competition does not entail that he is winning: it might be early in the race, and moreover a race of a kind in which only the inexperienced runner spurts ahead early. Again, the truth of "He will win" is neither necessary nor sufficient for the truth of "He is winning now." It is not necessary: a man who is winning may be shot by a spectator just before he crosses the finish line, and so in fact not win. And it is not sufficient: a man who is losing may put on a miraculous, sudden, last-minute rush of speed, and so in fact win. And similarly, it is not easy to say just what are the truth-conditions of "He is dying now". Everybody will die, so we should presumably ask instead whether or not "He will die soon" is necessary or sufficient for the truth of "He is dying now". And surely the answer is, neither. It is not necessary: a man who is dying might miraculously, spontaneously, recover, and so in fact not die soon. And it is not sufficient: a man who is not dying (he is in the pink of health) might be run down by a bus, and so in fact die soon.[2]

In any case, I shall suppose that a man's dying is identical with his death. And I shall suppose therefore that a causing of a dying is a causing of a death, and includes the death in including the dying.

4. To return. I suggested in section 2 that we ought to adopt

(S_1)   If y is an event, then z's causing of y contains y.

But things other than events are causable; and what if y is not an

---

[2] There is by now a considerable literature on the truth-conditions of "He is dead"; so far as I know, the only examination of the truth-conditions of "He is dying" is in Samuel Gorovitz, "Dealing with Dying," in *Medical Treatment of the Dying: The Moral Issues*, ed. M. Bayles and D. High, forthcoming.

event? Events should have only events as parts, so if *y* is not an event it should be no part of *z*'s causing of *y*.

What things other than events are causable? States of affairs, certainly. A man's overeating might cause his being overweight, for example, and his being overweight is a state of affairs. Anything else? I should think that facts are not causable, and that persons and chairs and tables are also not causable. I have no argument in hand, however, and will simply assume that only events and states of affairs are causable.

Well, then, what if *y* is a state of affairs?

In Chapter IX, I said that the verb "clean," for example, is a causal verb in that

> If *x* is a cleaning of *y* by *z*, then there is an α that is *y*'s being clean (or one of *y*'s being cleans) such that *x* is a causing of α by *z*;

and that a thing's being clean is a state of affairs rather than an event. I then drew attention to the possibility of saying

(S₃)   to cause a state of affairs is to cause an event that is an onset of that state of affairs.

(See Chapter IX, page 139.) It is time now to have a closer look at this idea.

If (S₃) is true, then so also is

(S₄)   *z* causes a state of affairs *y* just in case there is an event *E* such that Onset (*E*, *y*) and *z* causes *E*.

A natural desire for symmetry might lead one to regard (S₄) as plausible. What I have in mind is this. It was agreed (I hope) that an entity *z* causes *y* only if there is an event *C* that causes *y* (see Chapter X, section 1). Shouldn't we say also that *z* causes an entity *y* only if there is an event *E* that *z* causes? So that if an entity *z* causes an entity *y*, then an event *C* causes an event *E*. But if *y* is a state of affairs, then isn't it plausible to suppose that the event *z* must cause if it is to cause *y* is the event that is *y*'s onset? Better: an onset of *y*?

If (S₃) and (S₄) are true, then surely

(S₅)   If *y* is a state of affairs, then *z*'s causing of *y* is *z*'s causing of *E* for some event *E* such that Onset (*E*, *y*)

tells us what a causing of a state of affairs is.

But we can take (S₃), (S₄), and (S₅) to be true only if we can give an account of what 'onsets' of states of affairs are under which it is plausible that they are true.

Let us say that Onset (*x*, *y*) only if *x* is an event and *y* is a state of affairs. An onset of a state of affairs must surely occur at a time at which the state of affairs of which it is an onset starts to obtain. But what is 'a time at which a state of affairs starts to obtain'? Is it a point of time? I suppose some states of affairs may start to obtain at points of time, but it is not plain that all do. Suppose a floor was dirty all its life until I cleaned it, and then remained clean ever after. Is there a point of time t such that for all times before t the floor was not yet clean, and such that for all times at and after t it was already clean? Perhaps so, but let us not commit ourselves to its being so. Let us say

> Onset (x, y) only if x is an event and y is a state of affairs and there is a time t such that y starts to obtain at t and x occurs at t,

and allow the variable "t" to range over (more or less) fuzzy time-stretches as well as time-points.

If (S_4) is to be true, we must say also

> Onset (x, y) only if (C) $(C$ causes $x \supset C$ causes $y)$;

and it does in any case seem a plausible requirement on onsets of states of affairs that anything which causes an onset of a state of affairs itself causes that state of affairs.

It is important to notice that we must *not* also say

> Onset (x, y) only if (C) $(C$ causes $y \supset C$ causes $x)$.

The thing we have to remember is that states of affairs can obtain more than once. Consider the state of affairs 'my left thumb's being dirty', and suppose that that state of affairs obtained this morning and was caused by my pouring ink on my thumb, and suppose that it then ceased to obtain (I washed the thumb), and suppose that it then obtained again this evening and was caused by my pouring coffee on the thumb. I suppose that there was an event—let us call it "E"—which occurred this morning and which was an onset of my left thumb's being dirty. But the event which occurred this evening and which was my pouring coffee on the thumb, though it caused the thumb's being dirty, did not cause E, since it occurred some twelve hours after E.

Careful readers will have noticed a further consequence of the fact that states of affairs can obtain more than once. We are supposing that my left thumb's being dirty obtained this morning, and that it was caused by my pouring ink on the thumb. We are supposing also that I then washed the thumb, but that its being dirty obtained again this evening and was caused by my pouring coffee on the thumb. Let us suppose still further that my left thumb was photographed this evening shortly after the coffee-pouring, and that the thumb's being dirty caused a dark spot on the photograph. No doubt my pouring coffee on the thumb caused the thumb's being dirty, and thereby caused the dark spot on the photograph; but my pouring ink on the thumb (which event occurred this morning), though it caused the very same state of affairs, viz., the thumb's being dirty, surely did not cause the dark spot on the photograph.

In other words, what we have here is a breakdown of transitivity. I said at the beginning of Chapter V that causality is transitive, and I have relied on the assumption that it is at a great many places thereafter. Attention to the fact that states of affairs can obtain more than once brings home that that assumption calls for qualification. What we must say is, not that if x causes y and y causes z, then x causes z, but rather that if x causes y and y causes z, and y is an event, then x causes z. Energetic readers are invited to look back to see whether or not every argument that turned on the stronger assumption would also be valid if the stronger assumption were replaced by the weaker one.

What we have so far is this:

> Onset (x, y) only if x is an event and y is a state of affairs and there is a time t such that y starts to obtain at t and x occurs at t and (C) (C causes $x \supset$ C causes y).

What follows "only if" is unfortunately not sufficiently strong. Suppose E is in fact an onset of my left thumb's being dirty. And now consider the fusion of E and an irrelevant event F which is contemporaneous with E. (Let F be, for example, an explosion in a distant city.) The fusion of E and F is an event, and occurs when E occurs, and alas is such that everything which causes it causes my left thumb's being dirty. Alas, since although the fusion of E and F contains an onset of my left thumb's being dirty (in that it contains E), it should surely not itself be one.

But the difficulty is not serious: we already have in hand a way of dealing with it. Let us replace the last clause of what we have so far with something considerably stronger than it, viz.,

> (C) (C causes $x \supset$ C causes y by causing x).

Everything that causes the fusion of E and F also causes the thumb's being dirty; but I should imagine that nothing that causes the fusion of E and F causes the thumb's being dirty *by* causing that fusion—for the irrelevant event F is not on anything's route to the thumb's being dirty.

Acts and Other Events

Now I think that this is almost it: only one more constraint is needed.

It is compatible with what we have so far that a state of affairs should not only have lots of onsets, but that it should have lots of onsets each time it obtains. Suppose a state of affairs y starts to obtain at t. Then there may be several events x which occur at t, each of which is such that everything that causes it causes y by causing it—or at least, so it appears, nothing seems to rule it out. But it does seem a plausible requirement to impose that each time a state of affairs obtains it has a unique onset.

But the further constraint needed is obvious enough; and I suggest that what we should say is this:

(D_7)   Onset (x, y) just in case x is an event and y is a state of affairs and there is a time t such that y starts to obtain at t and x is the fusion of all events z such that z occurs at t and (C) (C causes $z \supset$ C causes y by causing z).

It seems to me that under this account of what an onset is we may plausibly take (S_3), (S_4), and (S_5) to be true.

It is worth noticing one consequence of this account of what it is to cause a state of affairs.

Suppose that a piece of chocolate was hard all its life until I melted it, and then remained liquid ever after. There was, then, exactly one event which was

(a)   my melting of the chocolate.

Since I caused the chocolate to become liquid, and did so only once, there was exactly one event which was

(b)   my causing of the chocolate's being liquid.

I am inclined to think that (a) is identical with (b): surely melting some chocolate *is* causing it to be liquid.

Now we know, from Chapter IX, that (a) is identical with

(c)   my causing of the chocolate's melting.

By hypothesis, there was exactly one event that was the onset of the chocolate's being liquid; let us call it "E". (S_5) tells us that (b) is identical with

(d)   my causing of E.

So (a) is identical with (b) only if (c) is identical with (d). But *is* (c) identical with (d)?

What seems to stand in the way of identifying (c) and (d) is this: (S_1) tells us that (d) contains E, but one is inclined to think that the chocolate's melting, and therefore (c) itself, precedes the chocolate's being liquid, and thus precedes E. Suppose that T is a point of time that is the first time at which that piece of chocolate is wholly liquid. Then, by (D_7), E occurs at T. One is inclined to think that although the chocolate's melting is going on at times t which are as close as you like to T, the chocolate's melting is not still going on at T—after all, T is a time at which the chocolate is wholly liquid.

But I think we really had better have (a) be identical with (b).

I asked you earlier to suppose that a floor was dirty all its life until I cleaned it, and then remained clean ever after. There was, then, exactly one event which was

(a′)   my cleaning of the floor.

There was also exactly one event which was

(b′)   my causing of the floor's being clean,

and we know, from Chapter IX, that (a′) is identical with (b′). There is no intransitive verb "clean" which stands to the transitive causal verb "clean" in the way in which the intransitive verb "melt" stands to the transitive causal verb "melt"; thus we could not say that, just as (a) is identical with (c), so is (a′) identical with

(c′)   my causing of the floor's cleaning.

But this is surely a mere accident of the language. And we surely must not say: if there had been such a verb, then (a′) would not have been identical with (b′)—it would instead have been identical with the (different) event (c′).

It is plausible to take it that the transitive causal verbs "clean" and "melt" function analogously. So it is plausible to take it that if (a′) is identical with (b′), then (a) is identical with (b).

As I said, (a) is identical with (b) only if (c) is identical with (d). And we *can* identify (c) and (d). Suppose (again) that T is a point of time which is the first time at which that piece of chocolate is wholly liquid. I said: one is inclined to think that although the chocolate's melting is going on at times t which are as close as you like to T, the chocolate's melting is not still going on at T—after all, T is a time at which the chocolate is wholly liquid. But suppose we say that the chocolate's melting *is* still going on at T. Suppose we say that T is the last time at which the chocolate's melting is still occurring. Then we can say that E is the 'termination' of the chocolate's melting, and thus is part of it. Then we can say that (c) does not precede E—indeed, we can say that (c) is identical with (d).

Acts and Other Events

There will be occasion to come back to this point again below. Meanwhile, however, I propose that the benefit is worth the cost. It is a consequence of (S_5) that (b) is identical with (d); and we know that (a) is identical with (c). The benefit of having (a) be identical with (b) is worth the cost of having (c) be identical with (d)—i.e., of having E be the termination of the chocolate's melting.

5. I suggested in section 2 that we ought to adopt
(S_1) If y is an event, then z's causing of y contains y.
I suggested in the preceding section that we ought to adopt
(S_5) If y is a state of affairs, then z's causing of y is z's causing of E for some event E such that Onset (E, y).
I said I would simply assume that only events and states of affairs are causable.[3] So we can return now to the question what is to be said about the nature of causings.

What we had so far was this:

> x is a causing of y by z just in case x is the fusion of all events C such that $Owns_{cause}$ (z, C) and C causes y and there is an α that causes y by causing C.

And we had noticed that this makes y be no part of z's causing of y—see page 178. So we need to make a change.

Suppose, for a moment, that states of affairs are not causable; i.e., suppose, for a moment, that only events are caused. Then all we need to do is replace "C causes y" with "(either C causes y or $C = y$)," so that what we have is:

> x is a causing of y by z just in case x is the fusion of all events C such that $Owns_{cause}$ (z, C) and (either C causes y or $C = y$) and there is an α that causes y by causing C.

Sirhan, for example, caused Kennedy's dying. Then the following is true:

> $Owns_{cause}$ (Sirhan, Kennedy's dying) and Kennedy's dying = Kennedy's dying and there is an α that causes Kennedy's dying by causing Kennedy's dying—

Sirhan himself caused Kennedy's dying by causing Kennedy's dying.

---

[3] If this assumption is false, then emendations in what follows are fairly easily made. For if an entity y is neither an event nor a state of affairs, then if it is nevertheless causable, it must surely 'come to obtain' in *some* appropriate sense. And then analogues of (S_5) will surely be constructible to cover it.

190

And Kennedy's dying therefore is, as it should be by (S_1), part of Sirhan's causing of it.

The reader will note that the change needed was very simple to make in light of our earlier decision to allow such sentences as

Sirhan caused Kennedy's dying by causing Kennedy's dying

to be true (see pages 173–174 above). This, in fact, is the first place at which it shows itself to be neater to allow them to be true.

Alas, states of affairs *are* causable. But we know, from (S_5), that if y is a state of affairs, z's causing of y is z's causing of an onset of y. So I suggest we say the following:

x is a causing of y by z just in case

(i) y is an event and x is the fusion of all events C such that $\text{Owns}_{\text{cause}}(z, C)$ and (either C causes y or $C = y$) and there is an α that causes y by causing C, or

(ii) y is a state of affairs and there is an event Y such that Y is an onset of y, and x is a causing of Y by z.

It would be very nice indeed if we could say we now have it. Unfortunately we do not. Two difficulties remain: I take one of them up in each of the two following sections.

6. Suppose some people approached me with the proposal that I get Smith to kill Jones. (For some reason, they want Smith, not me, to do the killing.) They offer a large sum of money, and I therefore accept— i.e., I decide to get Smith to kill Jones. The next day, I call in my henchmen and get them to kidnap Smith's children; I then tell Smith that my henchmen will kill his children unless he kills Jones. Smith then, and for that reason, kills Jones. Consider, now, the event

(b)   my deciding to get Smith to kill Jones.

That event, I suppose, caused Jones's death, for it caused the events that followed it which themselves caused Jones's death. Consider, next, the event

(a)   those people's offering me a large sum of money to get Smith to kill Jones.

It seems to me a very plausible idea that (a) caused Jones's death, and indeed, that (a) caused Jones's death by causing (b). Moreover, I surely cause everything (b) causes, and therefore 'own$_{\text{cause}}$' (b). If so, then (b) is an event C such that

Owns$_{cause}$ (I, C) and C causes Jones's death, and there is an α that causes y by causing C;

and therefore, if what we reached in the preceding section is true, (b) is part of my causing of Jones's death. Yet it really does not seem as if it should be. Surely (b) *precedes* my causing of Jones's death. Surely it is only *after* (indeed, the day after) I decide to get Smith to kill Jones that I start causing Jones's death.

If z caused y, then there plainly is a time-stretch t such that z caused y *during t*. For example, we may suppose that I caused Jones's death during the time-stretch that was the third week of May, 1976. Then I also caused it during the time-stretch that was May, 1976. And I also caused it during the time-stretch that was 1976. Let us say that z caused y IN t just in case z caused y during t and there is no time-stretch s such that s is in (and not identical with) t and z caused y during s. Then I did *not* cause Jones's death IN the time-stretch that was 1976, and I did *not* cause Jones's death IN the time-stretch that was May, 1976. Though we may suppose that I did cause Jones's death IN the time-stretch that was 9:05 A.M. Monday through 11:23 P.M. Friday of the third week of May, 1976.

I propose, then, that we say the following:

(T$_3^*$) x is a causing of y by z just in case there is a time-stretch t such that z causes y IN t, and

(i) y is an event and x is the fusion of all events C such that C occurs during t and Owns$_{cause}$ (z, C) and (either C causes y or C = y) and there is an α that causes y by causing C, or

(ii) y is a state of affairs and there is an event Y such that Y is an onset of y, and Y occurs during t, and x is a causing of Y by z.

The difficulty I drew attention to is now eliminated. Suppose

(b) my deciding to get Smith to kill Jones

occurred on a Sunday. Suppose I then began my enterprise of getting Smith to kill Jones at 9:05 the very next morning. The time IN which I caused Jones's death therefore does not include Sunday: nothing that happened on Sunday occurred during the time IN which I caused it. So in particular, (b) did not occur during the time IN which I caused Jones's death, and it follows, as it should, that (b) is not part of my causing of Jones's death.

It is easiest, I think, to say what time is a time IN which a *person* causes something. When did you cause Jones's death? "Last year." Well, let us suppose I did not cause Jones's death IN the time-stretch that was 1976. It is, all the same, easy enough to say what is a—indeed, the—time-stretch IN which I caused Jones's death: it began when I began (if I began by phoning my henchmen, then it began when I began phoning) and ended when Jones was dead. Again, when did you cause the house to be clean? "Monday, May 4; and then again on Monday, May 18." Well, I did not cause the house to be clean IN the time-stretch that was Monday, May 4, or IN the time-stretch that was Monday, May 18. But it is easy enough to give a time-stretch IN which I caused it to be clean: such a time-stretch began when I began (if I began by vacuuming, then it began when I began vacuuming) and ended when the house was first clean thereafter.

But times IN which *an event* causes something are not so transparent. When did your grating pepper onto that egg cause you to sneeze? There is nothing wrong with the question itself, and an answer might be forthcoming—the context in which it is asked might make plain that "last month," or "May 23," was both correct and acceptable. It is where the context suggests that what is wanted by way of answer is not just a time-stretch during which, but the time-stretch IN which, the pepper-grating caused the sneezing that one would feel at a loss. It was precisely such a context to which I drew attention on page 170 above.

Suppose the pepper-grating occurred at 3:15 and the sneezing at 3:16. One might (as in the cases above) try this: the time-stretch IN which the pepper-grating caused the sneezing began when the pepper-grating began causing the sneezing and ended with the sneezing. But when did the pepper-grating begin causing the sneezing? While it was itself occurring? Or only after it had occurred?

One can get at a (or the) time-stretch IN which something caused something from the opposite direction, viz., by looking to see what events had better turn out to be parts of the causing and by attending to their times. What was a time-stretch IN which I caused my house to be clean? Take a day on which I caused my house to be clean. I vacuumed, swept, dusted, etc.; plainly my vacuuming, my sweeping, my dusting, etc., had better turn out to be parts of my causing of my house to be clean, and we can find out what time is a time-stretch IN which I caused it to be clean by finding out the times of the vacuuming, the sweeping, the dusting, etc. Let us suppose that the way in which the pepper-grating caused the sneezing was this: the pepper-grating caused the sneezing by causing E_1, E_2, . . . which themselves caused the sneezing. It seems right that E_1, E_2, . . . should turn out to be parts of the pepper-grating's causing of the sneezing, for they are on the pepper-grating's route to the sneezing. But what about the pepper-grating itself? Should that turn out to be part of its own causing of the sneezing?

Perhaps some would say, off the cuff, that the pepper-grating itself should turn out *not* to be part of its own causing of the sneezing. (I after all am surely no part of my causing of the house's being clean.) And more generally, then, that no event is part of its own causing of something.

On the other hand, consider Bee again. Bee caused a certain sneezing—let us suppose it was that very sneezing that the pepper-grating caused. Bee, then, is the fusion of all events that caused that sneezing. It follows that there are no events E_1, E_2, . . . which are on *Bee's* route to the sneezing. We know, from

(S$_1$)   If y is an event, then z's causing of y contains y,

that

(c)   Bee's causing of the sneezing

contains

(d)   the sneezing.

Presumably (c) contains nothing that (d) causes. Now the only events outside both Bee and (d) are precisely events caused by (d). Then unless Bee, or some part of Bee, is part of (c), (c) is identical with (d). And I suspect that some would say, off the cuff, that (c) should turn out *not* to be identical with (d). More generally, that no event is identical with an event's causing of it.

Whatever one's preanalytic intuitions, there is what I take to be good reason to adopt the thesis

(S$_6$)   If z is an event, then z's causing of y contains z.

The first argument I gave for (S$_1$) began as follows. I drew attention to our old assumption

(III) C causes y if and only if C causes all of y's parts.

I said that in light of (III), the following thesis is very plausible:

(S$_2$) z's causing of an event y is the fusion of z's causing of y_1, z's causing of y_2, . . . , for all events y_1, y_2, . . . which are parts of y.

Consider now our old assumption

(IV) E is caused by y if and only if there is an x such that x is part

194

of y, and x causes E, and no part of E is part of y, and no part of E causes part of y.

Thus, if z is an event that causes y, there are events $z_1, z_2, \ldots$ which are parts of z and which cause y. In light of that, the following thesis is also very plausible:

(S_7)   an event z's causing of y is the fusion of z_1's causing of y, z_2's causing of y, . . . , for all events $z_1, z_2, \ldots$ which are parts of z and which cause y.

The pepper-grating is itself part of Bee (since it caused the sneezing, and Bee contains all events that caused the sneezing). By (S_7),

(e)   the pepper-grating's causing of the sneezing

is part of (c). Suppose, as I said, that the pepper-grating caused the sneezing by causing $E_1, E_2, \ldots$ which themselves caused the sneezing; I said that it seems right that $E_1, E_2, \ldots$ should turn out to be parts of the pepper-grating's causing of the sneezing, for they are on the pepper-grating's route to the sneezing. Then $E_1, E_2, \ldots$ are parts of (e) and therefore of (c). $E_1, E_2, \ldots$ caused the sneezing; so they are parts of Bee. So (c) contains at least *some* parts of Bee.

Suppose that onset of a desire for pepper on an egg caused the pepper-grating, and by causing the pepper-grating, caused the sneezing. Thus suppose that the pepper-grating is on that event's route to the sneezing. Then the pepper-grating is part of

(f)   onset of a desire for pepper on an egg's causing of the sneezing,

which, by (S_7), is part of (c); it follows that the pepper-grating is part of (c). So (c) contains yet another part of Bee.

I see no way of singling out some proper part of Bee of which it could plausibly be said that that and only that part of Bee is part of (c). But why should we try to find one? Some may have felt inclined to say—preanalytically—that an event should not turn out to be part of its own causing of something. (I, after all, am surely no part of my causing of the house's being clean.) It is at least as plausible—preanalytically—to say that no part of an event E is part of E's causing of something. (No part of me, after all, is part of my causing of the house's being clean.) But we now know that this is wrong, for we now know that at least part of Bee *is* part of (c). We may therefore allow ourselves to be moved by considerations of simplicity, which suggest we sweep the rest of Bee in too.

From the fact that Bee is part of (c), it by no means follows that the

Acts and Other Events

pepper-grating is part of (e). But if Bee *is* part of (c), then at least one event is part of its own causing of something, and the preanalytic intuition we began with is wrong. There being (as I take it) nothing else which stands in the way of taking an event to be part of its own causing of whatever it causes, we may allow ourselves to be moved a second time by considerations of simplicity, which suggest we take it that the pepper-grating *is* part of (e), and indeed, more generally, that

(S₆)   If z is an event, then z's causing of y contains z

is true.

And then it follows that we were right to take it—preanalytically— that (c) is not identical with (d). For while, from

(S₁)   If y is an event, then z's causing of y contains y,

we know that (c) contains (d), from (S₆) we know that (c) contains Bee as well.

And then, since we know that an event z is part of its own causing of y, we know that the time *IN* which z causes y includes the time of z. So finding the time-stretch *IN* which an event z caused y is not as hard as it first looked. Suppose, for example, that the pepper-grating occurred at 3:15 and the sneezing at 3:16. Then the time-stretch *IN* which the pepper-grating caused the sneezing includes both 3:15 and 3:16.

7. One difficulty remains. Given (S₆), Bee must turn out to be part of

(a)   Bee's causing of the sneezing.

But Bee, it will be remembered, is an uncaused event, and therefore the following is false:

there is an α that causes the sneezing by causing Bee.

And Bee therefore does not turn out to be part of (a) by (T₃*). [Notice that the pepper-grating is a caused event, and there surely is an α that causes the sneezing by causing the pepper-grating. The pepper-grating, in fact, does turn out to be part of the pepper-grating's causing of the sneezing by (T₃*).] This would not matter if Bee were divisible into parts, each of which is an event C that meets the conditions in (T₃*); but Bee is not plainly so divisible. I suggest, therefore, that we make a minor change in (T₃*), and that we have it read—I shall pretend it always did so read—as follows:

(T₃*) x is a causing of y by z just in case there is a time-stretch t such that z causes y *IN* t, and

(i) y is an event and x is the fusion of all events C such

196

that C occurs during t and Owns$_{cause}$ (z, C) and (either C causes y or $C = y$) and if there is an α that causes C, then there is an α that causes y by causing C, or

(ii) y is a state of affairs and there is an event Y such that Y is an onset of y, and Y occurs during t, and x is a causing of Y by z.

Bee now meets the required conditions on C (and, I think, nothing else does that should not). There is a time-stretch t such that Bee causes the sneezing IN t: since Bee is still occurring after the sneezing occurs, we can say that that time-stretch is the time of Bee itself. (If there does not come a time after which every event is caused by the sneezing, then the time of Bee is the time of the Super-Event, S-E.) Bee, then, occurs during that time-stretch. Moreover, Bee 'owns$_{cause}$' itself, and Bee causes the sneezing. And since there is nothing that causes Bee, the antecedent of

if there is an α that causes Bee, then there is an α that causes the sneezing by causing Bee

is false, and the conditional therefore is true.

I think we have it now. $(T_3{}^*)$, is, alas, and as I warned it would be, rather messy. But if $(T_3{}^*)$ is true, then we have what we wanted; i.e., we have an account of what causings are in terms of the two-term predicate 'x causes y' (a two-step account for causings of states of affairs), which does not trade on there being such things as activities.

XIII

Method and the Parts
of Some Events (III)

1. In Chapter X, section 4, I suggested that we can say

(T_4'')   x is a killing of y by z just in case

      (i)   there is an α that is y, or is y's dying, and x is a caus-
            ing of α by z, and

      (ii)   there is an event C such that $Owns_{kill}$ (z, C) and C
            kills y and PART (C, x).

I suggested that we can also say that for every causal verb, the result of
replacing it for "verb", its third-person singular for "verbs", its gerund
for "verb$_1$ing", and the gerund of some verb or verb-phrase for
"verb$_2$ing" in

(T-S_4)   x is a verb$_1$ing of y by z just in case

      (i)   there is an α that is y, or is (among) y's verb$_2$ing(s),
            and x is a causing of α by z, and

      (ii)   there is an event C such that $Owns_{verb}$ (z, C) and C
            verbs y and PART (C, x)

is a truth. By the use of (T-S_4), we are able to generate accounts of the
parts of a great many events: killings, meltings, sinkings, and so on.
But (as I said) this is not completely satisfactory. We had wanted to
know what killings, meltings, sinkings, and so on, are. Causings, how-

Method and Parts of Some Events (III)

ever, are no more transparent: as I had said, we are relatively at home with talk of killings and relatively unfamiliar with talk of causings. Yet the accounts of killings, meltings, sinkings, and so on, which are obtainable from (T-S$_4$) take 'x is a causing of y by z' as primitive.

Well, we now have an account of causings. And we can therefore give accounts of killings, meltings, sinkings, and so on, which do not take 'x is a causing of y by z' as primitive. Take killings, for example. We can say, straightway:

(T$_4$*) x is a killing of y by z just in case

(i*) there is an α that is y, or is y's dying, and [there is a time-stretch t such that z causes α IN t, and

(I) α is an event and x is the fusion of all events C such that C occurs during t and Owns$_{cause}$ (z, C) and (either C causes α or C = α and if there is a β that causes C, then there is a β that causes α by causing C, or

(II) α is a state of affairs and there is an event Y such that Y is an onset of α, and Y occurs during t, and x is a causing of Y by z] and

(ii*) there is an event C such that Owns$_{kill}$ (z, C) and C kills y and PART (C, x).

[I here merely replaced "x is a causing of α by z" in (T$_4$″) in accordance with (T$_3$*).] The expression "x is a causing of Y by z" occurs to the right of "just in case" in (T$_4$*). But this is no worry, for we know that it can be eliminated; i.e., we know that the conjunction of (i) and (ii) of (T$_4$″) is equivalent to the conjunction of

(i′) there is an α that is y's dying, and x is a causing of α by z

and (ii) of (T$_4$″)—see page 157 above. So we know that the conjunction of (i*) and (ii*) is equivalent to the conjunction of

(i′*) there is an α that is y's dying, and [there is a time-stretch t such that . . .]

and (ii*). But for any y you choose, y's dying is an event. So we can say, not merely (T$_4$*), but also

x is a killing of y by z just in case

(i′*) there is an α that is y's dying, and [there is a time-stretch t such that z causes α IN t, and α is an event and x is the fusion of all events C such that C occurs during t and Owns$_{cause}$ (z, C) and (either C causes α or C = α) and if there is a β that causes C,

199

then there is a β that causes α by causing C] and

(ii*) there is an event C such that $Owns_{kill}$ (z, C) and C kills y and $PART$ (C, x).

The transitive verb "clean" is a causal verb, and we can say, not merely (T_4''), but also

x is a cleaning of y by z just in case

  (i) there is an α that is y, or is y's being clean, and x is a causing of α by z, and

  (ii) there is an event C such that $Owns_{clean}$ (z, C) and C cleans y and $PART$ (C, x).

Proceeding in the same way, we obtain

x is a cleaning of y by z just in case

  (i*) there is an α that is y, or is y's being clean, and [there is a time-stretch t such that z causes α IN t, and

  (I) α is an event and . . . , or

  (II) α is a state of affairs and there is an event Y such that Y is an onset of α, and Y occurs during t, and x is a causing of Y by z] and

  (ii*) there is an event C such that $Owns_{clean}$ (z, C) and C cleans y and $PART$ (C, x).

Now an entity α is y's being clean only if it is *not* an event: a thing's being clean is a state of affairs. This means that we must eliminate "x is a causing of Y by z" from the brackets in a different way. But there is no difficulty; what we obtain is

x is a cleaning of y by z just in case

  (i'*) there is an α that is y's being clean, and [there is a time-stretch t such that z causes α IN t, and α is a state of affairs, and there is an event Y such that Y is an onset of α, and Y occurs during t, and x is the fusion of all events C such that C occurs during t and $Owns_{cause}$ (z, C) and (either C causes Y or $C = Y$) and if there is a β that causes C, then there is a β that causes Y by causing C] and

  (ii*) there is an event C such that $Owns_{clean}$ (z, C) and C cleans y and $PART$ (C, x).

I had said earlier that the following is true:

x is a causing of y by z just in case

  (i) there is an α that is y, or is y's dying, and x is a causing of α by z, and

(ii)   there is an event C such that Owns$_{cause}$ (z, C) and C
causes y and PART (C, x).

And in this too we can replace "x is a causing of α by z" in accordance with $(T_3{}^*)$. The result is:

   x is a causing of y by z just in case

(i*)   there is an α that is y, or is y's dying, and [there is a time-stretch t such that z causes α IN t, and

   (I) α is an event and x is the fusion of all events C such that C occurs during t and Owns$_{cause}$ (z, C) and (either C causes α or $C = \alpha$) and if there is a β that causes C, then there is a β that causes α by causing C, or

   (II) α is a state of affairs and there is an event Y such that Y is an onset of α, and Y occurs during t, and x is a causing of Y by z] and

(ii*)   there is an event C such that Owns$_{cause}$ (z, C) and C causes y and PART (C, x).

In light of the fact that the conjunction of (i) and (ii) is equivalent to the conjunction of

(i')   there is an α that is y, and x is a causing of α by z

and (ii), the conjunction of (i*) and (ii*) in what I wrote just above is equivalent to the conjunction of

(i'*)   there is an α that is y, and [. . .]

and (ii*). Plainly, then, what I wrote just above is equivalent to $(T_3{}^*)$ itself.

   These accounts are decidedly unlovely, and are so because $(T_3{}^*)$ is. However, their being true, if (as I hope) they are, is all that matters for our purposes.

2. It is worth noticing in passing, because we shall make use of the fact later, that a person's causing, killing, melting, cleaning, . . . of a thing may be identical with an event's causing, killing, melting, cleaning, . . . of that very same thing. Consider, for example, the event that was a killing of Kennedy by Sirhan, and the event that was a killing of Kennedy by Sirhan's shooting of Kennedy, i.e.,

(a)   Sirhan's killing of Kennedy

and

(b)   The shooting's killing of Kennedy.

By $(T_4{}^*)$, (a) contains the shooting, and (I should imagine) nothing prior to the shooting; but so also does (b) contain the shooting, and

Acts and Other Events

nothing prior to the shooting. Moreover, (a) contains the onset of hemorrhage; so also does (b) contain the onset of hemorrhage. (a) contains Kennedy's dying; so also does (b) contain Kennedy's dying. And so on. It comes out, then, that (a) is identical with (b). And this seems to me just as it should be.

3. There is a game you get to play if you do philosophy of action, a game that might be called Answering Wittgenstein's Question. Wittgenstein, it will be remembered, asked, "What is left over if we subtract the fact that my arm goes up from the fact that I raise it?" I am inclined to think that he did not mean for his question to *be* answered; I am inclined to think that he asked it in order to shock. In any case, I am not going to answer it: I have nothing at all to say in this book about facts and their constituents.

He might instead have asked a first cousin of that question, viz., "What is left over if we subtract the event that consists in my arm's rising from the event that consists in my raising of my arm?" And perhaps if he had, he would not have meant for *it* to be answered. Alas for the author of a joke that is taken seriously! We are now in a position to give it a quite serious answer. The verb "raise", as we know, is a causal verb. And the following is a truth:

x is a raising of y by z just in case

   (i)   there is an α that is y, or is among y's risings, and x is a causing of α by z, and

   (ii) there is an event C such that $\text{Owns}_{\text{raise}}$ (z, C) and C raises y and $PART$ (C, x)—

cf. (T-S$_4$). A thing's rising is an event; so we can make the appropriate replacements—by use of (T$_3$*)—as we did for killings. Then we shall have an account of raisings of things, and in particular, of raisings of arms. And we can say: what is left over if we subtract the event that consists in my arm's rising from the event that consists in my raising of it is the fusion of all events that are parts of my raising of my arm and discrete from my arm's rising.

XIV

Method (II)

I said in Chapter I that if there are acts it does no harm to suppose that

(1)   Sirhan killed Kennedy

and

(2)   Sirhan shot Kennedy

are rewritable as

(1.1) $(\exists x)$ Kills$_3$ $(x,$ Kennedy, Sirhan)

and

(2.1) $(\exists x)$ Shoots$_3$ $(x,$ Kennedy, Sirhan).

I said also that

(3)   Sirhan killed Kennedy by shooting him

entails (1) and (2); and that if we want it to do so by the rules of first-order logic, we can have it do so. We begin by noticing that (3) is equivalent to

(3′)   There was a shooting of Kennedy by Sirhan, which killed Kennedy.

Suppose that "kill" does not have different meanings according as it is predicated of a man or an event; then what (3′) predicates of a shooting is the same as what (1) predicates of Sirhan, so that (3′) entails

(3.1) $(\exists x)$ Kills$_3$ $(z,$ Kennedy, a shooting of Kennedy by Sirhan).

A shooting of Kennedy by Sirhan is just an event y such that

Shoots$_3$ (y, Kennedy, Sirhan);

so (3.1), and therefore (3'), entails

(3.2)   (∃y) (∃z) [Shoots$_3$ (y, Kennedy, Sirhan) & Kills$_3$ (z, Kennedy, y)].

But if, as I think, (3') is equivalent to (3), (3') also entails (1); and we can have that (3') entails (1) within first-order logic if we take (3') to be rewritable, not as (3.2) itself, but rather as

(3.3)   (∃x) (∃y) (∃z) [Kills$_3$ (x, Kennedy, Sirhan) & Shoots$_3$ (y, Kennedy, Sirhan) & Kills$_3$ (z, Kennedy, y)],

which entails both (1) and (2) within first-order logic. And if we wish to have that (3) entails both (1) and (2) within first-order logic, we need only suppose that (3) too is rewritable as (3.3).

So far so good, I think. When we try to generalize, however, we face trouble.

The insight that issued in this account of (3) seems to me very plausible. That is, it does seem to me plausible that the result of replacing "verb$_1$s" by an appropriate tensed form of a verb—a causal verb, at any rate—and replacing "verb$_2$ing" by the gerund of any transitive verb in

(T-S$_7$)   z verb$_1$s y by verb$_2$ing α just in case z's verb$_2$ing of α verb$_1$s y

is a truth. Or perhaps better, because the referring expression after "just in case" implies uniqueness, the result of making these replacements in

(T-S$_8$)   z verb$_1$s y by verb$_2$ing α just in case there is an x such that x is a verb$_2$ing of α by z and x verb$_1$s y

is a truth. Thus, for example, it seems to me plausible that

z killed y by shooting α just in case z's shooting of α killed y

is a truth; or, perhaps better, since

(3)   Sirhan killed Kennedy by shooting him,

for example, leaves the possibility that Sirhan shot Kennedy on other occasions than the one on which he killed him, that

z killed y by shooting α just in case there is an x such that x is a shooting of α by z and x killed y

is a truth. [Remember the proposal that (3) is equivalent to (3').] Again, it seems to me plausible that

z melted y by heating α just in case z's heating of α melted y

is a truth; or, perhaps better, since

(4)   I melted the chocolate by heating it,

for example, leaves it open that I heated the chocolate on other occasions than the one on which I melted it, that

> z melted y by heating α just in case there is an x such that x is a heating of α by z and x melted y

is a truth. Indeed, it seems to me plausible that

> z caused y by shooting α just in case z's shooting of α caused y

is a truth; or, perhaps better, since

(5)   Sirhan caused Kennedy's dying by shooting him,

for example, leaves it open that Sirhan shot Kennedy on other occasions than the one on which he caused Kennedy's death, that

> z caused y by shooting α just in case there is an x such that x is a shooting of α by z and x caused y

is a truth.

It seems to me, in fact, that we can treat (4) and (5) exactly as we treated (3), i.e., that we can rewrite them as:

(4.3) $(\exists x)\,(\exists y)(\exists z)$ [Melts$_3$ $(x,$ the chocolate, I) & Heats$_3$ $(y,$ the chocolate, I) & Melts$_3$ $(z,$ the chocolate, $y)]$,

(5.3) $(\exists x)\,(\exists y)\,(\exists z)$ [Causes$_3$ $(x,$ Kennedy's dying, Sirhan) & Shoots$_3$ $(y,$ Kennedy, Sirhan) & Causes$_3$ $(z,$ Kennedy's dying, $y)]$.

But (T-S$_8$) will not quite do. And we cannot generalize on this treatment of (3) through (5) and say that the results of replacing "α", "β", and "γ" by referring expressions, "verb$_1$s" by an appropriate tensed form of a causal verb, "verb$_2$ing" by the gerund of any transitive verb, and the schematic predicates with the relevant predicates, in

(T-S$_9$)   "α verb$_1$s β verb$_2$ing γ" is rewritable as

> "$(\exists x)\,(\exists y)\,(\exists z)$ [Verb$_1$s $(x,\ \beta,\ \alpha)$ &
> Verb$_2$s $(y,\ \gamma,\ \alpha)$ & Verb$_1$s $(z,\ \beta,\ y)]$"

are all true.

I have two difficulties in mind. The first is that accepting (T-S$_8$) and (T-S$_9$) commits us to the falsity of, for example,

(6)   Sirhan caused Kennedy's dying by causing Kennedy's dying.

Let us be sure this is so. (T-S$_9$) tells us that (6) is rewritable as

(6.3) $(\exists x)\,(\exists y)\,(\exists z)$ [Causes$_3$ $(x,$ Kennedy's dying, Sirhan) & Causes$_3$ $(y,$ Kennedy's dying, Sirhan) & Causes$_3$ $(z,$ Kennedy's dying, $y)]$.

But we know that any event y that is a causing of Kennedy's dying by

Acts and Other Events

Sirhan itself contains Kennedy's dying [see thesis (S_1) of Chapter XII]. It follows, by our old assumption

(II)   No event causes any of its parts; no event is caused by any of its parts,

that no such event y causes Kennedy's dying. It follows (see Chapter XI, section 2) that there is no event z that is a causing of Kennedy's dying by y. So (6.3) is false. So (6) is false. And that *is* a difficulty. For, as I said above, we should allow (6) to be true.

Of course, the only ground I gave for allowing (6) to be true was that it would prove to be neater to do so. (T-S_9) is itself pretty neat, so why change it? Why not instead reverse the decision, and accept the falsity of (6)?

Perhaps the reader will take my word for it that allowing (6) to be true will, in the long run, prove to be neater—my main reason for saying so will come out in Chapter XVII.

But the change needed is, after all, a very simple one to make. We must reject (T-S_9) in favor of

(T-S_{10})   "α verb$_1$s β by verb$_2$ing γ" is rewritable as

"($\exists x$) ($\exists y$) ($\exists z$) [Verb$_1$s (x, β, α) &

Verb$_2$s (y, γ, α) &

{Verb$_1$s (z, β, y) or $x = y$}]".

What (T-S_{10}) tells us is that (6) is rewritable as

(6.4)   ($\exists x$) ($\exists y$) ($\exists z$) [Causes$_3$ (x, Kennedy's dying, Sirhan) &

Causes$_3$ (y, Kennedy's dying, Sirhan) &

{Causes$_3$ (z, Kennedy's dying, y) or $x = y$}];

and (6.4) is true, for while its third clause is false, its fourth is true.

(T-S_{10}) tells us that (3) through (5) are rewritable in a similar way—(3), for example, as

(3.4)   ($\exists x$) ($\exists y$) ($\exists z$) [Kills$_3$ (x, Kennedy, Sirhan) &

Shoots$_3$ (y, Kennedy, Sirhan) &

{Kills$_3$ (z, Kennedy, y) or $x = y$}].

This seems entirely acceptable. While the fourth clause of (3.4) is false, its third clause is true; (3.4), therefore, is true—just as it should be, since (3) is true. And (3)'s being rewritable as (3.3) is no barrier to its also being rewritable as (3.4). (1), for example, may be rewritten, not merely as

($\exists x$) Kills$_3$ (x, Kennedy, Sirhan),

but also as

Kills$_2$ (Sirhan, Kennedy),

though it has not been, for our purposes, of any interest to do so.

(T-S$_8$) must of course also be revised if we are to have (6) be true. But it is easy enough to see how to revise it, in light of the availability of (T-S$_{10}$), and I shall not trouble to write it out.

The second difficulty I have in mind comes out if we look once again at an example I drew attention to earlier. I had asked you to suppose I cause Jones's death as follows: I tell Smith that my henchmen will kill his children (whom they hold as hostages) if he does not kill Jones, and Smith, then, to save his children, kills Jones. While waiting for Smith to kill Jones, I sit back and idly play the harmonica. Let (a) be the event that is the fusion of

> my threatening Smith

and

> my playing the harmonica.

(a) is an event, and it occurs during the time IN which I cause Jones's death. Moreover, I 'own$_{cause}$' (a). Since my threatening Smith causes Jones's death, (a) causes Jones's death. So we know, from (T$_3$*)—see page 196—that (a) is part of my causing of Jones's death if and only if the following is true:

> if there is an α that causes (a), then there is an α that causes Jones's death by causing (a).

Let us suppose that there is an event—I'll call it (b)—that is the fusion of

> its occurring to me that it would be a good idea to get Smith to kill Jones

and

> its occurring to me to play the harmonica while I wait for Smith to kill Jones,

and that (b) causes (a). Then (a) is part of my causing of Jones's death if and only if the following is true:

> there is an α that causes Jones's death by causing (a).

In particular, (a) is part of my causing of Jones's death if the following is true:

> (b) causes Jones's death by causing (a).

According to (T-S$_{10}$), we may rewrite this as follows:

$$(\exists x)\,(\exists y)\,(\exists z)\,[\text{Causes}_3\,(x,\ \text{Jones's death},\ (b))\ \&$$
$$\text{Causes}_3\,(y,\ (a),\ (b))\ \&$$
$$\{\text{Causes}_3\,(z,\ \text{Jones's death},\ y)\ \text{or}\ x = y\}].$$

Acts and Other Events

And this *is* true. For since (b) causes (a), and (a) causes Jones's death, (b) causes Jones's death, and there is therefore an x that is a causing of Jones's death by (b). Since (b) causes (a), there is a y that is a causing of (a) by (b). Since y is a causing of (a), y contains (a); since (a) causes Jones's death, y causes Jones's death; there is therefore a z that is a causing of Jones's death by y.

But surely (a) is *not* part of my causing of Jones's death. No doubt my threatening Smith is part of my causing of Jones's death. But surely my playing the harmonica is not.

Indeed, it was precisely in order to have that harmonica-playing not be part of my causing of Jones's death that I suggested we incorporate the 'by-clause' into what eventually became (T_3^*).

So we must make yet another emendation in $(T\text{-}S_9)$. Once again, however, the change needed is simple. We must reject both $(T\text{-}S_9)$ and $(T\text{-}S_{10})$ in favor of

$(T\text{-}S_{11})$ "α verb$_1$s β by verb$_2$ing γ" is rewritable as
"$(\exists x)\,(\exists y)\,(\exists z)\,[\text{Verb}_1\text{s}\,(x,\,\beta,\,\alpha)\,\&$
Verb$_2$s $(y,\,\gamma,\,\alpha)\,\&\,PART\,(y,\,x)\,\&$
$\{\text{Verb}_1\text{s}\,(z,\,\beta,\,y)\text{ or }x=y\}]$".

What $(T\text{-}S_{11})$ tells us is that
(b) causes Jones's death by causing (a)
is rewritable as

$(\exists x)\,(\exists y)\,(\exists z)\,[\text{Causes}_3\,(x,\,\text{Jones's death},\,(b))\,\&$
Causes$_3$ $(y,\,(a),\,(b))\,\&\,PART\,(y,\,x)\,\&$
$\{\text{Causes}_3\,(z,\,\text{Jones's death},\,y)\text{ or }x=y\}]$.

And this is *not* true. For since y is a causing of (a), y contains (a); y therefore contains my harmonica-playing. But x does not contain my harmonica-playing. It follows that $-PART\,(y,\,x)$.

We should have a second look at the claim I just made to the effect that x does not contain my harmonica-playing. We may depict (b), (a), and Jones's death in the diagram below.

(b)		(a)		
its occurring to me that it would be a good idea to get Smith to kill Jones	$\rightarrow$	my threatening Smith	$\rightarrow$	Jones's death
its occurring to me to play harmonica	$\rightarrow$	my harmonica-playing		

Method (II)

x is (b)'s causing of Jones's death. My threatening Smith is plainly part of x; so if my harmonica-playing is part of x, then (a) is part of x. Again, if (a) is part of x, then my harmonica-playing is part of x. So we can say that my harmonica-playing is part of x if and only if (a) is part of x. And why isn't (a) part of x? After all, (a) is an event, and it occurs during the time IN which (b) causes the death. Moreover, (b) 'owns$_{cause}$' (a), and (a) causes the death. So we know, from ($T_3{}^*$), that (a) is part of x if and only if the following is true:

> if there is an α that causes (a), then there is an α that causes Jones's death by causing (a).

Something causes (a). So (a) is part of x if and only if the following is true:

> there is an α that causes Jones's death by causing (a).

But nothing causes Jones's death by causing (a)—since (a) is no part of anything's causing of Jones's death.

It is obviously circular to argue that (a) is no part of x from the premise that there is nothing that causes Jones's death by causing (a), and then go on to argue that nothing causes Jones's death by causing (a) from the premise that (a) is no part of anything's—including (b)'s—causing of Jones's death. But it seems to me that this is not a vicious circle. Some may regard it as more obvious that nothing causes Jones's death by causing (a)—after all, (a) contains my harmonica-playing, and my harmonica-playing plays no role in anything's causing of Jones's death; I suggest that they are entitled to conclude that (a) is no part of anything's causing of Jones's death. Others may regard it as more obvious that (a) is no part of anything's causing of Jones's death—after all, (a) contains my harmonica-playing, and my harmonica-playing plays no role in anything's causing of Jones's death; I suggest that they are entitled to conclude that nothing causes Jones's death by causing (a). The intuitions, I suggest, are equivalent. Moreover, it seems to me that we are required to do no more than to incorporate both. And we *do* incorporate both if we, on the one hand, require for (a)'s being part of something's causing of Jones's death that something cause Jones's death by causing (a) [see ($T_3{}^*$)], and, on the other hand, require for something's causing Jones's death by causing (a) that that thing's causing of (a) be part of its causing of Jones's death [see (T-S_{11})], which *is* to require, if (a) is an event, that (a) itself be part of that thing's causing of Jones's death.

Further emendation in (T-S_8) to bring it into accord with (T-S_{11}) is easy enough, and I shall not trouble to write it out.

Acts and Other Events

$(T\text{-}S_{11})$ tells us that (3) through (6) are rewritable in yet another way—(3), for example, as

(3. 5) $(\exists x) (\exists y) (\exists z)$ [Kills$_3$ $(x,$ Kennedy, Sirhan) &
          Shoots$_3$ $(y,$ Kennedy, Sirhan) & PART (y, x) &
          {Kills$_3$ $(z,$ Kennedy, $y)$ or $x = y$}],

and (6) as

(6. 5) $(\exists x) (\exists y) (\exists z)$ [Causes$_3$ $(x,$ Kennedy's dying, Sirhan) &
          Causes$_3$ $(y,$ Kennedy's dying, Sirhan) & PART (y, x) &
          {Causes$_3$ $(z,$ Kennedy's dying, $y)$ or $x = y$}].

And this is quite all right: since, as we know, Sirhan's shooting of Kennedy is part of Sirhan's killing of Kennedy, (3. 5) is true, and since, as is plain, Sirhan's causing of Kennedy's dying *is* Sirhan's causing of Kennedy's dying, it is part of it, and (6. 5) is true.

One final point. Cases like the following are often enough pointed to in the literature. Jones knows how to tie his shoelaces. We ask him to show us the hand movements he makes in tying his shoelaces. Jones finds he cannot do this—until he unties his laces, and then ties them for us.[1] The writers I have in mind invite us to say:

(7)   Jones moved his hands by tying his shoelaces

is true in this case. Now by $(T\text{-}S_{11})$, (7) is rewritable as

(7. 5) $(\exists x) (\exists y) (\exists z)$ [Moves$_3$ $(x,$ his hands, Jones) &
          Ties$_3$ $(y,$ his shoelaces, Jones) & PART (y, x) &
          {Moves$_3$ $(z,$ his hands, $y)$ or $x = y$}].

But (7. 5) is false. For Jones's tying of his shoelaces is not part of his moving of his hands: his tying of his shoelaces contains the moving of the laces (since it is a causing of their moving), whereas his moving of his hands causes, and therefore does not contain, the moving of the laces.

But it seems to me that (7) itself is false. No doubt the point of Jones's lace-tying was to show us the hand movements one makes in lace-tying; but it does not follow from this that he moved his hands by tying his laces. What interests us now is *how*, i.e., by doing what, Jones did what he did, and not his intentions in doing what he did. And it seems plain that while his intention may have been to make, and thereby show us, hand movements, and he tied his laces only in order to do that, it was not by tying his laces that he moved his

---

[1] This example is from Annette Baier, "The Search for Basic Actions," *American Philosophical Quarterly,* 8 (1971), 161–170. [But she does not invite us to accept (7) in respect of it.]

210

Method (II)

hands—it was, rather, by moving his hands that he tied his laces.

It would be very nice indeed if we could say that we have it now. However the change we made in moving from $(T\text{-}S_{10})$ to $(T\text{-}S_{11})$ is going to make for trouble in connection with a kind of case we shall be turning to in the following chapter. One further revision will be called for.

XV

Omissions

It seems to me that there are no acts of omission.

Let us look at an example. At 8 A.M. last Monday, the neighbors told me they had to rush away for the week, and would I please feed their baby while they are gone? Every four hours, round the clock, starting at noon. I said, "Certainly, I'm on vacation this week." They then left. *I* then packed my bags, and left for the Cape for the week, thinking I never did much like that baby. It is now Sunday night, and the baby died this morning. If *ever* there was an act of omission, there was one this past week!

I am not the only one who did not feed that baby last week: Gerald Ford also did not feed it last week. So I should imagine there is a state of affairs consisting in Gerald Ford's not feeding the baby last week— i.e., Gerald Ford's possessing the property 'does not feed that baby last week'. (Compare the state of affairs consisting in John's possessing the property 'is (tenselessly) running at 10:07 A.M. February 8, 1975'.) This state of affairs obtained all last week. Indeed, it obtains all the time, for that is a property Gerald Ford possesses all the time. Again, I should imagine there is a state of affairs consisting in Gerald Ford's not feeding that baby—i.e., Gerald Ford's possessing the property 'not being feeding that baby'. (Compare the state of affairs consisting in John's possessing the property 'being running'.) This state of affairs

Omissions

also obtained all last week. Indeed, it too obtains all the time, for the fact is that Gerald Ford never at any time feeds that baby.

Similarly, I should imagine there is a state of affairs consisting in my not feeding it last week—i.e., my possessing the property 'does not feed that baby last week'—which obtains all the time; and a state of affairs consisting in my not feeding it—i.e., my possessing the property 'not being feeding that baby'—which obtains at all and only at those times at which I am not feeding it.

Now no state of affairs is itself an event. So neither the state of affairs consisting in Gerald Ford's not feeding the baby last week nor the state of affairs consisting in Gerald Ford's not feeding it is an event. Moreover, those who think there are acts of omission would say that Gerald Ford committed no act of omission last week (at least, no act of omission 'in respect of' that baby): i.e., there was no act of omission consisting in Gerald Ford's not feeding the baby. Presumably they would say also there was no event at all consisting in Gerald Ford's not feeding it, for if there had been such an event, would it not have been an act of omission? *Why* would they say there was no act of omission consisting in Gerald Ford's not feeding the baby? Well, Gerald Ford was not supposed to feed it. He had no duty or obligation to feed it. He was not committed to feeding it.[1]

By contrast, I *was* supposed to feed that baby. I did have a duty, an obligation, at least a commitment, to feed it, for I committed myself to feeding it by promising to feed it. So (it is concluded) there was an act of omission, and thus an event, consisting in my not feeding that baby. Not that the event was identical with the state of affairs consisting in my not feeding the baby. No event is itself a state of affairs. Rather that there was both an *event* consisting in my not feeding the baby and a *state of affairs* consisting in my not feeding it.

I will come back shortly to what it is that inclines people to want to say that while there was no act of omission consisting in Gerald Ford's not feeding the baby there was an act of omission consisting in my not feeding it. For the moment, what we want to look at is only whether or not it is true to say so.

Adopting the Principle of Event-Fusion committed us to the existence of some very peculiar events. Nevertheless, as I said, we would

[1] For more detail on 'acts of omission', see Eric D'Arcy, *Human Acts* (Oxford: Clarendon Press, 1963). See also David Sachs, "A Few Morals About Acts," *Philosophical Review*, 75 (1966), 91–98.

have reason to reject the principle only if we could not give the peculiar event-fusions to which it commits us a place among events, i.e., only if we could not give a plausible account of (i) what their temporal relations are to other events, (ii) what their causal relations are to other events, and (iii) what other events they have as parts and are parts of. Now it seems to me we cannot give a place among events to the putative act of omission consisting in my not feeding the baby: we cannot even assign it a time with any degree of plausibility.

When, after all, is the event, my not feeding the baby, supposed to have started? Surely not before 8 A.M. Monday, since it was only then that I took on the duty of feeding it. So perhaps the event started at or shortly after 8 A.M. But I was not supposed to start feeding it until noon, so perhaps the event started only at noon. Or did it start at 11 A.M., which was the time after which it was no longer possible for me to get back in time to feed the baby at noon?

Whether it started at 8 A.M. or at noon or at 11 A.M., it presumably was occurring at noon, if it occured at all, for it was at noon that I was supposed to give the baby its first feeding. Was it still occurring at 1 P.M.? Well, I was not supposed to be feeding the baby at 1 P.M., so perhaps it was not occurring then. Perhaps it was occurring only at noon, 4 P.M., 8 P.M., and so on, at four-hour intervals all week—i.e., perhaps it was a temporally discontinuous event. On the other hand, if a baby is supposed to be fed at noon, and you do not feed the baby at noon sharp, 12:05 will presumably do, and even 12:06, and even feeding it at 1:30 is better than not feeding it at all, so perhaps the event was occurring continuously from noon on.

And when did the event end? When the baby died? But why did the event end then? Perhaps the event ended when the baby died because the time of the baby's death is a time after which it is no longer possible for me to feed it. But it takes a good bit of time to get back to Boston from the Cape; so there was a time well before the baby's death after which it was no longer possible for me to feed it, and perhaps the event ended then.

Indeed, why should we even suppose that the event occurred last week? Well, perhaps it will be said that since I was supposed to feed the baby last week, it was last week that the event consisting in my not feeding it occurred. But why should we take this to follow?

It should be no wonder that (putative) acts of omission raise these difficulties. Consider the state of affairs consisting in my not feeding the baby. If my act of omission—i.e., my not feeding that baby—were supposed to be an event whose occurring is guaranteed by the obtaining of that state of affairs, then it would be plausible enough to take it to have the following temporal location: it occurs at all and only those times at which the state of affairs obtains. But in fact my act of omission is *not* supposed to be an event whose occurring is guaranteed by the obtaining of that state of affairs. After all, there is a state of affairs consisting in Gerald Ford's not feeding the baby, and there is supposed to be no act of omission consisting in Gerald Ford's not feeding the baby. An act of omission consisting in A's not feeding B is supposed to be an event that occurs only if (i) the state of affairs consisting in A's not feeding B obtains, *and* (ii) A is committed to feeding B. And it just is not clear what role the latter fact should be assigned in the guaranteeing of the occurring of an event, and therefore how it should be taken account of in assigning a time to the event.

Well, *why* take "act of omission" to have this use? Why make a difference between Gerald Ford and me in this respect? Why not say that since I did not feed that baby, there was an act of omission consisting in my not feeding it—*and* since Gerald Ford did not feed it, there was an act of omission consisting in his not feeding it? I think it is pretty plain why the writers I refer to do make a difference between Gerald Ford and me in this respect. The story I told being what it was, I caused that baby's death. (In fact, I killed the baby.) Now, as (I hope) everyone agrees, *I* cause *y* only if there is some event C, which causes *y*, and which I am responsible for in some strong sense. So there must be some event C, which I am responsible for in that strong sense, that caused the baby's death; and what else could that event C be but an event that consists in my not feeding the baby? By contrast, Gerald Ford did not cause the baby's death. So there need be no event C, which he is responsible for in that strong sense, that caused the baby's death. So there need be no event that consists in his not feeding it.

Again, and more simply, my not feeding it caused its death; so there had better be an event consisting in my not feeding it. But Gerald Ford's not feeding it did not cause its death; so whether or not there was an entity consisting in Gerald Ford's not feeding the baby, there need have been no event consisting in Gerald Ford's not feeding it.

But we should look more closely at these two arguments. *I* cause *y* only if there is some event C, which causes *y*, and which I am responsible for in some strong sense. I suggested in Chapter X that we should take this relationship of responsibility to be that of 'event-ownership', viz.,

(D_4)   Owns (x, y) just in case y is an event, and x causes everything y causes.

And I suggested that we say, quite generally,

(T_3) z causes y just in case there is an event C such that Owns (z, C) and C causes y.

So I caused that baby's death just in case there is an event C, which I 'own', and which caused the baby's death. If there were an event consisting in my not feeding the baby, then that would presumably do: i.e., that would presumably be an event I 'own', which caused the baby's death. But I have suggested that there is no such event, for we have not been able to give any such event a place among events. We may nevertheless take it that

(1)   I caused the baby's death

is true. For there surely were a good many physiological occurrences in the baby (things that happened as it starved) that I 'owned', which caused the baby's death. After all, I was committed to feeding that baby; and while it is not clear how that fact could be thought to contribute to the guaranteeing of the occurring of an event, it seems plain enough that the fact makes me an 'owner' of some physiological occurrences in the baby that caused its death.

By contrast, there surely are no events C such that Gerald Ford 'owns' them and such that they caused the baby's death. So it is open to us to mark the difference between Gerald Ford and me that the first argument wants marked—viz., that (1) is true and

(2)   Gerald Ford caused the baby's death

is false—without our having to say that there is an event consisting in my not feeding that baby but no event consisting in Gerald Ford's not feeding it.

Similarly, we may take it that

(3)   My not feeding that baby caused its death

is true even if there is no event consisting in my not feeding it. We have only to suppose that the subject of (3) refers to the state of affairs consisting in my not feeding the baby. For there surely were a good many physiological occurrences in the baby (things that happened as it starved) that that state of affairs 'owns', which caused the baby's death. After all, I was committed to feeding that baby; and that state of affairs consists in *my* not feeding it.

Omissions

By contrast, there surely are no events such that Gerald Ford's not feeding that baby 'owns' them, and such that they caused the baby's death. So it is open to us to mark the difference between Gerald Ford and me that the second argument wants marked—viz., that (3) is true and

(4)   Gerald Ford's not feeding that baby caused its death

is false—without our having to say there is an event consisting in my not feeding the baby but no event consisting in Gerald Ford's not feeding it.

It should be stressed that opting for the view that there was no event consisting in my not feeding the baby, and therefore that there was no such entity as the act of omission consisting in my not feeding the baby, leaves the moral issues entirely untouched. I did not merely cause that baby's death, I am responsible for it, I am to blame for it. And it is an excellent question what (if anything) more than the fact that you cause an event is required for it to be true that you are responsible for it and to blame for it. Fortunately our purposes do not require an answer to this question. In the case we are dealing with and quite generally in cases of the kind that incline people to appeal to acts of omission, the facts are plain enough. For example, if something more is required for the truth of "She is responsible for, and to blame for, that baby's death" than "She caused that baby's death", it lies in the fact that I was committed to feeding it—and that remains a fact even if there is no such entity as the act of omission consisting in my not feeding that baby.

But opting for this view has a consequence that makes trouble for what was said in the preceding chapter. Consider

(5)   I caused the baby's death by not feeding it.

Let us invent a new verb, viz., "unfeed": z unfeeds y just in case z does not feed y. Thus we can say, for example, that Gerald Ford and I both unfed that baby last week; and I take it we can also say that (5) is equivalent to

(5′)   I caused the baby's death by unfeeding it.

Now the account of method we reached in the preceding chapter yields that (5′) is rewritable as

(5′.1) $(\exists x)\,(\exists y)\,(\exists z)\,[\text{Causes}_3\,(x, \text{ the baby's death, me})\,\&$
             $\text{Unfeeds}_3\,(y, \text{ the baby, me})\,\&\, PART\,(y, x)\,\&$
             $\{\text{Causes}_3\,(z, \text{ the baby's death, } y) \text{ or } x = y\}]$—

see (T-S$_{11}$). I did cause the baby's death, so there was an x consisting in my causing of the baby's death, so the first clause is true. I did unfeed the baby, so there was a y consisting in my unfeeding the baby. Since x is a causing of something, x is an event. But y, which is my unfeeding the baby, i.e., is my not feeding the baby, is not an event— it is a state of affairs. We know, however, that no state of affairs is part of any event; indeed, "PART (y, x)" is false. So $(5'.1)$ is false. So $(5')$ is false if $(5')$ is rewritable as $(5'.1)$. But surely (5) ought to be true.

I suggest, then, that we need to make yet one more revision in our account of method. I suggest we say that the results of replacing "α", "β", and "γ" by referring expressions, "verb₁s" by an appropriate tensed form of a causal verb, "verb₂ing" by the gerund of any transitive verb, and the schematic predicates with appropriate predicates, in—not $(T\text{-}S_{11})$—but

$(T\text{-}S_{12})$ "α verb₁s β by verb₂ing γ" is rewritable as
 "$(\exists x)(\exists y)(\exists z)$ [Verb₁s (x, β, α) &
 Verb₂s (y, γ, α) &
 {PART (y, x) or y is a state of affairs} &
 {Verb₁s (z, β, y) or $x = y$}]"

are all true. On this account of the matter $(5')$ is rewritable—not as $(5'.1)$—but rather as

$(5'.2)$ $(\exists x)(\exists y)(\exists z)$ [Causes₃ $(x,$ the baby's death, me$)$ &
 Unfeeds₃ $(y,$ the baby, me$)$ &
 {PART (y, x) or y is a state of affairs} &
 {Causes₃ $(z,$ the baby's death, $y)$ or $x = y$}].

The first and second clauses of $(5'.2)$ are true. Its third clause is false, but its fourth clause is true. Since, as we know, (3) is true, the fifth clause of $(5'.2)$ is true. And $(5'.2)$ is therefore true.

Since (2) and (4) are false, however, the first and fifth clauses of

$(6'.2)$ $(\exists x)(\exists y)(\exists z)$ [Causes₃ $(x,$ the baby's death, Gerald Ford$)$ &
 Unfeeds₃ $(y,$ the baby, Gerald Ford$)$ &
 {PART (y, x) or y is a state of affairs} &
 {Causes₃ $(z,$ the baby's death, $y)$ or $x = y$}]

are false; since y is a state of affairs and x an event, the third and sixth clauses of $(6'.2)$ are also false. Therefore $(6'.2)$ is false—which is just as it should be, since

(6) Gerald Ford caused the baby's death by not feeding it
is false.

XVI

Noncausal Verbs

At the beginning of Chapter IX I asked, "In virtue of what is an event a killing?" We now have an answer to that question. Indeed, we have an answer to every question of the form

(S)　　In virtue of what is an event a verbing?

in which the gerund of a casual verb replaces "verbing". But what about questions of this form in which the gerund of a noncausal verb replaces "verbing"?

For some noncausal verbs, the question that results from replacing "verbing" in (S) by the verb's gerund is easily answered. Consider, for example, the following verbs:

believe, know, doubt,
expect, intend, wish, hope, want,
love, hate, prefer, detest, fear,
precede, postdate.

In virtue of what is an event a believing, a knowing, a . . . ? The answer is: nothing, because necessarily not. I have no doubt that there are such facts as the fact that so and so believes such and such, the fact that so and so knows such and such, etc., and such states of affairs as so and so's believing, knowing, etc., such and such. But it is plain that nothing that is a believing, knowing, etc. ever *occurs*. Alfred's believ-

Acts and Other Events

ing what Bert said, Charles's knowing David, etc., may exist; they cannot occur. And I take it to follow that no event is, indeed no event can be, a believing, knowing, etc.

Again, consider the incomplete verbs.[1] The expressions that result from replacing "verbing" in (S) by the gerund of an incomplete verb are also easily dealt with. Consider, for example,

> In virtue of what is an event a putting?

This is a nonsense, and hence not a question, and hence calls for no answer at all. (It should be stressed that what makes it a nonsense is not absence of 'subject and object'. Thus, "In virtue of what is an event a believing that the earth is round by John?" is not a nonsense, and is easily answered; "In virtue of what is an event a putting of a book by John?" is a nonsense.)

But if we restrict ourselves to those noncausal verbs such that the results of replacing their gerunds for "verbing" in

$(T\text{-}S_{13})$ It is possible that there is an event that is a verbing

are true—or, as I shall put it, to those noncausal verbs that satisfy $(T\text{-}S_{13})$—then it seems to me that the questions resulting from replacement in (S) are very hard to answer. In any case, I shall not offer answers to any of them.

On the other hand, it will pay us to note some distinctions among the noncausal verbs that satisfy $(T\text{-}S_{13})$.[2] I draw attention to them in order to indicate the great variety of verbs that fall into this category, and to serve a purpose that will come out in Chapter XVIII.

1. All causal verbs are transitive, but, as we saw, not all transitive verbs are causal. It will be remembered that a necessary condition for a verb to be a causal verb is that it accept events as subjects. The transitive verb "kick", then, is not causal, since it is not possible for an event to kick anything. Some other transitive verbs like the transitive verb "kick" in this respect are

punch, shove, slap,
kiss, stroke, pat,
eat, bite, drink, swallow.

All of these verbs satisfy $(T\text{-}S_{13})$.

They have something else in common as well. Notice that you kick

---

[1] See pp. 144–147 above.

[2] I have been much helped in writing this chapter by Zeno Vendler's "Verbs and Times," *Linguistics in Philosophy* (Ithaca, N.Y.: Cornell University Press, 1967).

a thing only if you move something (you have to move your foot); you punch a thing only if you move something (your fist); you kiss something only if you move something (your lips); and so on.

Moreover, suppose you kicked Alfred at 10 A.M. last Wednesday. You moved your foot at 10 A.M. last Wednesday. It seems very plausible that the event that was a kicking of Alfred by you just was a moving of your foot by you. In fact, it seems very plausible that every event that is a kicking of something is a moving of a foot. Or, suppose you ate an apple this morning. Then you moved something this morning. In particular, I suppose you moved the apple successively to and away from your mouth a number of times; you moved your jaws up and down; you moved whatever the muscles are that are such that it is by moving those muscles that you swallow. I think it very plausible that the event that occurred this morning, which was your eating of an apple, just was your moving of those things—i.e., that the event which was your eating of that apple was the fusion of the events that were your movings of the apple, your jaws, and your throat muscles. I think, more generally, that it is plausible to say that for every one of the verbs so far mentioned in this section, the result of replacing its gerund for "verbing" in

> If an event x is a verbing of y by z, then x is a moving of something by z or a fusion of movings of things by z

is a truth. Since a moving of something by z is itself a fusion of movings of things by z, I shall say that for every one of the verbs so far mentioned in this section, the result of replacing its gerund for "verbing" in

(T-S$_{14}$)   If an event x is a verbing of y by z, then x is a fusion of movings of things by z

is a truth.

This is true of some causal verbs too. The transitive verb "move", for example, is itself a causal verb; and plainly it satisfies (T-S$_{14}$) too. Let us say that a verb is a 'transitive motion verb' just in case it is transitive and satisfies both (T-S$_{13}$) and (T-S$_{14}$);[3] what interests us now is that all of the *non*causal verbs so far mentioned in this section are transitive motion verbs.

[3] We might want to revise this in such a way as to allow that certain completed verbs, e.g., "put ____ on the table" and "place ____ in my Bible", are also transitive motion verbs. (Or at any rate, that they are transitive motion 'verbals', as we might put it, for a completed verb is not itself a verb.) Certainly, if an event x is a putting of y on the table by z, then x is a fusion of movings of things by z; and so on.

Acts and Other Events

Every event that is a kicking of something by you is an event that is a moving of something by you; but not every event that is a moving of something by you is an event that is a kicking of something by you. First, and most obviously, it has to be your foot that you move. Again, there has to be something in the path of your foot. Can we say

> An event x is a kicking of y by z just in case x is a moving of z's foot by z, and there is a path p on which z's foot travels during the time IN which x occurs, and y is on p?

No. In the first place, we should have to add that the path must not be vertically downward (stamping on a man's foot is not kicking him). Again, we should have to add that the foot must move at a certain minimal rate of speed (if you bring your foot slowly to rest against a man's ankle you have not really kicked him); and what is that minimal rate of speed? I am sure there are other objections too. I suspect, in fact, that there is not going to be any such thing as finding a thesis comparable to those we got for causal verbs—comparable to, e.g., $(T_4{}^*)$—for kickings.

The complexities are even greater in the case of some of the other verbs I mentioned. Take "eat". Just what do you have to move, and how, if you are to have eaten an apple? It seems even less likely that anyone will produce a thesis comparable to $(T_4{}^*)$ for eatings.

Nevertheless, it is not nothing to know that any event that is a kicking of y by z is a moving of something by z, and that any event that is an eating of y by z is a fusion of movings of a variety of things by z.

The transitive verb "move" is a causal verb. Indeed, an event that is a moving of α by z is a causing by z of α's moving, and an event that is a fusion of movings of α, β, and γ by z is a fusion of a causing by z of α's moving and a causing by z of β's moving and a causing by z of γ's moving. So, for example, if I am right in thinking that Bert's kicking of Alfred is Bert's moving of his foot, then Bert's kicking of Alfred is a causing of something by Bert. If I am right in thinking that Charles's eating of an apple is a fusion of movings of things by Charles, then Charles's eating of an apple is a fusion of causings of things by Charles. More generally, we can say that every transitive motion verb satisfies.

(T-S$_{15}$)   If an event x is a verbing of y by z, then x is a fusion of causings of things by z.

And this is a useful point to have in hand—we shall come back to it in Chapter XVIII.

Noncausal Verbs

2. A particularly interesting class of noncausal transitive verbs is the class of noncausal transitive illocutionary-act-verbs. Here again are the noncausal illocutionary-act-verbs listed earlier—with the exception of "apologize", which is intransitive:

assert, declare, state, remark, predicate, deny,
criticize, praise,
admit, confess,
ask, answer,
command, order, request, demand,
promise.

These verbs plainly satisfy

(T-S$_{13}$) It is possible that there is an event that is a verbing.

Do they satisfy

(T-S$_{14}$) If an event x is a verbing of y by z, then x is a fusion of movings of things by z?

I think not. Perhaps you and I only assert, declare, state, . . . a thing if we move something, our mouths (to make sounds), or our hands (to write words, or wave flags, . . .); and if so, our asserting, declaring, stating, . . . of a thing presumably just is our moving of whatever it is that we move. But it seems possible that there should be people who communicate without moving anything. We might imagine that Martians communicate by making their foreheads glow in patterned ways.

On the other hand, it does seem to me that all of these verbs satisfy

(T-S$_{15}$) If an event x is a verbing of y by z, then x is a fusion of causings of things by z.

Perhaps a Martian might assert something by making his forehead glow first green and then red; making your forehead glow green and then red is causing your forehead to glow green and then red, so if that is what his asserting of what he asserts consists in, then his asserting of what he asserts is a fusion of causings of things.

But perhaps it is not obvious that *all* of these verbs satisfy (T-S$_{15}$). What I have in mind is that someone may ask why it should not be possible to (as it might be) answer a question by doing nothing at all. For at least some of these verbs, this sort of thing is plainly impossible. Take "demand", for example. Suppose Alfred says to Bert: "If you really very much, and very urgently, want me to give you back your wallet, don't do anything at all. If you don't care, make some sign." And suppose that Bert does not do anything at all. Has Bert demanded that Alfred give him back his wallet? I should think it plain he has not: I should think that his not doing anything (his neither moving his mouth nor waving a flag nor making his forehead glow) might be taken to show that he really very much, and very urgently, wants Alfred to give back his wallet, but that he has not *demanded* that Alfred give it back.

But now consider "answer". Suppose Alfred says to Bert: "Do you want pudding for dessert? Waggle your thumb if you do, and don't waggle your thumb if you don't." And suppose Bert does not waggle his thumb. Has Bert answered Alfred's question? *I* think not: I think that his not waggling his thumb might be taken to show that he does not want pudding for dessert, but I think also that he has not *answered* the question asked him. But it would not surprise me if there were those who thought that Bert might be taken to have answered. Now if Bert has answered, then his answering presumably just *was* his not waggling his thumb. But Bert's not waggling his thumb is not an event (compare my not feeding the baby), and a fortiori is not a fusion of causings of things. So it may appear that if Bert has answered, then "answer" does not satisfy $(T\text{-}S_{15})$.

But in fact this does not follow. If Bert has answered, then, since his answering *was* his not waggling his thumb, his answering was itself not an event. And for "answer" to satisfy $(T\text{-}S_{15})$, it is required only that if an *event* x is an answering of something by someone, then x is a fusion of causings of things by z.

So while *I* am inclined to think that you cannot answer a question by doing nothing at all (just as you cannot demand anything by doing nothing at all), and indeed that every answering is an event (just as every kicking, punching, shoving, . . . is an event), "answer" satisfies $(T\text{-}S_{15})$ even if I am mistaken—i.e., even if some answerings are not events (e.g., Bert's answering of the question Alfred asked him), every answering that is an event is a fusion of causings of things. And, for present purposes, this is all that matters.

With which fusion of causings of things is a given event that is an asserting, declaring, stating, . . . to be identified? I suspect there is not going to be any such thing as finding theses comparable to $(T_4{}^*)$ that tell us. One thing that would make finding such theses difficult is the fact that all of these verbs involve intentionality. That is, if the suggestion I made just above was right, then if a noncausal transitive illocutionary-act-verb is main verb in a sentence of the form "z verbed y",

Noncausal Verbs

the sentence requires for its truth that the thing to which the expression that replaces "z" refers caused something intentionally. Thus, for example,

(1)   Bert answered the question Alfred asked

entails

(2)   Bert caused something intentionally.

Of course, if I was mistaken, (1) entails, not (2), but rather

(3)   Either Bert intentionally caused something or Bert intentionally refrained from causing something.

Either way, it is very hard to see what could be taken to set the limits. People might answer by intentionally moving (or refraining from moving) all sorts of different things, including the various different movable parts of their bodies; Martians might answer by intentionally making their foreheads glow.

The fact that these verbs involve intentionality may be expressed in yet another way: we may put it (if I am right) that all of them satisfy—not merely $(T\text{-}S_{13})$ and $(T\text{-}S_{15})$—but also

$(T\text{-}S_{15}')$ If an event x is a verbing of y by z, then x is a fusion of causings of things by z, and among those causings is an intentional causing,

and that they do is of interest. But it should be noticed that they are not the only verbs that do. So do a great many transitive verbs that are not illocutionary-act-verbs, such as, for example, "forge" (as in "John forged a check") and "murder". But it should be stressed that no causal verb does. There need be no intentionality in your killing of a man: you may kill a man in your sleep. More generally, it will be remembered that a verb is causal only if it accepts events as subjects; and clearly no event ever does anything intentionally.

3. The verb "hit" plainly satisfies

$(T\text{-}S_{13})$ It is possible that there is an event that is a verbing:

there not only may be, but actually have been, any number of events that were hittings.

Suppose that Alfred punched Bert in the nose. Then there was an event that was a hitting of Bert by Alfred, and I should think that it was a moving of something (Alfred's fist) by Alfred. So we might suppose we can say that "hit" also satisfies

$(T\text{-}S_{14})$ If an event x is a verbing of y by z, then x is a fusion of movings of things by z.

Acts and Other Events

But other hittings are different. Suppose my car hit the side of a mountain. Certainly my car moved. But my car did not move any part of itself—e.g., its fender or bumper—so the car's hitting the side of the mountain cannot have been its moving any part of itself. Of course the car might well have moved the side of the mountain (compressing it in toward the center of the mountain). But I am inclined to think that the car's hitting the side of the mountain occurred at the time at which the car first touched the side, and that if the car moved the side of the mountain, its moving the side of the mountain did not start until after the time at which the car first touched the side. If so, then the car's hitting the side of the mountain cannot have been its moving any part of the mountain. And it then seems plausible to suppose that the car's hitting the side of the mountain was not its moving anything at all.

This difference may be accommodated in a number of ways. For convenience (and for convenience only[4]), I suggest we say that there are two verbs "hit". One verb "hit" is such that if (as it might be)

(1)   Alfred hit Bert

contains it, then (1) entails "Alfred moved something into contact with Bert," but is compatible with the falsity of "Alfred came into contact with Bert". (Picture, for example, Alfred's hitting Bert with a stick rather than his fist.) The second verb "hit" is such that if (1) contains it, then (1) entails "Alfred came into contact with Bert," but is compatible with the falsity of "Alfred moved something into contact with Bert". (Picture, for example, Alfred's landing on Bert after being thrown out of a plane.) Again, I shall say that there are two sentences

My car hit the side of the mountain;

but I take it that only one of them can have been true.

The first of the two verbs "hit" is transitive and satisfies (T-S$_{13}$) and (T-S$_{14}$), and thus is a transitive motion verb. The second of the two verbs "hit" satisfies (T-S$_{13}$), but not (T-S$_{14}$); it instead satisfies

(T-S$_{16}$)   If an event x is a verbing of y by z, then x is an onset of a state of affairs.

What I have in mind is this. Suppose I drove a car fast into the side of a mountain, and that it exploded shortly after making contact. Suppose also that there was a time-point—call it "T"—such that the car was in contact with the mountain at T but at no time before T. Then

---

[4] See footnote 3, Ch. IX.

T was a time at which the state of affairs that consists in the car's being in contact with that mountain started to obtain; and since that state of affairs obtains only once, there is a unique event which is

(a)   the onset of the state of affairs that consists in the car's being in contact with the mountain,

which, by (D$_7$) of Chapter XII above, occurred at T. It seems plausible to conclude that

(b)   the event that consisted in the car's hitting the side of the mountain

itself occurred at T and is identical with (a).

Was there such a time as T? Perhaps there was no *point* of time that was the first time at which the car was in contact with the mountain; perhaps we should take the car's being in contact with the mountain to have started to obtain, not at a point of time, but instead at a (more or less) fuzzy stretch of time. No matter. It still seems plausible to identify (b) with (a).

This example is worth stopping over a bit longer—a counterintuitive consequence of something said earlier comes out particularly clearly here.

In Chapter XII, section 4, I invited you to suppose that a piece of chocolate was hard all its life until I melted it, and then remained liquid ever after. So the state of affairs that consists in the chocolate's being liquid obtains only once, and there is a unique event which is

(a′)   the onset of the state of affairs that consists in the chocolate's being liquid.

I said that we shall need to suppose that (a′) is the termination of

(c′)   the chocolate's melting.

Analogous reasoning brings out that we shall need to suppose that (a) is the termination of

(c)   the car's moving toward the mountain.

For we know, from Chapter IX, that my moving the car toward the mountain is my causing of (c); and my moving the car toward the mountain had better be identical with my causing of its being in contact with the mountain and therefore with my causing of (a).

Now we plainly cannot say about a time *t* both that it is a time at which A is moving toward B and that it is a time at which A is not moving toward B. The time of (a) is, by hypothesis, a time at which the car is in contact with the mountain; thus the time of (a) is presumably a time at which the car is not still moving toward the mountain.

Acts and Other Events

So if (a) is to be part of (c), (c) must be still occurring at a time at which the car is not moving toward the mountain. But surely the following principle is intuitively very plausible:

> A's moving toward B is occurring at *t* only if A is moving toward B at *t*.

If the principle is true, however, (c) is not still occurring at the time at which (a) occurs, and (a) is therefore no part of (c).

If we wish to have (a) be the termination of (c), we do have to give up that principle. We have to say that if a car's moving toward a thing ends in contact with that thing, then the car's moving toward that thing has a part, viz., its termination, which occurs at a time at which the car is not moving toward the thing. But I do think the benefit to be got by having (a) be the termination of (c) is worth this cost. And perhaps the cost is not, after all, too great: it is only very special times which we hereby take to be exceptions to the principle, namely times of terminations.

In any case, it seems very plausible that the event that consisted in the car's hitting the side of the mountain is an onset of a state of affairs.

Let us call a verb a 'transitive onset verb' just in case it is transitive and satisfies both (T-S$_{13}$) and (T-S$_{16}$). Then while the first of the two verbs "hit" is a transitive motion verb, the second of the two verbs "hit" is a transitive onset verb.

Compare also the transitive verb "reach"—as in "I reached the top of the mountain at 10 P.M." It too is a noncausal transitive onset verb. So also is "win".

The verb "touch" is particularly interesting. If you are given the order "Touch your nose with your forefinger!" and decide to obey it, you will touch your nose with your forefinger, i.e., you will move your forefinger up until it is in contact with your nose. *Your* touching your nose is a moving of something (your forefinger) by you. But what about your *forefinger's* touching your nose? I am inclined to think there was an event consisting in your forefinger's touching your nose, which was an onset of a state of affairs (viz., the state of affairs consisting in your forefinger's being in contact with your nose). And I am inclined to think also that there is a state of affairs consisting in your forefinger's touching your nose (and which is identical with the state of affairs consisting in your forefinger's being in contact with your nose), which obtains for a longer or shorter period of time. I suggest, then,

228

Noncausal Verbs

that we say I was wrong to speak as I did just above of *the* verb "touch". I suggest, that is, that we say there are three verbs "touch". One of them is a transitive motion verb, and is such that if

(2)   A touched B

contains it, (2) entails that A moved something into contact with B. The second is a transitive onset verb, and is such that if (2) contains it, (2) entails that A came into contact with B, but is compatible with A's not having moved anything into contact with B. The third is neither a transitive motion verb nor a transitive onset verb, since it does not satisfy $(T-S_{13})$—if the gerund in "your forefinger's touching your nose" is the gerund of the third verb "touch", the expression refers to a state of affairs rather than an event.

To return to the transitive verbs "hit". One, as I said, is a transitive motion verb, and thus if its gerund is replaced for "verbing" in

$(T-S_{14})$ If an event x is a verbing of y by z, then x is a fusion of movings of things by z,

the result is a truth, and thus if its gerund is replaced for "verbing" in

$(T-S_{15})$ If an event x is a verbing of y by z, then x is a fusion of causings of things by z,

the result is a truth. The other, however, is a transitive onset verb; and it seems plausible to suppose that if *its* gerund is replaced for "verbing" in either $(T-S_{14})$ or $(T-S_{15})$, the result is not a truth. Indeed, it seems plausible to suppose, more generally, that the result of replacing the gerund of any transitive onset verb in

There is no event x that is a verbing of y by z, and that is a fusion of causings of things by z

is itself a truth.

4. Some transitive onset verbs are such that the result of replacing referring expressions for "z" and "y", and the gerund of the verb for "verbing", in

z's verbing of y

is plausibly said to be referring to a mental event whenever it refers to an event. Consider, e.g., the transitive verbs

recall, recognize, notice, spot,
discover, find,
infer, deduce,
guess, estimate,
decide, resolve, choose,
forgive.

These verbs plainly satisfy

(T-S₁₃)   It is possible that there is an event that is a verbing.

And I think they also satisfy

(T-S₁₆)   If an event x is a verbing of y by z, then x is an onset of a state of affairs.

Alfred's recalling thus and such is an onset of the state of affairs that is his remembering thus and such; Bert's recognizing so and so is an onset of the state of affairs that is his being aware of who or what so and so is; Charles's noticing thus and such is an onset of the state of affairs that is his being aware of thus and such; etc. If these statements are true, the verbs are transitive onset verbs. Now Alfred's recalling thus and such is surely a mental event; so also is Bert's recognizing so and so, and Charles's noticing thus and such; etc. Let us call a verb a 'transitive mental verb' just in case it is transitive and satisfies both (T-S₁₃) and

(T-S₁₇)   If an event x is a verbing of y by z, then x is a mental event.

Then if I am right in thinking that the verbs I listed above are transitive onset verbs, the class of transitive onset verbs has members in common with the class of transitive mental verbs.

But there are transitive mental verbs that are not transitive onset verbs. Consider, for example,

watch, observe, listen to, attend to,
rejoice in,
dream of.

Alfred's watching something, Bert's observing something, etc. are not onsets of states of affairs; hence these verbs, though transitive, and though they satisfy (T-S₁₃), are not transitive onset verbs. Yet Alfred's watching something, Bert's observing something, etc. surely are mental events.

What about "see", "hear", "feel", "taste", "smell"? I am inclined to think that these verbs do not satisfy (T-S₁₃). Thus in particular, that although it may be true that Alfred now sees his hand, and that there therefore is such a thing as Alfred's seeing his hand, Alfred's seeing his hand is a fact or state of affairs, and not an event. And similarly for Bert's hearing the music, Charles's feeling the bump on David's head (and David's feeling the pain in David's head), etc. No doubt Alfred's catching sight of, or spotting, or noticing his hand may occur, and therefore is an event; but it seems to me that Alfred's *seeing* his hand is not something that occurs. If these verbs do not satisfy (T-S$_{13}$), then they are not transitive mental verbs—and are not transitive onset verbs, and are not transitive illocutionary-act-verbs, and are not transitive motion verbs. Fortunately, however, we do not have to worry about them. For we are concerned only with noncausal verbs that satisfy (T-S$_{13}$).

As I said, some transitive onset verbs are transitive mental verbs. I think that no transitive motion verb is a transitive mental verb. Certainly it is plain that none of the transitive motion verbs mentioned in section 1 are transitive mental verbs: Alfred's kicking Bert, Charles's punching David, Edward's kissing Frances, etc.—all of them may well be events, but none of them is at all plausibly thought to be a mental event. What about the transitive illocutionary-act-verbs? I said that a person asserts, declares, states, etc. something only if he causes something intentionally (or intentionally refrains from causing something). Does this mean that a person's (as it might be) asserting that today is Wednesday is a mental event? Does it mean that any part of a person's asserting that today is Wednesday is a mental event? No doubt a person's forming an intention to do this or that may be a mental event, and indeed, it may be a mental event that causes his then (intentionally) doing the this or that. No doubt a person's thinking about this or that may be a mental event, and his (intentionally) doing this or that may be accompanied by, and part of it even caused by, his thinking about what he thinks about. But it seems to me that your (intentionally) moving your mouth, for example, as in saying the words "today is Wednesday", just is your (intentionally) causing your mouth to move; and that *that* event is not, and need not even contain, a mental event.

It is worth noticing, however, that while it appears that no transitive motion verb is a transitive mental verb, it *may* be the case that all transitive mental verbs that are not transitive onset verbs satisfy

(T-S$_{15}$)   If an event x is a verbing of y by z, then x is a fusion of causings of things by z.

Some philosophers take the view that every mental event is identical with some physical event. It is open to them also to take the view that all mental events (which are not onsets of states of affairs) are identical with physical events of a quite particular kind, viz., fusions of causings of physical events or states of affairs. Thus, e.g., that

Alfred's watching a moving finger consists in Alfred's causing of certain events in his brain, or at any rate, in his head. If this view is right, then all transitive mental verbs that are not transitive onset verbs satisfy (T-S$_{15}$). I leave open whether or not it is right.

5. There are noncausal transitive verbs that satisfy

(T-S$_{13}$)   It is possible that there is an event that is a verbing

but are neither transitive motion verbs nor transitive illocutionary-act-verbs nor transitive onset verbs nor transitive mental verbs. But we have looked at enough such verbs to bring out the only really important point for our purposes, viz., that for some such verbs, the results of making appropriate replacements in

           z's verbing of *y*

always refer to a fusion of causings of things by *z* (the transitive motion verbs and—if *I* am right—the transitive illocutionary-act-verbs), and that for some such verbs, the results of making the appropriate replacements in it never refer to a fusion of causings of things by *z* (the transitive onset verbs), whereas for other such verbs, the results of making the appropriate replacements in it may or may not refer to a fusion of causings of things by *z* (the transitive mental verbs).

Before we turn to the intransitive verbs, we should look briefly at what settles whether a verb is transitive or intransitive.

If we want the verb in

(1)   Alfred ate

to be the same as the verb in

(2)   Alfred ate my apple,

then we cannot say that a verb is transitive just in case it has a direct object in every sentence in which it is main verb. For the verb in (2) should surely turn out to be transitive.

On pages 135–136 above, I suggested that we should take the verb in a sentence of the form "*x* verbed" to be transitive if the sentence entails the relevant sentence of the form "*x* verbed something". Under that policy, the verb in (1) is transitive, since (1) entails

(3)   Alfred ate something.

And then if, as seems plausible, we can say that the verb in (1) is the same as the verb in (2) and (3), we can conclude that the verb in (2) and (3) is transitive, since the verb in (1) is.

But this gives us only a sufficient condition for transitivity. The verb in

Noncausal Verbs

(4)   I liked Bert,

for example, should surely turn out to be transitive. Yet there is no such sentence as

(5)   I liked,

and a fortiori, no such sentence which entails

(6)   I liked something;

so we cannot conclude from the fact that (5) entails (6) that the verb in (5), and therefore the verb in (4) and (6), is transitive—there is no such fact.

I gather that it is common practice among linguists to tie transitivity to availability of passive transformations, and we might as well follow them.[5] Thus I gather they would say that the verb in

(7)   John's house cost $75,000

is not transitive in that there is no such sentence as "$75,000 was cost by John's house". Let us say, then, that a verb is transitive just in case there are sentences of the form "x verbed y" in which it is main verb, and every such sentence has a passive transform. I should imagine that the verb in (4) and (6), for example, passes this test; and I should imagine also that if a verb satisfies the sufficient condition I laid out above, then it satisfies this test too.[6]

I gather that linguists would say that the verb in (7) is also not intransitive, and we might as well follow them here too. If we do, we

---

[5] I am grateful to Jerrold J. Katz for drawing my attention to transformation into the passive, and for information about the practice of linguists on this matter. "Cost" is his example.

[6] "Alice married" entails "Alice married something"; but does

(i)   Alice married Bert

have a passive transform? Certainly

(ii)   The minister married Bert

has a passive transform; more precisely, (ii) has a passive transform if it contains the causal verb "marry", i.e., the one such that if (ii) contains it, then (ii) is not equivalent to "Bert married the minister". Let us suppose that (i) does not contain the causal verb "marry": i.e., let us suppose that (i) is equivalent to

(iii)   Bert married Alice.

Does (i) have a passive transform? Suppose that the verb in

(iv)   Bert was married by Alice,

is a passive of the verb in (i); is (iv) a sentence? No doubt it would be odd to say (iv); would that be because (iv) is not a sentence? If so, the test for transitivity which I gave in the text above must be revised. But I think that (iv) is a sentence, and that what makes it odd to say (iv) is the very fact that (i) is equivalent to (iii): i.e., if it is Bert who concerns you, and thus Bert whom you want to talk about, you have available, not merely the passive of (i), viz., (iv), but also the simpler, active, (iii). (I am indebted to George Boolos for the question, and to Allan Gibbard for the answer.)

233

cannot say that a verb is intransitive just in case it is not transitive. Let us say, then, that a verb is intransitive just in case there are nonelliptical sentences of the form "x verbed" in which it is main verb, and none of them entails the relevant sentence of the form "x verbed something". In that there are no such sentences as "John's house cost", the verb in (7) fails this test. And so also does the verb in (1) fail it. By contrast, the verb in "I slept" surely passes it: "I slept" plainly does not entail "I slept something".

The verb in (7) fails both of these tests, and hence is neither transitive nor intransitive.[7] Are there any verbs which pass both tests, and hence are both transitive and intransitive? Well, consider the verb in

(8)   John melted the ice cube;

I should imagine it passes our test for transitivity. I should imagine that the verb in

(9)   The ice cube melted

passes our test for intransitivity—(9), for example, certainly does not entail "The ice cube melted something". So if the verb in (8) is the same as the verb in (9), then it is a verb which is both transitive and intransitive.

I said in Chapter IX that we *could* say there is just one verb "melt", and thus that the verb in (8) is the same as the verb in (9). But if we do say this, we must surely say that it occurs transitively (but not intransitively) in (8), and intransitively (but not transitively) in (9). More generally, we must surely first define, not "transitive verb" and "intransitive verb", but rather "transitive occurrence of a verb" and "intransitive occurrence of a verb". (Then, if we liked, we could go on to say that a verb is transitive if it has transitive occurrences, and intransitive if it has intransitive occurrences; the verb "melt" would thus be both transitive and intransitive. Or we could go on to say that a verb is transitive if it has only transitive occurrences, and intransitive if it has only intransitive occurrences; the verb "melt" would thus be nei-

[7] Plainly all incomplete verbs fail both of these tests, and that is surely as it should be. (Remember that while "Bert refrained" certainly does not entail "Bert refrained something", "Bert refrained" is elliptical.) But we could get certain completed verbs to pass analogous tests. E.g., we could get "put ____ on the table" and "let ____ die" to be transitive verbs (better, transitive 'verbals') in that such sentences as "I put the book on the table" and "I let him die" have passive transforms. And we could get "put the book on the table" and "refrain from smiling" to be intransitive verbs (better, intransitive 'verbals') in that "I put the book on the table" and "Bert refrained from smiling" are nonelliptical sentences and do not entail "I put the book on the table something" and "Bert refrained from smiling something".

ther transitive nor intransitive. Still other policies would be available too.)

I said, however, that it would be less cumbersome for our purposes if we said that the verb in (8) is not the same as (though it 'matches') the verb in (9). (Among other things, we were thereby enabled to speak of 'causal verbs' as opposed to 'causal occurrences of verbs'.) If we do say this then we are able to say that the verb in (8) does not merely have a transitive occurrence in (8), but that it is a transitive verb, and that it is not also an intransitive verb; and we are able to say that the verb in (9) does not merely have an intransitive occurrence in (9), but that it is an intransitive verb, and that is it not also a transitive verb. For simplicity, I shall continue to speak in this way.

6. The verb "cost" is neither transitive nor intransitive; and no event can be, for example, a costing of $75,000 by John's house. I hazard a guess that *no* verb that is neither transitive nor intransitive satisfies $(T-S_{13})$ It is possible that there is an event that is a verbing, and therefore that we need concern ourselves now only with intransitive verbs.

A great many intransitive verbs match causal verbs. Consider, e.g., the intransitive verbs "melt", "sink", and so on—see page 134 for some causal verbs that are matched by intransitive verbs. The intransitive verb "sleep" is not matched by any causal verb, but it could have been: remember the mother who says to the babysitter as she leaves, "Sleep Albert as soon after 7:30 as you can." Indeed, I should imagine that every intransitive verb could have been matched by a causal verb, and that the distinction between those that are, and those that are not, matched by causal verbs is not of any great theoretical interest.

What is of interest for our purposes is that some intransitive verbs are very like what I called 'transitive motion verbs'. Consider, that is, the intransitive verbs

walk, swim, jump, kick,
talk, grumble, growl, groan, moan,
laugh, giggle,
yawn, sneeze, wink, blink, breathe, cough, shudder,
smile, scowl.

Presumably you walk only if you move something (you have to move your feet); you swim only if you move something (your arms or legs);

and so on. Moreover, it seems very plausible to suppose that the event that was a walking by you just was a moving of your feet by you; and similarly for the other verbs on this list. Let us say that a verb is an 'intransitive motion verb' just in case it is intransitive and satisfies both (T-S₁₃) and

(T-S₁₄*) If an event x is a verbing by z, then x is a fusion of movings of things by z.

It is plausible to say that all of the verbs in the list above are intransitive motion verbs.

What about the verb "run"? Well, we shall have to say that there is no such thing as *the* verb "run". We shall have to say that the verb in

(1)   I ran the engine all afternoon

is not the same as the verb in

(2)   I ran:

for we shall want to have it that the verb in (1) is transitive (and causal), whereas the verb in (2) is intransitive. Can we say that the verb in (2) belongs on the list I set out above? Certainly I run only if I move something, and it does seem plausible that any event that is a running by me is a fusion of movings of things by me. But is the verb in (2) the same as the verb in

(3)   The engine ran?

If (3) is true, then presumably some part of the engine moved; but I should imagine that the truth of (3) is compatible with the engine's not having, itself, moved anything, and if so, then an engine's running is not (at least not in general) a fusion of movings of things by it. It will come as no surprise that I suggest we say that the verb in (2) is not the same as the verb in (3). After all, it seems plausible to say that (2) entails "I moved something", and that (3) does not entail "the engine moved something". (Compare the verbs "hit", page 229 above.) If this is acceptable, then we can say that the verb in (2)—but not the verb in (3)—belongs on the list I set out above.

Just as every transitive motion verb satisfies (T-S₁₅), every intransitive motion verb satisfies

(T-S₁₅*) If an event x is a verbing by z, then x is a fusion of causings of things by z.

I should imagine that the intransitive illocutionary-act-verbs also satisfy (T-S₁₅*). Consider "apologize": If an event x is an apologizing by z, then x is a fusion of causings of things by z. Indeed, we can also say that if an event x is an apologizing by z, then x is a fusion of causings of things by z, and among those causings is an intentional causing.

Consider, next, the intransitive verbs "arrive", "stop", "start". These verbs are intransitive, and they satisfy both (T-S$_{13}$) and

(T-S$_{16}$*) If an event x is a verbing by z, then x is an onset of a state of affairs.

For obvious reasons, I shall therefore call them 'intransitive onset verbs'.

There are also verbs we might call 'intransitive mental verbs', such as "think", "wonder", "meditate", "reminisce", "worry", "suffer", "mope", "hesitate".

There are noncausal transitive verbs that satisfy (T-S$_{13}$), but that are neither transitive motion verbs nor transitive illocutionary-act-verbs nor transitive onset verbs nor transitive mental verbs; so also are there intransitive verbs that satisfy (T-S$_{13}$), but that are neither intransitive motion verbs nor intransitive illocutionary-act-verbs nor intransitive onset verbs nor intransitive mental verbs. Consider, for example, the intransitive verbs

melt, sink, move,[8] break, bend,
rise, drift, fall, run,[9]
rust, decay, fade,
sleep, die:

these satisfy (T-S$_{13}$), but fall into none of the groups mentioned. I am sure it would be of interest to look more closely at these verbs and to attend to the differences among them. For our purposes, however, it is enough to notice that none of the ones I listed is such that the result of replacing its gerund for "verbing", and a referring expression for "z", in

z's verbing

refers to a fusion of causings of things by z.

More generally, what is of interest for our purposes is this: for some intransitive verbs that satisfy (T-S$_{13}$), the results of making the appropriate replacements in

z's verbing

always refer to a fusion of causings of things by z (the intransitive mo-

---

[8] The verb "move" in "The piano moved"—not the verb "move" in "I moved because you told me to". (The latter verb is transitive.)

[9] The verb "run' in (3)—not the verb "run" in (2). (The latter verb is an intransitive motion verb.)

tion verbs, and [I should imagine] the intransitive illocutionary-act-verbs), and that for some such verbs, the results of making the appropriate replacements in it never refer to a fusion of causings of things by z (the intransitive onset verbs and the verbs on the list in the preceding paragraph), whereas for other such verbs, the results of making the appropriate replacements in it may or may not refer to a fusion of causings of things by z (the intransitive mental verbs).

XVII

Method (III)

I suggested in Chapter XV that the results of replacing "α", "β", and "γ" by referring expressions, "verb$_1$s" by an appropriate tensed form of a *causal verb*, "verb$_2$ing" by the gerund of any transitive verb, and the schematic predicates with appropriate predicates, in

(T-S$_{12}$)   "α verb$_1$s β by verb$_2$ing γ" is rewritable as

"$(\exists x)\,(\exists y)\,(\exists z)$ [Verb$_1$s (x, β, α) &

Verb$_2$s (y, γ, α) &

{PART (y, x) or y is a state of affairs} &

{Verb$_1$s (z, β, y) or $x = y$}]"

are all true. We must now attend to method and the noncausal verbs.

1. The transitive verb "kick" is noncausal. It seems plain enough that

(1)   John kicked Jim by moving his foot

is is true if John kicked Jim. Suppose John kicked Jim, so that (1) is true. Then certainly

$(\exists x)$ [Kicks$_3$ $(x, $ Jim, John) & x is an event]

and

$(\exists y)$ [Moves$_3$ $(y, $ John's foot, John) & y is an event]

are true. Moreover, some such y is surely part of some such x, and thus

PART (y, x)

is true. Now one thing we know is that

$(\exists z)$ Kicks$_3$ $(z,$ Jim, $y)$

is *not* true: nothing that is a moving of a foot by John can have kicked Jim, for only what has feet can kick, and nothing that is a moving of a foot by John has feet. But "kick", as we saw, is a transitive motion verb (see pages 220–221); i.e., any event x that is a kicking of Jim by John is a fusion of movings of things by John. Presumably any event x that is a kicking of Jim by John in fact is a moving of John's foot by John. So if an event x is a kicking of Jim by John, there is an event y such that y is a moving of John's foot by John, and such that $x = y$. We can therefore say that if (1) is true, then so also is

(1.1) $(\exists x)(\exists y)(\exists z)$ [Kicks$_3$ $(x,$ Jim, John) &

Moves$_3$ $(y,$ John's foot, John) &

{PART (y, x) or y is a state of affairs} &

{Kicks$_3$ $(z,$ Jim, $y)$ or $x = y$}].

It seems plain enough also that if (1.1) is true, (1) is true. And that we can say that (1) is rewritable as (1.1).

It was precisely out of a desire for a simple generalization that I suggested we insert the identity-clause into

(T-S$_9$)   "α verb$_1$s β by verb$_2$ing γ" is rewritable as

"$(\exists x)(\exists y)(\exists z)$ [Verb$_1$s $(x,$ $\beta,$ $\alpha)$ &

Verb$_2$s $(y,$ $\gamma,$ $\alpha)$ & Verb$_1$s $(z,$ $\beta,$ $y)$]"

of page 205. If we say that the results of making the appropriate replacements in (T-S$_9$) are true, then

(2)   Sirhan caused Kennedy's dying by causing Kennedy's dying

is false. Well, some people would prefer to have it false, so why not? On the other hand, (1) might well be true. We could, of course, distinguish, and say that the rewriting appropriate to sentences of the form

α verb$_1$s β by verb$_2$ing γ.

when their first verb is causal, is different from the rewriting appropriate to such sentences when their first verb is noncausal. But there is no need to say so. If we are prepared to allow that (2) is true—and, as I said, I see no good reason not to do so—then we have a simple generalization available to us. I.e., I suggest we can say that the results of replacing "α", "β", and "γ" by referring expressions, "verb$_1$s" by an appropriate tensed form of *any transitive verb*, "verb$_2$ing" by the gerund of any transitive verb, and the schematic predicates with appropriate predicates, in (T-S$_{12}$) are true.

Of course we shall then have to allow that

Method (III)

(3)   John kicked Jim by kicking Jim

is true if John kicked Jim. But it is hard to see how anyone can object to (3) who is prepared to accept (2).

We shall have to allow also that

(4)   John moved his foot by kicking Jim

is true if John kicked Jim, and this will probably strike some people as more objectionable than (2) and (3). That *may* be because they take (4) to say that John's intention in kicking Jim was to move his foot, which (I suppose) could be true but, at least mostly, is not. But it must be remembered that sentences of the form we are now considering say nothing at all about anyone's intentions. (1), for example, would be true if John kicked Jim in his sleep. Again, it *may* be because they think a by-clause of method should tell us the method—and how can kicking have been the method of the foot-moving when the kicking was identical with the foot-moving? But notice that this would work equally well against (2) and (3), and we are allowing these to be true. Indeed, it would work equally well against (1): how can foot-moving have been the method of the kicking when the foot-moving was identical with the kicking? I am not denying that if asked "How did John move his foot?" it would be (in the most usual sort of case) an odd business to say (4) in reply. More odd, even, than to say

(5)   John moved his foot by moving his foot.

[Compare saying (2) in reply to the question "How did Sirhan cause Kennedy's dying?"] But I can see no good reason to reject (4) as *false*.

More interesting, we shall have to allow also that

(6)   Jack ate a bean by putting it in his mouth

is false—for Jack's putting a bean in his mouth does not itself eat a bean (only what has a mouth can eat), and is not itself identical with Jack's eating of any bean (putting a bean in your mouth is only part of eating it). This seems to me to be entirely right. You do not eat a bean by putting it in your mouth; you eat a bean by putting it in your mouth *and* chewing it *and* swallowing it. Suppose we say that you VERB a thing just in case you put it in your mouth and chew it and swallow it. Then your VERBING of a bean is a fusion of your putting that bean in your mouth and your chewing it and your swallowing it. Then I think we can say, not (6), but

John ate a bean by VERBING it:

certainly his VERBING of that bean does not eat it, but his VERB-ING of that bean is *his* eating of it.

241

More generally, it seems to me that a sentence of the form

α verb$_1$s β by verb$_2$ing γ,

in which the first verb is noncausal, is true only if the result of making the relevant replacements in

there is an entity that is both a verb$_1$ing of β by α and a verb$_2$ing of γ by α

is true. If so, then the identity-clause is needed not just to allow for sentences in which a by-clause of method attaches to "kick" and "eat", but for every sentence in which a by-clause of method attaches to a noncausal verb. And this does seem independently plausible. What is characteristic of causings is that, as we might put it, events themselves do most of the work. If you shoot a man, for example, you may yourself do anything or nothing after the shooting, and if the shooting itself causes your man's death, then *you* cause his death, and perhaps also kill him. You may die in midstream of a killing, and the killing nevertheless occur. By contrast, you have to keep your foot moving until it connects if you are to kick a man, you have to go on chewing and then swallow if you are to eat a bean, and if you die in midstream of a kicking or an eating no kicking or eating occurs. In the case of a causal verb, then, there always is an activity such that your engaging in that activity is your method and is not your act; in the case of a noncausal verb, it is plausible to suppose that any activity such that your engaging in that activity is your method is also such that your engaging in that activity is your act.

"Kick" is a noncausal transitive motion verb. What about noncausal transitive illocutionary-act-verbs? Well,

Bert answered Alfred's question by waving a flag

obviously makes for no trouble. But suppose Alfred says to Bert: "Do you want pudding for dessert? Waggle your thumb if you do, and don't waggle your thumb if you don't." And suppose Bert does not waggle his thumb. Has Bert answered Alfred's question? *I* think not: I think that his not waggling his thumb might be taken to show that he does not want pudding for dessert, but I think also that he has not *answered* the question asked him, and thus that

(7)   Bert answered Alfred's question

is false. If I am right, then so also is

(8)   Bert answered Alfred's question by not waggling his thumb

false. Now the instructions I gave for use of (T-S$_{12}$) tell us that (8) is rewritable as

Method (III)

(8.1) $(\exists x)\,(\exists y)\,(\exists z)$ [Answers$_3$ $(x$, Alfred's question, Bert) &
Not-waggles$_3$ $(y$, Bert's thumb, Bert) &
$\{PART\,(y,\,x)$ or y is a state of affairs$\}$ &
$\{$Answers$_3$ $(z$, Alfred's question, $y)$ or $x = y\}]$.

If I am right in thinking that (7) is false, the first clause of (8.1) is false, and (8.1) is therefore itself false. So my view makes no trouble for the instructions I gave for use of (T-S$_{12}$).

On the other hand, I said earlier that I would not be surprised if there were those who thought that (7) is true in such a case, and they would presumably say that (8) too is true. But their view too makes no trouble for the instructions I gave for use of (T-S$_{12}$). On their view, there was such a thing as Bert's answering of Alfred's question; but that thing presumably just *was* Bert's not waggling his thumb. Now Bert's not waggling his thumb is a state of affairs. So if their view is right, (8.1) is true.

Does it seem a serious objection that opting for (T-S$_{12}$) and the instructions I gave for use of it commits us to the truth of

(9)   The car hit the side of the mountain by hitting the side of the mountain

if the car hit the side of the mountain? A car's hitting the side of a mountain is an event that is not a causing of anything; so how can anything at all be the *method* by which a car hit the side of a mountain? Well, how can kicking have been the method of a kicking? I do not myself regard (9) as any more objectionable than

(3)   John kicked Jim by kicking Jim.

But anyone who does may rule (9) out by restricting the range of permissible replacements in (T-S$_{12}$)—i.e., by requiring that "verb$_1$s" be replaced by an appropriate tensed form, not of just any transitive verb, but of any transitive verb that is not a transitive onset verb—and adopting the further thesis that every sentence of the form

α verb$_1$s β by verb$_2$ing γ,

in which the first verb is a transitive onset verb, is false.

What of the fact that opting for (T-S$_{12}$) and the instructions I gave for use of it commits us to the truth of

(10)   Alfred watched the moving finger by watching the moving finger

if Alfred watched the moving finger? I do not myself regard (10) as any more objectionable than (3). But anyone who does may rule (10) out in a manner analogous to that indicated in the preceding paragraph.

Acts and Other Events

But here a certain caution is called for. Some philosophers say that every mental event is identical with a physical event; and I said that I would leave it open whether or not every mental event (which is not an onset of a state of affairs) is identical, not merely with a physical event, but with a physical event that is a fusion of causings of things. If this should turn out to be right, then we shall want to allow for the possibility that

Alfred watched the moving finger by causing A

(where "A" is the name of the fusion of some events in Alfred's head) is true. And if we do want to leave this open as a possibility, we should not, now, declare that every sentence of the form

α verb$_1$s β by verb$_2$ing γ,

in which the first verb is a transitive mental verb, is false—or even that every sentence of the form

α watched β by verb$_2$ing γ

is false.

What about transitive verbs that do not satisfy

(T-S$_{13}$)   It is possible that there is an event that is a verbing?

We have no trouble with, as it might be,

John believed what Jim said by waggling his thumb:

a thumb-waggling is an event, a believing is not an event, so a thumb-waggling is no part of a believing, and use of (T-S$_{12}$) yields the result that this sentence is false, which is just as it should be. Unfortunately, use of (T-S$_{12}$) yields that

(11)   John believed what Jim said by believing what Jim said

is true if John believed what Jim said. I do not myself regard (11) as any more objectionable than (3). But anyone who does may rule (11) out in a manner analogous to that indicated in connection with (9). Thus it could be said that replacements for "verb$_1$s" in (T-S$_{12}$) are restricted to transitive verbs that satisfy (T-S$_{13}$) and the further thesis adopted that every sentence of the form

α verb$_1$s β by verb$_2$ing γ,

in which the first verb fails to satisfy (T-S$_{13}$) is false. And here there would be no need for caution on the kind of ground indicated above. Perhaps a man's watching a moving finger is identical with his causing of something in his head; a man's believing something, since it is not an event, is not his causing of anything at all.

Incomplete verbs are not transitive; and (T-S$_{12}$) tells us nothing about what is said by such sentences as "John put the book on the

Method (III)

table by moving his hand". But I should imagine it would be easy enough to construct a thesis-schema for such sentences analogous to (T-S$_{12}$).

2. By-clauses of method attach to intransitive verbs too. It is possible, for example, that

(1)   John apologized by sending that box of chocolates

is true. I suggest we say that the results of replacing "α" and "β" by referring expressions, "verb$_1$s" by an appropriate tensed form of *any intransitive verb*, "verb$_2$ing" by the gerund of any transitive verb, and the schematic predicates with appropriate predicates, in

(T-S$_{12}$') "α verb$_1$s by verb$_2$ing β" is rewritable as

"$(\exists x)\,(\exists y)\,(\exists z)$ [Verb$_1$s (x, α) &

Verb$_2$s (y, β, α) &

{PART (y, x) or y is a state of affairs} &

{Verb$_1$s (z, y) or $x = y$}]"

are all true. What this tells us is that (1) is rewritable as

(1.1) $(\exists x)\,(\exists y)\,(\exists z)$ [Apologizes$_2$ $(x, $ John) &

Sends$_3$ $(y, $ that box of chocolates, John) &

{PART (y, x) or y is a state of affairs} &

{Apologizes$_2$ (z, y) or $x = y$}],

and since (as I should imagine) (1) is true if and only if John's apologizing *was* his sending that box of chocolates, it does seem plausible to take it that (1) is true if and only if (1.1) is.

It is easy to construct a further schema (T-S$_{12}$'') to deal with such sentences as

John apologized by smiling,

and I therefore do not take space to lay it out.

3. On page 235, I said I hazard a guess that no verb that is neither transitive nor intransitive satisifies

(T-S$_{13}$)   It is possible that there is an event that is a verbing.

I therefore suggest that we declare that every sentence of the form

α verb$_1$s (β) by verb$_2$ing (γ),

in which the first verb is neither transitive nor intransitive, is false. This yields that

John's house cost $50,000 by waving a flag,

for example, is false—hardly ground for complaint.

4. Are there any basic acts? I indicated in Chapter XI that the most familiar explications of the notion 'basic act' are unacceptable, and why (see in particular page 168). Nevertheless one does have a rough idea what its friends have in mind; and while I think there is not going to be any such thing as finding acceptable necessary and sufficient conditions for the use of the term "basic act", it is perhaps worth stopping for a moment to bring out that it is possible—compatibly with what has been said in this and the preceding chapters—to lay out a thesis-schema from which it is easy to construct (not entirely uninteresting) sufficient conditions for an event's *not* being a basic act.

Let us begin with this. Sirhan killed Kennedy by shooting him, and Sirhan's killing of Kennedy is a paradigm of an act that is not a basic act. Why? What makes it a paradigm? Consider the sentence

(1)   Sirhan killed Kennedy by shooting him.

(T-S$_{12}$) tells us that (1) is rewritable as

(1.1) $(\exists x) (\exists y) (\exists z)$ [Kills$_3$ $(x,$ Kennedy, Sirhan) &
        Shoots$_3$ $(y,$ Kennedy, Sirhan) &
        {PART (y, x) or y is a state of affairs} &
        {Kills$_3$ $(z,$ Kennedy, $y)$ or $x = y$}].

Now (1.1) is true. Notice, however, that (1.1) is not true in that an event that was a shooting of Kennedy by Sirhan was identical with an event that was a killing of Kennedy by Sirhan: no shooting of Kennedy by Sirhan was identical with any killing of Kennedy by Sirhan. (1.1) is true in that an event that was a shooting of Kennedy killed Kennedy. I suggest it is *that* fact that makes Sirhan's killing of Kennedy a paradigm of an act that is not a basic act.

Consider, now, another case:

suppose I caused my arm to move. How? Well, suppose I caused my muscles to tense. How did I do that? If I caused them to tense in the ordinary way—i.e., in the way in which one does this when one moves one's arm in the ordinary way—then there does not *seem* to be any answer to the question how I caused them to tense. There does not in such a case seem to be anything I did, by doing which I caused them to tense.

(See pages 166 and 173 above.) Well, we have (I hope) agreed that even in such a case as is indicated in the extract, it would be true all the same to say

(2)   I caused my muscles' tensing by causing my muscles' tensing.

Method (III)

Let us abbreviate and call the event that took place then, which was my muscles' tensing, "M". Then we may rewrite (2) as

I caused M by causing M.

(T-S$_{12}$) tells us that we may rewrite this as follows:

(2.1) $(\exists x)(\exists y)(\exists z)$ [Causes$_3$ (x, M, me) &
Causes$_3$ (y, M, me) &
{$PART$ (y, x) or y is a state of affairs} &
{Causes$_3$ (z, M, y) or $x = y$}].

Now since there was an event x on that occasion that was a causing of M by me, (2.1) is true. But (2.1) is not true in that there was an event y that was a causing of M by me, which was part of x, and which was such that y itself caused M: if y is a causing of M, it contains M, and cannot therefore have caused M. (2.1) is true in that there was an event y that was a causing of M by me, which was identical with x. I suggest that, the case being what it was, the result of replacing the gerund of a verb-phrase for "verbing" in

I caused M by verbing

is true only if the result of replacing its gerund for "verbing" in

My causing of M *was* my verbing

is also true. I suggest, in any case, that it is only if one supposes that this is so that one supposes my causing of M was a basic act.

It seems a plausible idea, then, that the results of making appropriate replacements in

If x is a verb$_1$ing of β by α, and there are a y and a z such that y is a verb$_2$ing by α, and $PART$ (y, x), and z is a verb$_1$ing of β by y, then x is *not* a basic act

are true. Thus, for example, that the following are true:

If x is a causing of Kennedy's dying by Sirhan, and there are a y and a z such that y is a causing of Kennedy's dying by Sirhan, and $PART$ (y, x), and z is a causing of Kennedy's dying by y, then x is *not* a basic act;

If x is a killing of Kennedy by Sirhan, and there are a y and a z such that y is a shooting of Kennedy by Sirhan, and $PART$ (y, x), and z is a killing of Kennedy by y, then x is *not* a basic act;

If x is a causing of M by me, and there are a y and a z such that y is a causing of M by me, and $PART$ (y, x), and z is a causing of M by y, then x is *not* a basic act.

Sirhan's killing of Kennedy is a causing of Kennedy's dying by Sirhan, but there are no y and z related to it as prescribed in the antecedent of the first conditional, for nothing can both be a causing of Kennedy's dying and cause Kennedy's dying; so the first conditional leaves it open that Sirhan's killing of Kennedy may be a basic act. However, Sirhan's killing of Kennedy is a killing of Kennedy by Sirhan, and there are events y and z related to it as prescribed in the antecedent of the second conditional; so we can conclude that Sirhan's killing of Kennedy is *not* a basic act. My causing of M is a causing of M by me, but there are no y and z related to it as prescribed in the antecedent of the third conditional, for nothing can both be a causing of M and cause M; so the third conditional leaves it open that my causing of M may be a basic act. We do not in this way get the result that my causing of M *is* a basic act; but we at least do not in this way get the result that it is not one.

It should be stressed that this is the best that can be done along these lines. That is, what we have is a battery of sufficient conditions for not being a basic act; we cannot turn what we have into a battery of necessary and sufficient conditions for being a basic act. For we cannot, for example, say that an event x is a basic act if and only if there are verbs and verb-phrases such that the results of making the relevant replacements of them in such and such a schema are true—for presumably there might well have been basic acts and no verbs or verb-phrases at all.

XVIII

Agency: Causality (II)

At the beginning of Chapter III, I said that if acts are to be singled out from all other events by

(D$_{2a}$)   Act (y) just in case y is an event and there is an x such that Agent (x, y),

we must do better at saying what this 'agent-relation' is than we had done in Chapter II.

Which events is a person agent of? Some writers take the view that intentionality is the mark of action; on their view, a man who kills while in an epileptic fit, or while asleep, is *not* agent of the event that is his killing of his victim, and that event is *not* an act, since such a man does nothing intentionally. Others suppose that a man who kills while in an epileptic fit, or while asleep, *is* agent of the event that is his killing of his victim, and that event *is* an act. It seems to me that neither is right and neither is wrong, and that there simply are two quite distinct notions 'agency,' and therefore two quite distinct notions 'act,' at work here. (See Chapter III.) Intentionality is, of course, of much interest, and we shall have a look at it in the following chapter. For the time being, however, it is the second notion 'agency' that interests us. The intuition it issues from seems to be right. It really does seem as if a man's killing of a man—whether in an epileptic fit, or while asleep, on the one hand, *or* fully intentionally, on the other hand—is a very different sort of event from a man's falling asleep and

Acts and Other Events

from the fall of a book or a tree. There really does seem to be *some* sense in which a man who kills another is plausibly said to be agent of an event, whereas a man who merely falls asleep is not, and *some* sense in which a killing is plausibly said to be an act, and a falling asleep is not. But what are those senses?

At the end of Chapter III, I suggested that we shall want to appeal to causality in order to make them out, and that the best way to begin is with this:

(D_{3i})   Agent (x, y) just in case y is a causing of something by x.

It is plain now that (D_{3i}) is very different from

(D_{3d})   Agent (x, y) just in case x causes y.

Sirhan's killing of Kennedy, for example, is a causing of something by Sirhan (in fact, it is a causing of Kennedy's death by Sirhan); but its being so is compatible with Sirhan's not having caused Sirhan's killing of Kennedy. Again, Sirhan's shooting of Kennedy caused Kennedy's death; but Kennedy's death is not a causing of something by Sirhan's shooting of Kennedy—as we know, whatever is a causing of something by Sirhan's shooting of Kennedy itself contains Sirhan's shooting of Kennedy, and Kennedy's death plainly does not contain it.

It seems to me that a great many cases that should be captured are captured by (D_{3i}). Thus Sirhan's killing of Kennedy is a causing of something by Sirhan, and it seems right that Sirhan turn out to be agent of it. Suppose Alfred killed Bill while in an epileptic fit, or while asleep; still, Alfred did kill Bill, so there was an event that was Alfred's killing of Bill, and that event was a causing of something by Alfred, so Alfred turns out to be agent of it by (D_{3i}), which is as it should be. Take any causal verb you choose. If the result of replacing "x" by a man's name, "verbing" by the gerund of the causal verb, and "y" by some referring expression in

> x's verbing of y

refers to an event, then the event it refers to is a causing of something by the man whose name replaces "x," and he turns out to be agent of it by (D_{3i}), which seems to be as it should be.

What if "verbing" is replaced by the gerund of some *non*causal verb? Consider again the transitive motion verbs. I suggested we say that a verb is a transitive motion verb just in case it is transitive and satisfies both

($T\text{-}S_{13}$)   It is possible that there is an event that is a verbing

and

Agency: Causality (II)

$(T-S_{14})$ If an event x is a verbing of y by z, then x is a fusion of movings of things by z.

Since the transitive verb "move" is a causal verb, transitive motion verbs also satisfy

$(T-S_{15})$ If an event x is a verbing of y by z, then x is a fusion of causings of things by z.

Some noncausal verbs are transitive motion verbs. Take the verb "eat," for example: "eat" is noncausal ("eat" does not accept events as subjects), yet it is a transitive motion verb. Now I should imagine that if

> Charles's eating of his apple

refers to an event, then Charles should turn out to be agent of it. Does (D_{3i}) allow him to do so? Well, is the event a causing of something by Charles? It certainly is a fusion of causings of things by Charles, and I should imagine that every event that is a fusion F of causings of things is itself a causing of something (a causing of the fusion G of the things such that each causing in the fusion F is a causing of one or more of them). But there is no need to dwell on the matter. Since every event that is a causing of something is itself a fusion of causings of things, we may simply replace (D_{3i}) with

(D_{3j}) Agent (x, y) just in case y is a fusion of causings of things by x.

If we do so, it turns out not merely that Sirhan is agent of his killing of Kennedy, not merely that Alfred is agent of his killing of Bill, but also that Charles is agent of his eating of his apple.

It turns out, moreover, that if

> John's running

refers to an event, then John is agent of it. More precisely, if the word "running" in it is the gerund of the intransitive motion verb "run," then the event is a fusion of movings of things by John, and hence a fusion of causings of things by John, and hence, by (D_{3j}), an event which John is agent of. By contrast, Jim's sleeping (if there is such an event) is not an event which Jim is agent of, for it is not a fusion of causings of things by Jim. Jack's falling asleep (if there is such an event) is not an event which Jack is agent of, for it is not a fusion of causings of things by Jack. And a certain ice cube's melting (if it melts) is not an event which the ice cube is agent of, for it is not a fusion of causings of things by the ice cube. These results are surely exactly as they should be.

251

Acts and Other Events

What about a man's watching a moving finger? What about a man's meditating? These are mental events, and I left it open whether or not they are identical with any physical events. If they are, then I should imagine that we really would wish to have the man himself as agent of the events just in case those events are causings of things by him. If they are not physical events, then it is not clear what they are; nevertheless I hazard a guess that we should all the same hold that the man himself is agent of the events just in case those events are causings of things by him.

I shall not canvass the other noncausal verbs. It seems to *me* that—worries about mental events apart—this second notion 'agency' with which we are here concerned really is captured by (D_{3j}). And so also, then, the notion 'act' that (D_{2a}) defines in terms of it.

But I italicized the word "me" for a reason. For we should notice now that (D_{3j}) allows inanimate objects to be agents of events, and (D_{2a}) then allows the events which they are agents of to be acts. Consider, for example, Sirhan's shooting of Kennedy. That event killed Kennedy; so there was an event that was a killing of Kennedy by it. Every killing is a causing. Therefore the event that was a killing of Kennedy by Sirhan's shooting of Kennedy is a fusion of causings of things, and therefore, by (D_{3j}), Sirhan's shooting of Kennedy is agent of it, and therefore, by (D_{2a}), it is an act. But *should* Sirhan's shooting of Kennedy be agent of anything? *Should* its killing of Kennedy be an act?

I am inclined to think there is no good reason to rule that inanimate objects cannot be agents of events, and those events acts. Obviously, no inanimate object thinks about what it is doing or ever does anything intentionally. But an inanimate object's doing of something may be very like an animate being's doing of something.

Indeed, an inanimate object's doing of something may be identical with an animate being's doing of something—identical even with a doing of something by an animate being which is on any view an act. Consider the event that was a killing of Kennedy by Sirhan's shooting of Kennedy. That event is identical with Sirhan's killing of Kennedy (see page 202). And Sirhan's killing of Kennedy is on any view an act.

It could, of course, be insisted that (D_{3j}) is wrong, and that what one wants is, instead,

(D_{3k}) Agent (x, y) just in case y is a fusion of causings of things by x and x is an animate being.

Then it would be Sirhan, and only Sirhan, who is agent of the event that is both Sirhan's killing of Kennedy and the shooting's killing of Kennedy.

And perhaps we should revise

(D_{2a})   Act (y) just in case y is an event and there is an x such that Agent (x, y)

also? After all, if we accept (D_{3k}), then the event that is both Sirhan's and the shooting's killing of Kennedy does have an agent, viz., Sirhan; and if we also accept (D_{2a}), then that event is an act—i.e., even if the shooting is not agent of its killing of Kennedy, still its killing of Kennedy is an act. So perhaps we should say, not merely that (D_{3j}) is wrong, but also that (D_{2a}) is wrong. Perhaps, that is, we should take the predicate "x is an act" to be intensional and say that it does not follow from the fact that Sirhan's killing of Kennedy is an act, and is identical with the shooting's killing of Kennedy, that the shooting's killing of Kennedy is an act.

But I see nothing to be gained by these two moves. If we want to keep plainly before our minds the fact that Sirhan is animate, and the shooting is not, we can do this without making animatedness a requirement for agency. We need merely announce to ourselves from time to time that Sirhan is an *animate* agent of, and the shooting only an *inanimate* agent of, the event that is both Sirhan's, and the shooting's, killing of Kennedy.

I suspect that anyone who feels a desire to make these two moves simply does not find the notion 'agency' I have been attending to of interest—what *he* wants is an account of the other notion 'agency', the one according to which an event does not have an agent, and is not an act, unless it involves intentionality. Which of the two notions 'agency' is of greater interest, I cannot say, and do not now really care.[1] But it is just worth pointing out that if you are interested in the other notion 'agency,' it will not pay you to tinker with (D_{3j}). (D_{3k}), for example, is no more what you want than (D_{3j}) is: for a man (who is

---

[1] However, I cannot forbear drawing attention to the fact that it is by no means obvious that the notion 'agency' I have not dealt with is any more important for ethics than is the notion 'agency' I have dealt with. No doubt a great many good acts and a great many evil acts are intentional, and a moral philosopher does need to know something about what intentionality is. But in the first place, what we are responsible for is by no means restricted to what we bring about in a way that involves intentionality. And in the second place, it is a plausible hypothesis that causings will turn out to be central, and intentionality at most peripheral, to a theory of rights—i.e., to a theory about what we have a right to do and why we have a right to do it.

therefore animate) may kill a man while in an epileptic fit, or while asleep, and the event that is his killing of his victim therefore involve no intentionality, yet according to (D_{3k}) he is agent of that event.

So I suggest that those who are interested only in the other notion 'agency' leave (D_{3j}) and (D_{2a}) alone. The rest of us are then free to adopt them as accounts of one of the pairs of notions 'agency' and 'act,' and to accept as itself of interest that an inanimate being may be agent of an event in the very same sense of the word as that in which a person may be agent of an event.

XIX

Intentionality

1. I said in the preceding chapter that if you are interested in the other notion 'agency'—i.e., that notion 'agency' according to which a person is not agent of an event unless that event involves intentionality—it will not pay you to tinker with

(D_{3j})   Agent (x, y) just in case y is a fusion of causings of things by x.

Quite to the contrary: (D_{3j}) itself, as it stands, turns out to be a useful piece of equipment for one who wants to find an account of intentionality.

What I have in mind is this: it is a very plausible idea that the results of replacing "α" (and "β") by referring expressions, and "verbed" by an appropriate tensed form of a verb, in

α verbed (β) intentionally

are true only if the results of making the appropriate replacements in

Agent (α, α's verbing (of β))

are true. You can kill, melt, sink, or cause a thing intentionally, and I should think the same is true for any causal verb. You can eat a thing or run intentionally, and I should think the same is true for any transitive or intransitive motion verb. But you cannot love someone or sleep or fall downstairs intentionally—though of course you can intentionally cause yourself to love someone or to sleep or to fall downstairs. Why not? It seems right to say that it is because neither your loving someone nor your sleeping nor your falling downstairs is a fusion of causings of things. It seems right to say that an intentional act is always a fusion of causings.[1]

But the next step is very much harder, for there are many events which a person is agent of in the sense of (D_{3j}) that are nevertheless not intentional acts of his. For example, a man may be asleep when he kills another; he is agent of the event that is his killing of his victim, yet it would be false to say that he killed his victim intentionally.

What is missing if you kill while asleep? Presumably desire and belief. Or better, hope, since "desire" and "belief" really are rather strong. It suggests itself, then, as a first approximation, that

(1)   Alfred killed Bert intentionally,

for example, is rewritable as

(1.1) $(\exists w)$ [Kills$_3$ $(w$, Bert, Alfred) & Agent (Alfred, w) &
           Throughout the time IN which w occurs
           {Alfred hopes that Kills$_3$ $(w$, Bert, Alfred)}].

Every killing is a causing of a death, and *a fortiori* a fusion of causings of things, so the 'agent-clause' in (1.1) could have been omitted; I include it only for the sake of the generalization to come.

I am inclined to think that the truth of (1.1) really is sufficient for the truth of (1). If there is an event which you are agent of, and which is a killing of a man by you, then it seems to me that if also you hope throughout the occurrence of that event that it is a killing of that man by you, then you do kill that man intentionally.

On the other hand, it is probably plain enough that the truth of (1.1) is not necessary for the truth of (1). It is, as we know, possible for Alfred to have killed Bert even though Alfred died before Bert died. We may suppose, for example, that Alfred shot Bert, thereby wounding him fatally, and that although Bert lingered for a while before dying, Alfred was himself straightway killed by Bert's bodyguards. Now I should imagine that the fact that Alfred died before Bert no more makes it false to say he killed Bert intentionally than it makes it false to

---

[1] We are more relaxed about these matters than I suggest in the text above. If your friend, who won the game, says "I won the game intentionally", we do not say "False!" or "Asterisk!" Yet his winning the game was not a fusion of causings of things by him. But I think that a strict speaker does not say such things. What should be said about your friend is, not that he won intentionally, but that he intentionally brought about that he won. (Compare "I intentionally arrived at 3 P.M." and "I intentionally brought about that I arrived at 3 P.M.")

say he killed Bert. But then the truth of (1) is compatible with the falsity of (1.1)—for if Alfred dies before the killing ends, he plainly does not go on having hopes about it throughout the time IN which it occurs.

This case itself suggests what is wanted. It suggests we should say that if there is an event which Alfred is agent of—such as a shooting of Bert by Alfred—and if also Alfred hopes throughout the time of *its* occurrence that it will be *part of* a killing of Bert by him, and if also what Alfred hopes will come true does come true, then, whether or not Alfred dies before Bert, Alfred kills Bert intentionally. I.e., the case suggests we should say that the truth of

(1.2) $(\exists w)\,(\exists x)$ [Kills$_3$ $(w,$ Bert, Alfred) & Agent (Alfred, w) &
            Agent (Alfred, x) & PART (x, w) &
            Throughout the time IN which x occurs
            {Alfred hopes that $(\exists z)$ (Kills$_3$ $(z,$ Bert, Alfred) & PART $(x,$
            $z))$}]

is sufficient for the truth of (1).

It will be noted that (1.2) leaves much room for 'mistake' on Alfred's part; but I think it should. Suppose that Alfred shot Bert, hoping throughout about his shooting of Bert that it would be part of a killing of Bert by him; and suppose that what he hoped would come true did come true. (1.2), then, is true. But suppose also that Alfred killed Bert in a manner in which Alfred had not expected to. Suppose, for example, that instead of causing hemorrhage (which Alfred expected), the shooting so startled Bert that it caused Bert to have a fatal heart attack (which Alfred did not expect). Is (1) true in this case? I am inclined to think we should allow that it is.

On any view, a killer surely does not have to be right about *every* step in the process by which he kills in order for it to be true to say he killed his victim intentionally. Suppose that Alfred is rather confused about physiology. He thinks hemorrhage kills in the following way: when you lose too much blood, your chest muscles contract so that you cannot breathe any more. Suppose, now, that Alfred shot Bert in a place such that he thinks that shooting a man there causes hemorrhage, and did so hoping throughout about his shooting of Bert that it would be part of a killing of Bert by him. And suppose that what he hoped would come true did come true. The fact that Alfred was mistaken as to how hemorrhage causes death is no ground at all for supposing that he did not kill Bert intentionally.

Acts and Other Events

Of course, in some cases there is too much mistake. As I said, I take it that Alfred did kill Bert intentionally in both of the two cases just mentioned. Consider, by contrast, a third case. Alfred shot Bert, hoping throughout about his shooting of Bert that it would be part of a killing of Bert by him. But suppose that Bert did not die of the wound: suppose that Alfred left Bert for dead, but that Bert was in fact killed by an unexpected stroke of lightning.[2] In this case, I think, there is too much mistake: Alfred did not kill Bert intentionally. But then this is a case in which Alfred did not kill Bert, and there was therefore no event that was a killing of Bert by Alfred, and (1.2) is therefore false.

Consider a fourth case. Alfred shot Bert, hoping throughout about his shooting of Bert that it would be part of a killing of Bert by him. But suppose that his shooting of Bert itself did not proceed as he had expected it to. Suppose, for example, that (unbeknownst to Alfred) there was a sheet of glass between Alfred and Bert, and that the bullet was deflected as it went through. Suppose, further, that there was a rock in the path along which the bullet was deflected, and that the rock deflected the bullet toward a brick wall, which deflected the bullet into Bert's back, thereby killing Bert. It is perhaps not obvious that (1.2) is true in this case. There are a w and an x such that

$Kills_3$ (w, Bert, Alfred) & Agent (Alfred, w) &

Agent (Alfred, x) & $PART$ (x, w),

since Alfred surely killed Bert, and his shooting of Bert was part of his killing of Bert. But is there an x that meets that condition and *also* meets the following condition:

Throughout the time IN which x occurs

{Alfred hopes that ($\exists z$) ($Kills_3$ (z, Bert, Alfred) & $PART$ (x, z))})?

I should think yes. Admittedly, Alfred was mistaken as to how his shooting of Bert proceeded: he thought it took less time than it in fact did, and he thought his bullet went straight through though it in fact did not. But you certainly can have hopes about a thing whose nature you are mistaken about. (You might have hopes about a person whose nature you are mistaken about.) So it seems acceptable to suppose that Alfred did throughout hope about the very event that was a shooting of Bert by him, that *it* would be part of a killing of Bert by him.

[2] Adapted from a case of Roderick M. Chisholm's. See his "Freedom and Action," in *Freedom and Determinism*, ed. Keith Lehrer (New York: Random House, 1966).

So (1.2) is true in this case. But is (1) true in it? I think we should allow that Alfred did kill Bert intentionally in this case. As I said, a killer surely does not have to be right about *every* step in the process by which he kills in order for it to be true to say he killed his victim intentionally. In particular, you can be mistaken about the internal mechanism of your gun and still have killed a man intentionally with it. And it seems to me, similarly, that you can be mistaken about the path your bullet takes and still have killed a man intentionally with it.

I suggest, then, that we accept the truth of (1.2) as really sufficient for the truth of (1).

Perhaps we can take the truth of (1.2) to be also necessary for the truth of (1)? I said earlier that the truth of

(1.1) $(\exists w)$ [Kills$_3$ (w, Bert, Alfred) & Agent (Alfred, w) &
         Throughout the time IN which w occurs
         {Alfred hopes that Kills$_3$ (w, Bert, Alfred)}]

is sufficient for the truth of (1). It seems to me a plausible idea that if Alfred hopes about an event w that w is a killing of Bert by him, then Alfred hopes that there is a killing of Bert by him and that w is identical with, and therefore part of, it. If so, then if (1.1) is true, so is (1.2). So taking the truth of (1.1) to be sufficient for the truth of (1) would be no barrier to taking the truth of (1.2) to be both necessary and sufficient for the truth of (1).

But I think we really should opt for a considerably weaker rewriting of (1). Suppose, for example, that Alfred wants to kill Bert and knows that Bert is in Omaha, but does not know precisely where. Alfred thinks: "I'll destroy the whole city!" After the bomb has been dropped, and the city leveled, Alfred says: "You see, I hoped that destroying the city would include destroying Bert." We can, I think, say that Alfred hoped about his dropping of the bomb that it would be part of a killing of Bert by him, and thus that (1.2) really is true in this case. But there is no need to argue the matter.

(1.3) $(\exists w)$ $(\exists x)$ [Kills$_3$ (w, Bert, Alfred) & Agent (Alfred, w) &
         Agent (Alfred, x) & PART (w, x) &
         Throughout the time IN which x occurs
         {Alfred hopes that $(\exists z)$ (Kills$_3$ (z, Bert, Alfred) & PART (z,
         x))}]

is plainly true in this case, and I see no reason why we should not take the truth of (1.3) also to be sufficient for the truth of (1).

And shouldn't we make room for people with queer beliefs about the part-whole relationships among events? Suppose that Alfred thinks that when you kill a man by shooting him your killing of him does not contain, but is instead contained by, your shooting of him. Suppose, then, that Alfred shoots Bert, and thereby kills him. But suppose that, in light of his queer belief, what he hoped about his shooting of Bert was that a killing of Bert by him would be part of it. What he hoped would come true did not come true; but it seems to me that we should allow all the same that he did kill Bert intentionally.

It is plausible, then, that we should take (1) to be rewritable, not as (1.2), not as the disjunction of (1.2) and (1.3), but rather as

(1.4)　　$(\exists w)\,(\exists x)$ [Kills$_3$ $(w,$ Bert, Alfred$)$ & Agent (Alfred, w) & Agent (Alfred, x) & {PART $(x,\,w)$ or PART $(w,\,x)$} & Throughout the time IN which x occurs {Alfred hopes that $(\exists z)$ (Kills$_3$ $(z,$ Bert, Alfred$)$ & PART $(x,\,z)$) or Alfred hopes that $(\exists z)$ (Kills$_3$ $(z,$ Bert, Alfred$)$ & PART $(z,\,x)$)}].

Alas, one further weakening is required. Suppose that Alfred is suffering from amnesia and does not now know that he is Alfred. If Alfred does not now know that he is Alfred, we may suppose that he does not now hope about any event at all that it is part of, or contains, a killing of Bert *by Alfred*. Yet he might nevertheless be in process of killing Bert, and intentionally at that. So I suggest we instead take (1) to be rewritable as

(1.5)　　$(\exists w)\,(\exists x)$ [Kills$_3$ $(w,$ Bert, Alfred$)$ & Agent (Alfred, w) & Agent (Alfred, x) & {PART $(x,\,w)$ or PART $(w,\,x)$} & $(\exists y)$ ($y =$ Alfred & Throughout the time IN which x occurs {y hopes that $(\exists z)$ (Kills$_3$ $(z,$ Bert, $y)$ & PART $(x,\,z)$) or y hopes that $(\exists z)$ (Kills$_3$ $(z,$ Bert, $y)$ & PART $(z,\,x)$)})].

One thing to be stressed about (1.5) is that I *may* not mean by "hopes" what you mean by it. What I have in mind is this. I take it that you might shoot a man, *knowing* throughout about your shooting of him that it is part of a killing of him by you. And I take it that your knowing this is perfectly compatible with its being the case that you kill your man intentionally. Could it be said of you that you *hope* throughout about your shooting of him that it is part of a killing of him by you? "Hope" suggests uncertainty. But I am inclined to think that this is a mere suggestion (as opposed to an entailment). In any case, *I* am throughout so using "hopes" as to be compatible with "knows".

If I am right in thinking that (1) is rewritable as (1.5), then the rest is easy enough.

What holds of "kill" in this respect surely also holds of "melt", "sink", "cause", and so on, whatever causal verb you choose. Consider a case of the kind pointed to on page 210. Jones knows how to tie his shoelaces. We ask him to show us the hand movements he makes in tying his shoelaces. Jones finds he cannot do this—until he unties his laces, and then ties them for us. I said that it seems to me that

> Jones moved his hands by tying his shoelaces

is false in that case. Nevertheless

> Jones moved his hands intentionally

is surely true. And what stands to it as (1.5) stands to (1) is also true. For there is an event x which Jones is agent of, and which Jones's moving of his hands was part of—viz., his tying of his shoelaces—such that throughout its occurence, he hoped there would be a moving of his hands which was part of it.

It is worth stressing that cases of omission make for no trouble in connection with causal verbs. In Chapter XV, I caused a baby's death (indeed, I killed the baby) by not feeding it. I did not write it into the story that I caused the baby's death intentionally. All I said was that, having promised the neighbors I would feed their baby, I then packed my bags and left for the Cape for the week, thinking I never did much like that baby. Suppose I had thought, not merely that I did not much like the baby, but that I positively disliked it; suppose in fact that I went to the Cape positively hoping that the baby would starve to death. Then

(2)   I caused the baby's death intentionally

is certainly true. Consider, now, what stands to (2) as (1.5) stands to (1):

(2.5) $(\exists w)(\exists x)$ [Causes$_3$ (w, the baby's death, me) & Agent (I, w) &

Agent (I, x) & {PART (x, w) or PART (w, x)} &

$(\exists y)$ (y = me & Throughout the time IN which x occurs

{y hopes that $(\exists z)$ (Causes$_3$ (z, the baby's death, y) & PART (x, z)) or

y hopes that $(\exists z)$ (Causes$_3$ (z, the baby's death, y) & PART (z, x))})].

Since I did cause the baby's death, there was a w that was a causing of the baby's death by me, and I was therefore agent of w. Since I hoped the baby would starve to death, and it did, there was an event x—a causing of certain physiological occurrences in the baby—that I hoped would be part of a causing of the baby's death by me, and that was. Since I was the one who was supposed to feed the baby, I was agent of x. Therefore (2.5) is true, just as it should be.

What about the noncausal verbs? What stands to

Charles kicked David intentionally

as (1.5) stands to (1) is surely true if and only if Charles kicked David intentionally. Indeed, it seems to *me* that we can say that the results of replacing "α" and "β" by referring expressions, "verbs" by an appropriate tensed form of *any transitive verb*, and the schematic predicates with appropriate predicates, in

(T-S$_{18}$)   "α verbs β intentionally" is rewritable as
"$(\exists w)$ $(\exists x)$ [Verbs (w, β, α) & Agent (α, w) &
Agent (α, x) & {PART (x, w) or PART (w, x)} &
$(\exists y)$ $(y = \alpha$ & Throughout the time IN which x occurs
{y hopes that $(\exists z)$ (Verbs (z, β, y) & PART (x, z)) or
y hopes that $(\exists z)$ (Verbs (z, β, y) & PART (z, x))})]"

are all true. Consider, for example, the transitive verb "love". I said at the outset that you cannot love someone intentionally, and this because your loving someone is not a fusion of causings of things. Well, (T-S$_{18}$) tells us we may rewrite

(3)   John loves Mary intentionally

as

(3.5) $(\exists w)$ $(\exists x)$ [Loves$_3$ $(w,$ Mary, John) & Agent (John, w)
& . . .],

which of course is false.

But I italicized the word "me" for a reason. Consider, again, Bert, who was asked by Alfred if he wants pudding for dessert and told to waggle his thumb if he does and to not waggle his thumb if he does not. Suppose Bert does not waggle his thumb. On my view, Bert does not answer Alfred's question, and so certainly does not answer it intentionally: i.e.,

(4)   Bert answered Alfred's question intentionally

is false. But then on my view, so also is

(4.5) $(\exists w)$ $(\exists x)$ [Answers$_3$ $(w,$ Alfred's question, Bert) & . . .]

false, so all is well. But as I said, others may take the view that Bert did answer Alfred's question, and indeed that (4) may well be true. But if Bert did answer Alfred's question, his doing so *was* his not waggling his thumb; and since Bert's not waggling his thumb is no event, it is not a causing of anything, and

Intentionality

(4.5) $(\exists w)\,(\exists x)$ [Answers$_3$ $(w$, Alfred's question, Bert$)$ & Agent
(Bert, w) & . . .]

is therefore still false.

More generally, on my view, cases of omission make no more trouble for noncausal verbs than they do for causal verbs. On their view, cases of omission do make trouble for some noncausal verbs at any rate. Anyone who adopts their view, then, will have to constrain the range of permissible replacements in thesis-schema (T-S$_{18}$): he must replace "any transitive verb" by something more complicated—perhaps "any causal verb, and any noncausal transitive verb such that the results of making the appropriate replacements in

α verbed β by refraining from doing something

cannot be true". And to cover the exceptions, he must adopt a further thesis—a highly complicated thesis, I suspect, for it will have to allow that (4) may be true in cases in which Bert's answering is an event (as, e.g., if he answers by uttering some words) as well as in cases in which Bert's answering is not an event. I shall from here on simply ignore the difficulty that faces anyone who disagrees with me on this matter; in fact I shall from here on pretend that no one does.

If I am right about (T-S$_{18}$), it is easy enough to construct a schema for intransitive verbs, and I shall not take space to do so.

Three final points. First, I should stress that I do not pretend that the logic of sentences of the form

$(\exists x)\,(\exists y)\; y$ hopes that $...x...$

is at all clear. "Alfred hopes that ......" is an intensional context. But it should be no surprise that an account of intentionality makes use of intensional expressions: intentionality, after all, *is* intensional. You may kill Bert intentionally and not kill the mayor intentionally, even though Bert is the mayor, for you may not know that Bert is the mayor.[3] We could hardly wish for an account of intentionality that does not preserve this feature. And in fact, (T-S$_{18}$) does preserve intensionality just where it is wanted. "Bert", for example, appears in an intensional context in (1.5), and hence cannot be substituted for, just as in the case of (1) itself; "Alfred", by contrast, appears only in extensional contexts in (1.5), and hence can be substituted for, just as in the case of (1) itself.

Second, it will be plain that this account of certain attributions of intentionality has nothing to say about the causes of an act. I.e., many

---

[3] But of course if you kill Bert intentionally, and Bert is the mayor, then you kill, intentionally, the man who in fact is the mayor, whether you know it or not.

writers have tried to find an account of what it is for an act to be intentional in terms of what causes it. So, for example, it has been suggested that Alfred's killing of Bert is an intentional act just in case it had a certain kind of causal history, the job being to say precisely what kind. I do not myself rate the chances of success in this enterprise as very high. Causality certainly does seem to me to be involved, but in a much more subtle way—i.e., the way in which it is involved in the notion 'agency' that I use throughout this chapter. On the other hand, I want to stress that nothing I say here is incompatible with anyone's finding an account of intentionality in which causality enters more directly: nothing I say here is incompatible with there being a certain kind of causal history such that an act is intentional just in case it has a causal history of that kind.

Third, I rate as nonexistent the chances of success in the enterprise of trying to get from (T-S$_{18}$) to an account of what it is for an event to be an intentional act.[4] Similarly for the chances of success in getting from this schema to an account of that other notion 'agency', according to which a person is not agent of an event unless that event involves intentionality. Similarly for the chances of success in getting from this schema to an account of the notion 'act' that is first cousin to that notion 'agency'. Clearly, there is no direct route from this schema to accounts of those notions. For example, one certainly cannot say

> Intentional act (x) just in case there is a verb such that the results of making the appropriate substitutions in . . . are all true:

for there could have been intentional acts even if there had been no verbs. (Cats, for example, act intentionally; and I should imagine there is a possible world in which cats are the highest form of animal life.) And I doubt very much that there is any indirect route that will work any better.[5]

2. An account of intentionality should certainly include more than an account of simple ascriptions of intentionality of the form

α verbed (β) intentionally.

For example, it might be true to say "John intentionally killed Jim at precisely 3 P.M."; nothing in the preceding section tells us what it says. Again, consider sentences whose main verb is an incomplete verb,

[4] Unless one quantifies over activities.
[5] Unless one takes an indirect route that involves quantifying over activities.

such as "John put the book on the table intentionally" and "John made his mother cry intentionally"; we need an account of what these say too.

I suspect that these sentences present no new theoretical problem. But other sentences whose main verb is an incomplete verb do. What I have in mind is sentences such as "I intentionally let the baby die" and "Bert intentionally refrained from waggling his thumb". On any view, intentional omissions are puzzling. If there are no acts of omission—if omissions are states of affairs rather than events—then accommodating these sentences requires giving a place to the notion 'intentional state of affairs', and it is (to say the least) not obvious how this is to be done. Having nothing useful to say on the matter, I shall simply pass it by.

3. An account of intentionality should also include an account of what it is to intend to do something, and what it is to form an intention. The question what these are is large and hard, and I shall not go into it.[6] But there is a class of sentences which would be of interest to anyone with an interest in that question, and which we already have equipment in hand for dealing with.

Consider, for example,

(1)   Alfred shot Bert with the intention of killing him.

(1) plainly entails

(2)   Alfred shot Bert intentionally;

so since we know—from (T-S_{18})—that (2) is rewritable as

(2.5)   ($\exists w$) ($\exists x$) [Shoots$_3$ (w, Bert, Alfred) & Agent (Alfred, w) &
          Agent (Alfred, x) & {PART (x, w) or PART (w, x)} &
          ($\exists y$) (y = Alfred & Throughout the time IN which x occurs
          {y hopes that ($\exists z$) (Shoots$_3$ (z, Bert, y) & PART (x, z)) or
          y hopes that ($\exists z$) (Shoots$_3$ (z, Bert, y) & PART (z, x))})],

we also know that (1) is true only if (2.5) is.

What more is required for the truth of (1)? Surely it has to be the case, not merely that Alfred hopes throughout x that there will be a shooting of Bert by him that x is part of (or that is part of x), it has to be the case also that Alfred hopes throughout w itself that there will be a killing of Bert by him that w is part of (or that is part of w). More precisely, the truth of (1) also requires the truth of

[6] Some very interesting suggestions are made by Gilbert Harman, in "Practical Reasoning," *The Review of Metaphysics*, 29 (1976), 431–463.

Acts and Other Events

Throughout the time IN which w occurs

$\{y$ hopes that $(\exists z)$ $(Kills_3$ $(z,$ Bert, $y)$ & $PART$ $(w, z))$ or

y hopes that $(\exists z)$ $(Kills_3$ $(z,$ Bert, $y)$ & $PART$ $(z, w))\}$.

I am inclined to think that this is enough: i.e., that we can take what we now have to be a rewriting of (1). But I think also that what makes it possible for us to rewrite (1) in this way is the fact that if there does turn out to be a killing of Bert by Alfred, then it will itself be an event which Alfred is agent of. What I have in mind is that it seems to me very plausible, not merely that an intentional act is always a fusion of causings, but also that you can only intend to do something if your doing of it (i.e., if you succeed, and actually carry out your intention) would itself be a fusion of causings. Thus, for example, it seems to me that

John kicked Jim with the intention of getting even with him

could well be true, but that

John kicked Jim with the intention of being even with him

could not.[7] If so, then since people have queer beliefs and hopes, and since we are in search of a generalization, we must add a further clause, viz.,

& (z) $(Kills_3$ $(z,$ Bert, Alfred) $\supset$ Agent (Alfred, z)).[8]

I suggest, then, that we can say that the results of replacing "α", "β", and "γ" by referring expressions, "verb$_1$s" by an appropriate tensed form of any transitive verb, "verb$_2$ing" by the gerund of any transitive verb, and the schematic predicates with the appropriate predicates, in

(T-S$_{19}$) "α verb$_1$s β with the intention of verb$_2$ing γ"

is rewritable as

"$(\exists w)$ $(\exists x)$ [Verb$_1$s (w, β, α) & Agent (α, w) &

Agent (α, x) & $\{PART$ (x, w) or $PART$ $(w, x)\}$ &

$(\exists y)$ $(y = \alpha$ & Throughout the time IN which x occurs

$\{y$ hopes that $(\exists z)$ (Verb$_1$s (z, β, y) & $PART$ $(x, z))$ or

y hopes that $(\exists z)$ (Verb$_1$s (z, β, y) & $PART$ $(z, x))\}$ &

Throughout the time IN which w occurs

$\{y$ hopes that $(\exists z)$ (Verb$_2$s (z, β, y) & $PART$ $(w, z))$ or

---

[7] Compare "I moved the pawn with the intention of bringing about that I win" and "I moved the pawn with the intention of winning"; and see footnote 1 above.

[8] The connective in this clause—and in the last clause of (T-S$_{19}$)—should really be stronger than the horseshoe; i.e., we do not want the clause made true by falsity of antecedent.

266

y hopes that $(\exists z)$ (Verb$_2$s (z, β, y) & PART $(z, w))\})] \, \&$
(z) (Verb$_2$s $(z, \beta, \alpha) \supset$ Agent $(\alpha, z))$"

are all true.

It should be noticed that on this account of the matter, the truth of (1) does not require that Alfred at any time knew he was actually succeeding in shooting Bert. This seems to me not to be a worry. Anyone who is worried about it may prefer to add a clause requiring knowledge that there was a shooting as well as hope that there would be one.

It should also be noticed that on this account of the matter,

(3)   Alfred killed Bert with the intention of killing Bert

is true if Bert killed Alfred intentionally, and moreover, that the truth of (3) is compatible with the truth of

> Alfred killed Bert with the intention of annoying Bert's father,

and that the truth of both is compatible with the truth of

> Alfred killed Bert with the intention of getting even with Bert's father.

These results seem to me to be exactly as they should be; i.e., it seems to me that the expression "the intention" in sentences of the form we are looking at does not imply uniqueness. People may (and perhaps mostly do) have, as we might put it, 'nested' intentions. We do sometimes say such things as that *the* intention with which Alfred killed Bert was. . . . And when we do, I suppose we do mean to imply uniqueness. Perhaps *the* intention with which a person acts is to be picked out by picking out the hope he has in acting, such that all of the other hopes he has in acting *are* hopes he has because he has that hope. But I leave it open.

4. What is it to carry out an intention? Suppose, for example, that

(1)   Alfred shot Bert with the intention of killing him

is true. What is required for the truth of

(2)   Alfred shot Bert with the intention of killing him and carried out that intention?

Well, certainly (2) is true only if (1) is. Certainly also, (2) is true only if Alfred does in fact kill Bert. But we cannot say that (2) is equivalent to

(2')   Alfred shot Bert with the intention of killing him, and Alfred killed Bert.

For suppose that Alfred shot Bert with the intention of killing him, and that Bert did not die of the wound. We may suppose that Alfred nevertheless did later kill Bert, but by (perhaps) drowning him. No doubt it would be misleading to say (2') if that was what had happened, but it would be true to say it all the same. But (2) surely is not true: surely Alfred did not carry out the intention with which he shot Bert.

One thing that went wrong in the preceding case is this: Alfred killed Bert by drowning him, and not by shooting him. But even

(2″)   Alfred shot Bert with the intention of killing him, and Alfred killed Bert by shooting him

is not equivalent to (2). For suppose that Alfred shot Bert with the intention of killing him and that Bert did not die of that wound. We may suppose that Alfred nevertheless did later kill Bert by shooting him—for example, Alfred might have decided that, having failed on the first try, he had better practice his shooting, and it might turn out that Bert was in fact sunbathing right next to the target. No doubt it would be misleading to say (2″) if that was what had happened, but it would be true to say it all the same. But (2) surely is not true: surely Alfred did not carry out the intention with which he shot Bert on that first occasion.

The more that is required for the truth of (2) comes out if we attend, once again, to (1). (T-S_{19}) tells us that (1) is rewritable as

(1.5)   ($\exists w$) ($\exists x$) [Shoots$_3$ (w, Bert, Alfred) & . . . &

          ($\exists y$) (y = Alfred & . . . & Throughout the time IN which w occurs

          {y hopes that ($\exists z$) (Kills$_3$ (z, Bert, y) & PART (w, z)) or

          y hopes that ($\exists z$) (Kills$_3$ (z, Bert, y) & PART (z, w))})]

          & . . . .

(See pages 266–267 above.) It seems to me a very plausible idea that for Alfred to have carried out the intention that (1) attributes to him is for one or the other of those two hopes to come true—for it is only by virtue of the fact that he has one or the other of those two hopes that his intention in shooting Bert is what it is. Thus I suggest that we should take (2) to be rewritable as

(2.5)   ($\exists w$) ($\exists x$) [Shoots$_3$ (w, Bert, Alfred) & Agent (Alfred, w) &

          Agent (Alfred, x) & {PART (x, w) or PART (w, x) } &

          ($\exists y$) (y = Alfred & Throughout the time IN which x occurs

          {y hopes that ($\exists z$) (Shoots$_3$ (z, Bert, y) & PART (x, z)) or

          y hopes that ($\exists z$) (Shoots$_3$ (z, Bert, y) & PART (z, x))} &

Throughout the time IN which w occurs
$\{y$ hopes that $(\exists z)$ (Kills$_3$ $(z,$ Bert, $y)$ & PART $(w, z))$ or
y hopes that $(\exists z)$ (Kills$_3$ $(z,$ Bert, $y)$ & PART $(z, w))\}$ &
$\{(\exists z)$ (Kills$_3$ $(z,$ Bert, $y)$ & PART $(w, z))$ or
$(\exists z)$ (Kills$_3$ $(z,$ Bert, $y)$ & PART $(z, w))\})]$ &
(z) (Kills$_3$ $(z,$ Bert, Alfred) $\supset$ Agent (Alfred, $z))$.

If Alfred killed Bert by shooting him, then it is plain enough that the fourth 'hope-clause' did not come true. If Alfred hoped that it would, he was bound to be disappointed. But that does not matter. If I am right in thinking that (1) is rewritable as (1.5), the fact that he was bound to be disappointed in that hope shows only that he carried out his intention in a different manner from that in which he hoped he would.

In fact, since (2) leaves much room for 'mistake' on Alfred's part, it is right that (2.5) should do so too. Suppose that Alfred shot Bert, hoping thereby to cause hemorrhage and thereby to kill Bert. (People, as we noted, may have 'nested' intentions.) Then

(1)   Alfred shot Bert with the intention of killing him

and

(3)   Alfred shot Bert with the intention of causing hemorrhage

are both true. Suppose, now, that Alfred did not cause hemorrhage: suppose that instead of causing hemorrhage, the shooting so startled Bert that it caused Bert to have a fatal heart attack. Then

(4)   Alfred shot Bert with the intention of causing hemorrhage and carried out that intention

is false. But

(2)   Alfred shot Bert with the intention of killing him and carried out that intention

is nevertheless true—Alfred has simply carried out the intention attributed to him by (1) in a different manner from that in which he hoped he would.

The fact that (2) leaves this room for 'mistake' counts in favor of the thesis of section 1 above. What I have in mind is this. I should imagine that if the result of making appropriate replacements in

      α verb$_1$ed β with the intention of verb$_2$ing and carried out that intention

is true, then so also is the result of making the appropriate replacements in

      α verb$_2$ed intentionally.

Thus, in particular, if (2) is true, so also is

(5)   Alfred killed Bert intentionally.

Now under my accounts of (2) and (5), (2) does entail (5). For if (2.5) is true, then so also is

(5.5) $(\exists w)\,(\exists x)$ [Kills$_3$ $(w, \text{Bert}, \text{Alfred})$ & Agent (Alfred, w) & Agent (Alfred, x) & {PART (x, w) or PART (w, x)} & $(\exists y)\,(y = \text{Alfred}$ & Throughout the time IN which x occurs {y hopes that $(\exists z)$ (Kills$_3$ (z, Bert, y) & PART $(x, z))$) or y hopes that $(\exists z)$ (Kills$_3$ (z, Bert, y) & PART $(z, x))$)})],

and (T-S$_{18}$) of section 1 tells us that if this is true, then (5) is true. The fact that, under my accounts of them, (2) entails (5) lends weight to both of those accounts. But more important for present purposes is this: since (2) leaves room for 'mistake', and (2) entails (5), (5) must also leave room for 'mistake'—and it was not only not a mark against my thesis about (5) in section 1 that it does make (5) leave this room, its doing so counts in favor of it.

A generalization of the thesis that (2) is rewritable as (2.5) is easy enough to construct, and I shall not take space to do so.

5. Some moral philosophers think that the difference between intending to cause a thing and merely expecting that you will cause it is morally significant. Others think that this is false. Still others think that dispute about the matter is premature: they think we should not ask whether the difference between these is morally significant until we have in hand an account of what that difference is.

It seems to me that the difference is obvious enough. Consider

(1)   Charles operated on his dog with the intention of causing it pain

and

(2)   David operated on his dog in the belief that he would thereby cause it pain.

According to (T-S$_{19}$), (1) tells us that throughout w (which is an operating on his dog by Charles), Charles hopes there will be a causing of his dog's being in pain by him, and that w will be part of it (or that it will be part of w). I should imagine that (2) attributes to David the very same thing, except that in it, "David" replaces "Charles", and "believes" replaces "hopes".

It may seem a plausible idea, then, that the difference between intending and expecting does make a moral difference. No doubt, if (2) is true, David believes his dog will be in pain; but if (1) is true, Charles hopes his dog will be in pain. It can hardly be thought a nice thing to act in thus and such a way, believing that you will thereby cause pain; but it surely is worse to act in that very same way, positively hoping that you will!

But to be told that (1) and (2) are true is not to be told very much about what Charles and David did. And (I should imagine) it may even be that neither acts badly. Suppose, for example, that there are a dozen children, whose lives can be saved only if they are given an injection of a certain material produced in the skin of the tip of a dog's ear. That material, let us suppose, is produced only while the dog is in pain; thus to get the material you have to cause the dog pain. It is a very serious business to cause pain. Nevertheless, I take it that the lives of a dozen children are more important than the pain of a dog. So if Charles operates on the dog without anesthetic, with the intention of causing pain, and thereby being able to get the material, and thereby being able to save the children, we cannot complain of what he does: he does not act badly. Again, suppose that there are a dozen children, whose lives can be saved only if they are given an injection of a certain material normally present in the skin of the tip of a dog's ear. David is a good person, and it goes without saying that he would prefer to operate on the dog with an anesthetic. But David has no anesthetics. It is a very serious business to cause pain. Nevertheless, I take it that the lives of a dozen children are more important than the pain of a dog. So if David operates on the dog without anesthetic, believing that he will thereby cause it pain, but with the intention of being able to get the material and thereby being able to save the children, we cannot complain of what he does: he does not act badly.

I should imagine, as I say, that if these things are true, then neither Charles nor David acts badly if he acts. Does one act even a tiny bit better than the other by virtue of the fact that one intends the pain and the other only expects it? I should have thought the answer was, simply, No.[9]

[9] I drew attention earlier to the fact that my account of sentences of the form "α verbed (β) intentionally" is in one way nonrestrictive: it leaves a considerable amount of room for mistake. This is perhaps the place to draw attention to the fact that my account of these sentences is in another way restrictive, more restrictive than some would like. Gilbert Harman, for example, says: "One can do something intentionally even though one does not intend to do it, if one does it in the face of what ought to be a reason not to do it and . . . does it as a foreseen consequence of something else that one intends to

Acts and Other Events

Again, if the difference between intending and expecting makes a moral difference, we should surely expect it to be possible that that difference be outweighed. What I have in mind is this. Suppose that Edward knows of a dozen children whose lives can be saved only if they are given an injection of one or the other of two materials produced in the skin of the tips of certain dogs' ears. One of those materials is normally present in terriers; and Edward has a terrier; but he has no anesthetic to deaden the pain of operating. The other of those materials is produced in spaniels—and Edward has a spaniel—but only while the dog is in pain. One would expect that if the difference between intending and expecting makes a moral difference then there should be some difference in amount of pain that will outweigh that difference and make it morally *in*different which dog Edward attacks. But is there? Surely if one dog will have even a little less pain, then that is the dog Edward must attack, and it would be wrong for him to flip a coin.[10]

There is more to be said about this issue; but going further would take us too far outside the theory of action. It is no surprise that a student of the theory of action finds himself or herself, sooner or later, straying into ethics: one can hardly think that acts *are* this or that without wondering what, then, are the things that make some acts good and some acts bad. I have thought it best, however, to segregate the ontological questions: we can have confidence in the ontological conclusions we bring to ethics only to the extent that they are independently plausible.

---

do" ("Practical Reasoning," p. 434). Suppose, then, that David goes ahead; on Harman's view,

(S)   David caused his dog's being in pain intentionally

is true. But on my account of the matter, (S) is false. Indeed, I confess to thinking it counts in favor of (T-S$_{18}$) that, rewritten as (T-S$_{18}$) prescribes, (S) is false.

[10] These examples are the property of the Society for Ethical and Legal Philosophy.

Index

Index

Verbs:
  completed, 145-147, 221, 234
  illocutionary-act-verbs, 140-142, 223-225, 231, 236, 242

incomplete, 144-147, 220, 234, 244
perlocutionary-act-verbs, 138

Wolterstorff, Nicholas, 114, 119-122

Library of Congress Cataloging in Publication Data
(For library cataloging purposes only)

Thomson, Judith J
    Acts and other events.

    (Contemporary philosophy)
    Includes index.
    1. Events (Philosophy) 2. Act (Philosophy) 3. Agent (Philosophy)
4. Causation. I. Title. II. Series.
B105.E7T47   122   77-4791
ISBN 0-8014-1050-9